FM 3-04.113 (FM 1-113)

Utility and Cargo Helicopter Operations

December 2007

DISTRIBUTION RESTRICTION: Approved for public release; distribution is unlimited.

Headquarters, Department of the Army

Published by Books Express Publishing
Books Express Publishing, 2011
ISBN 978-1-78039-906-5

Books Express publications are available from all good retail and online booksellers. For
publishing proposals and direct ordering please contact us at: info@books-express.com

Field Manual
No. 3-04.113 (1-113)

Headquarters
Department of the Army
Washington, DC, 7 December 2007

Utility and Cargo Helicopter Operations

Contents

Distribution Restriction: Approved for public release; distribution is unlimited.

*This publication supersedes FM 1-113, 12 September 1997.

Figures

Tables

Preface

Field manual (FM) 3-04.113 is intended for use by commanders, staffs, and United States (U.S.) military personnel expecting to operate and employ Army aviation assault and/or general support (GS) helicopter units.

This FM is the Army's doctrine for how to fight and sustain assault helicopter battalions (AHBs) and general support aviation battalions (GSABs). The operational concepts described in this manual are based on Army doctrine as established in FM 1, FM 3-0, and FM 3-04.111. Emphasis is placed on modular force structure and the enhanced operational capability provided by Army aviation transformation.

FM 3-04.113 applies to regular Army and reserve component units. It builds on collective knowledge and experience gained through recent operations, numerous exercises, and the deliberate process of informed reasoning. This publication is rooted in time-tested principles and fundamentals, while accommodating new technologies, and evolving responses to the diverse threats to our national security. This manual also assists Army proponent schools in teaching utility and cargo helicopter operations.

FM 3-04.113 lays out the "how-to" of assault and GS helicopter organizations, missions, command and control (C2), tactical employment, and sustainment. It describes the responsibilities and duties of key personnel during training, operations, and combat. This manual is authoritative but not considered inflexible. Each situation in combat must be resolved by an intelligent interpretation and application of the doctrine set forth herein. Standardized battalion and company operations are necessary for effective employment of aviation battalion task forces (ABTFs). To this end, like companies should follow similar operational and employment procedures.

Finally, FM 3-04.113 furnishes a foundation for assault and GS helicopter doctrine, force design, materiel acquisition, professional education, and individual and unit training.

This publication applies to the Active Army, the Army National Guard/Army National Guard of the United States, and the United States Army Reserve, unless otherwise stated.

The proponent of this publication is Headquarters, United States Army Training and Doctrine Command (TRADOC). Send comments and recommendations on Department of the Army (DA) Form 2028 (Recommended Changes to publications and Blank Forms) to Commander, United States Army Aviation Warfighting Center, ATTN: ATZQ-TDD-D, Fort Rucker, Alabama 36362-5263 or complete the Directorate of Training and Doctrine (DOTD) electronic change request form at https://www.us.army.mil/suite/doc/7288766. Comments may be e-mailed to the DOTD at av.doctrine@us.army.mil. Other doctrinal information can be found on the Internet at the Aviation Doctrine Branch homepage (https://www.us.army.mil/suite/page/394729), Army Knowledge Online (AKO).

This publication has been reviewed for operations security (OPSEC) considerations.

Chapter 1

Missions and Organization

AHBs and GSABs are organized and equipped to support Army and joint, interagency, and multinational (JIM) operations. These units conduct continuous maneuver, support, and maneuver sustainment missions across the depth and breadth of the operational environment. Each unit focuses on time-tested fundamentals to achieve success. This chapter discusses these fundamentals in relation to the type of battalion and outlines the basic organization, principal mission focus, and capabilities of the AHB and GSAB. The organization description for each unit is based on the official table of organization and equipment (TOE). Operationally, all units are resourced according to a modified table of organization and equipment (MTOE), so organizations may be different than described in the TOEs in this FM.

SECTION I – OVERVIEW

COMBINED ARMS

1-1. Combined arms is the synchronized and simultaneous application of warfighting functions (WFF) to achieve an effect that is greater than if each arm were used in sequence. It is the full integration of a unit's differing capabilities in such a way that, to counteract one, the enemy must become

<table>
<tr><td colspan="2" align="center">Contents</td></tr>
<tr><td>Section I – Overview</td><td>1-1</td></tr>
<tr><td>Section II – Missions</td><td>1-3</td></tr>
<tr><td>Section III – Organization</td><td>1-4</td></tr>
</table>

more vulnerable to another. Combined arms employs all the WFF and their supporting systems. Combined arms multiply the effectiveness of Army forces in all operations.

1-2. Employing combined arms is simple in concept; however, it requires highly trained Soldiers, skilled leadership, effective staff work, and integrated information systems. Combined arms operations must be synchronized so the effects of combat power occur simultaneously. Synchronization is defined as arranging activities in time, space, and purpose to mass maximum relative combat power at a decisive place and time (joint publication [JP] 1-02). Through synchronization, commanders arrange WFF to mass the effects of combat power at the chosen place and time to overwhelm an enemy or dominate the situation.

1-3. Combined arms is achieved through organizational design (standing organizations) and temporary reorganization (tailored and task-organized units). For example, units organic to brigade combat teams (BCTs) perform all WFF; however, the BCT does not organically include Army aviation. When required, capabilities are added through the temporary tailoring and task-organizing of subordinating elements of different units under one commander.

1-4. Aviation battalions plan, coordinate, and execute operations thereby creating opportunities for commanders to disrupt the enemy's decisionmaking process. This process forces the enemy to make decisions that disrupt its initial plans. The battalion—through coordination, liaison, C2, situational awareness (SA), and situational understanding (SU)—assists in setting conditions for the force's success.

FUNDAMENTALS

ARMY WARFIGHTING FUNCTIONS

1-5. Battalion commanders and staffs must be fully aware of the six Army WFF (see field manual interim [FMI] 5-0.1). Table 1-1 provides examples of tasks the AHB and GSAB may perform in support of each warfighting function.

Table 1-1. Assault helicopter battalion and general support aviation battalion roles in Army warfighting functions

Army WFF	AHB and GSAB Role
Movement and Maneuver	Insert and augment ground forces to find, fix, and/or destroy the enemy. Transport personnel, equipment, and supplies. Insert engineers and survivability materiel. Emplace Volcano minefields.
Intelligence	Assist commander and staff in conducting intelligence preparation of the battlefield (IPB). Provide higher headquarters (HQ) SA. Confirm/deny elements of the intelligence, surveillance, and reconnaissance (ISR) plan and priority intelligence requirements (PIR).
Fires	Transport indirect fire systems, forward observers, and ground designation teams. Assist in planning joint suppression of enemy air defenses (J-SEAD) fires and electronic warfare (EW).
Sustainment	Conduct air movement operations of personnel, supplies, and equipment. Perform aircraft recovery. Support forward arming and refueling point (FARP) emplacement or resupply. Perform aeromedical evacuation or casualty evacuation (CASEVAC).
Command and Control	Provide air and ground commanders the ability to rapidly traverse and see the battlefield. Provide battle command on the move (BCOTM), Army Airborne Command and Control System (A2C2S), and retransmission. Provide air traffic services (ATS).
Protection	Transport air defense artillery (ADA) systems. Transport fortification supplies, support deception by false insertions. Support chemical, biological, radiological, and nuclear (CBRN) surveys.

TYPES OF OPERATIONS

Decisive Operations

1-6. Decisive operations directly accomplish the mission assigned by higher HQ. Decisive operations do not require the presence of overwhelming forces; they simply require the massing of overwhelming firepower and other effects against the enemy. The AHB and GSAB enhance and extend the capabilities of commanders to initiate, conduct, and sustain combat operations. These units provide tactical air movement of troops, as well as internal and external lift of weapon systems, supplies, and equipment at corps and lower echelons to negate the effects of complex terrain. AHBs and GSABs support decisive operations through—

- Air assaults.
- Inserting/extracting engineer, Pathfinder, and infantry elements to increase the tempo of reconnaissance and security.
- Minefield emplacement at chokepoints along primary enemy avenues of counterattack or along enemy avenues of withdrawal to cut-off the enemy's retreat.
- C2 support.
- Air movement to reinforce success.
- Aerial emplacement and sustainment of FARPs.

Shaping Operations

1-7.   Shaping operations establish and preserve conditions for success of the decisive operation by manipulating the battlefield. Shaping includes lethal and nonlethal operations that—

- Make the enemy vulnerable to attack.
- Impede or divert the enemy's attempts to maneuver.
- Provide combat support to facilitate the maneuver of friendly forces.
- Enhance deception or otherwise dictate the time and place for decisive battle.

1-8.   Through shaping, commanders gain the initiative, preserve momentum, and control the tempo of combat. Shaping operations may occur with, before, or after initiation of decisive operations and involve any combination of forces. AHBs and GSABs support shaping operations through—

- Air assault and air movement to seize terrain or attack enemy units, facilities, or equipment.
- Insertion and extraction operations in support of special operating forces and conventional units to conduct raids, long-range surveillance (LRS), or reconnaissance.
- Volcano operations to turn, block, and otherwise delay the enemy.
- C2 support.
- Aerial emplacement and sustainment of FARPs and forward operating bases (FOBs).
- Psychological operations (PSYOP) with leaflet drops or loudspeaker missions.

Sustaining Operations

1-9.   Sustaining operations generate and maintain combat power. Sustaining operations at any echelon are defined as those assisting the decisive and shaping operations by ensuring freedom of action and continuity of operations. Sustaining operations include base security, maintenance, movement control, terrain management, and protection of lines of communications (LOC) and HQ. AHBs and GSABs support sustaining operations through—

- Air movement.
- Aeromedical evacuation.
- CASEVAC.
- Downed aircraft recovery.
- Personnel recovery (PR) operations.

SECTION II – MISSIONS

1-10. The missions of utility and cargo helicopter units are air assault, air movement, C2 support (GSAB), aeromedical evacuation (GSAB), CASEVAC, ATS (GSAB), and PR.

ASSAULT HELICOPTER BATTALION

1-11. The AHB's primary missions are to conduct air assault and air movement operations to extend the tactical reach of the maneuver commander, negate effects of terrain, seize key nodes, achieve surprise, and isolate or dislocate enemy forces. These missions encompass numerous other functions including:

- Insertion/extraction operations.
- Pathfinder operations (medium divisions only).
- Artillery raids.
- Aerial mine delivery operations (Volcano).
- CBRN surveys.
- PSYOP missions (leaflet drop and speaker missions).
- Wet Hawk and Fat Hawk refueling operations.

GENERAL SUPPORT AVIATION BATTALION

1-12. The GSAB's primary missions include air assault, air movement, aeromedical evacuation, C2 support, and ATS. Specific functions of the GSAB are the same as an AHB with the addition of CH-47 and HH-60 capabilities. Some of these functions include—

- BCOTM.
- Air movement of supplies, equipment, and personnel including logistics-over-the-shore when applicable.
- Wet Hawk, Fat Hawk, and Fat Cow refueling operations.
- Air crash rescue support.

1-13. Due to the CH-47's capabilities, heavy helicopter units enhance mission success with—

- High-altitude operations.
- Oversized, heavy, and special equipment movement.

SECTION III – ORGANIZATION

BATTALION STAFF ORGANIZATION

1-14. The battalion staff (figure 1-1, page 1-5) is organized into personal staff, special staff, and coordinating staff (refer to FM 6-0). The battalion staff consists of officers and enlisted personnel who plan, supervise, and synchronize operations according to the battalion commander's concept and intent. Except in scope, duties, and responsibilities, the battalion staff is similar to those of higher echelon staff. Key personnel must be positioned on the battlefield where they can effectively carry out their duties. Refer to chapter 2 for more information on staff duties and responsibilities.

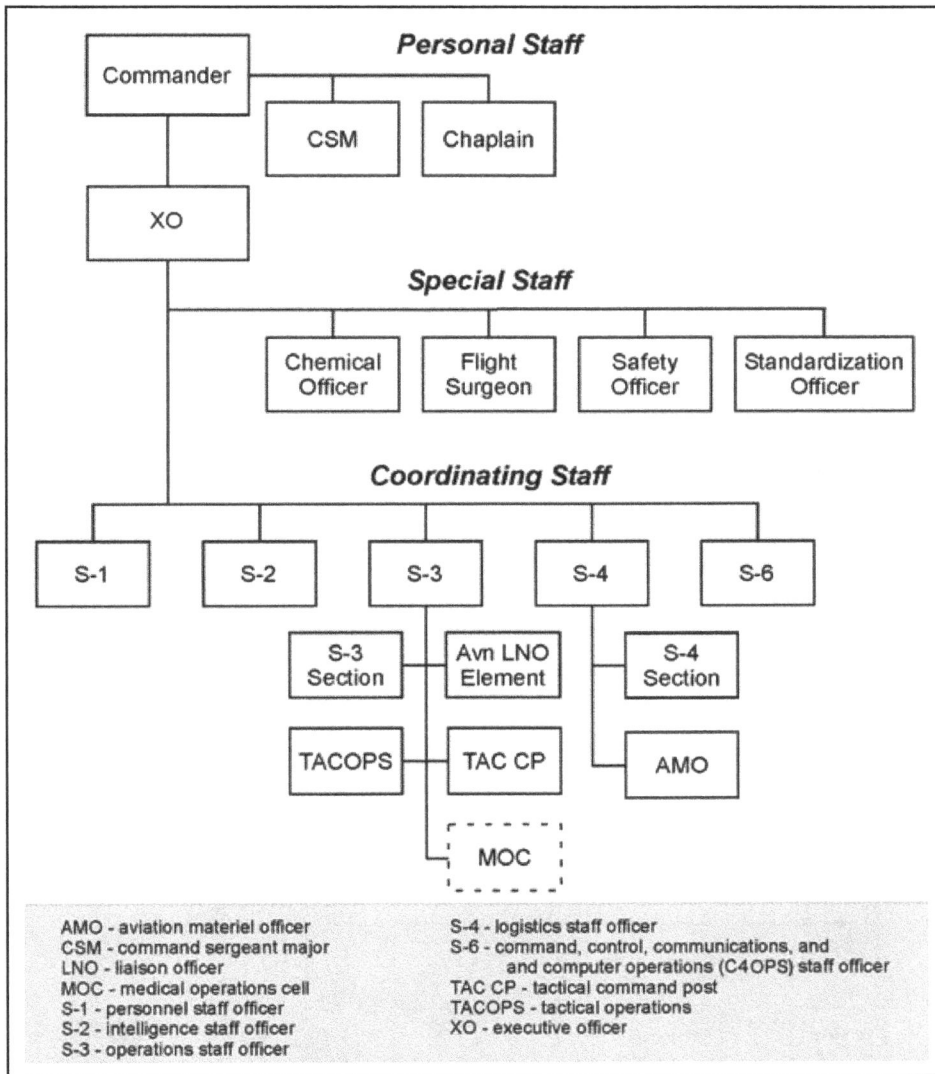

Figure 1-1. Battalion staff organization

PERSONAL STAFF

1-15. The personal staff works under the commander's immediate control but may work through the executive officer (XO) or a specific coordinating staff officer for coordination and control purposes. Members of the personal staff normally have a direct line of communication to the commander due to the confidential nature and broad scope of their assigned duties.

SPECIAL STAFF

1-16. Special staff officers help the battalion commander and other staff members perform their functional responsibilities.

COORDINATING STAFF

1-17. The coordinating staff is composed of the commander's principal assistants responsible for one or a combination of broad fields of interest (personnel, intelligence, operations, logistics, planning, and communications). Coordinating staff members help the commander coordinate and supervise execution of plans, operations, and activities. Collectively through the XO, they are accountable for the commander's entire field of responsibility.

Note. The GSAB also has a medical operations cell (MOC) that provides assistance with communication between higher echelons of medical C2.

ASSAULT HELICOPTER BATTALION

1-18. Division aviation brigades have one AHB, while theater assault aviation brigades have three AHBs. The air assault division is unique in that it has two aviation brigades, each with its own AHB. The AHB (figure 1-2) at all echelons consists of a headquarters and headquarters company (HHC), a forward support company (FSC), three assault helicopter companies (AHCs), and an aviation maintenance company. Each medium division AHB also has a Pathfinder company.

1-19. The AHB is dependent on the combat aviation brigade (CAB) or division for additional maintenance support, Airspace command and control (AC2), weather, legal, finance, and specific personnel and administrative services. Unlike attack/reconnaissance helicopter battalions, the AHB does not have an organic FS element and is reliant on the CAB for this support when formed as an ABTF HQ.

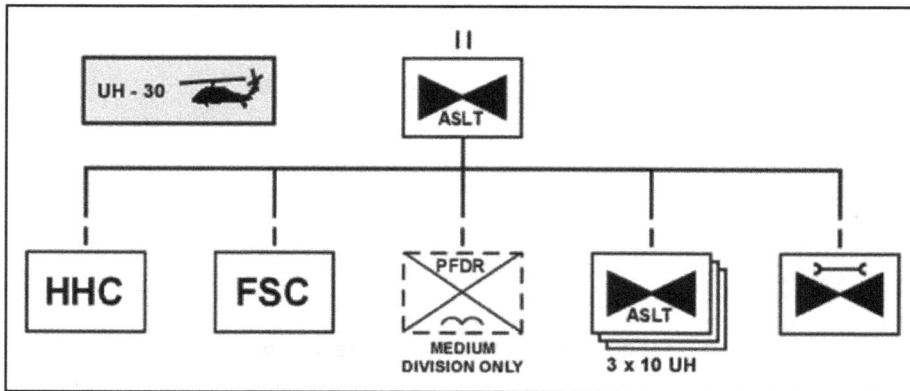

Figure 1-2. Assault helicopter battalion organization

HEADQUARTERS AND HEADQUARTERS COMPANY

1-20. The AHB HHC (figure 1-3, page 1-7) consists of the command group, staff, company HQ section, supply section, communications/automation section, medical treatment squad, and unit ministry team (UMT). The HHC provides personnel and equipment for the C2 functions of the battalion, and security and defense of the command post (CP). The HHC also provides the following types of support: unit-level personnel service, UMT, logistics, medical, and CBRN. Refer to chapter 4 for additional information.

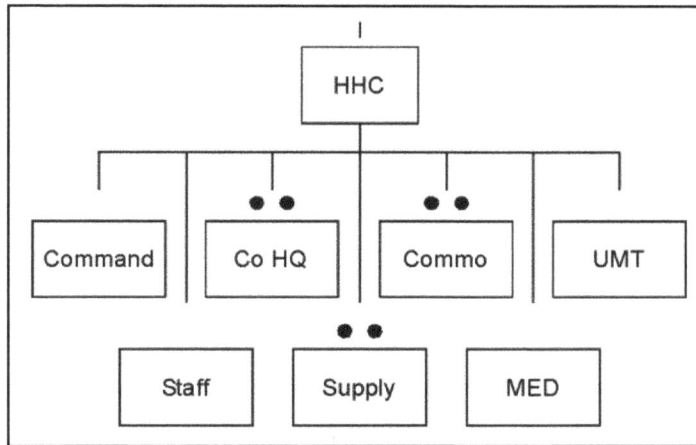

Figure 1-3. Assault helicopter battalion headquarters and headquarters company organization

FORWARD SUPPORT COMPANY

1-21. The AHB FSC (figure 1-4) has a company HQ, field feeding section, distribution platoon, and ground maintenance platoon. The FSC provides field feeding, transportation, refueling, ground maintenance support, and coordinates with the aviation support battalion (ASB) for additional support as required. Refer to chapter 4 for additional information.

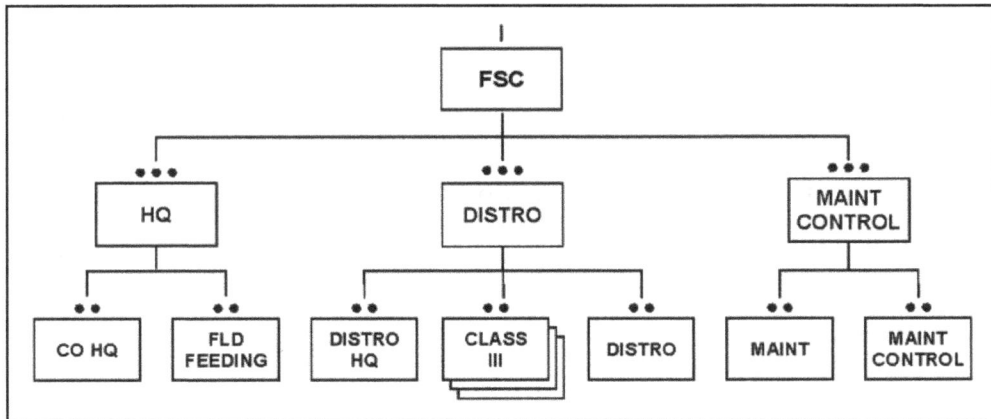

Figure 1-4. Assault helicopter battalion forward support company organization

ASSAULT HELICOPTER COMPANY

1-22. The AHC (figure 1-5, page 1-8) consists of a company HQ and two assault helicopter platoons with five UH-60 aircraft each.

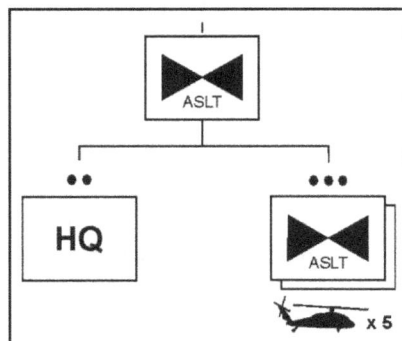

Figure 1-5. Assault helicopter company organization

Headquarters Section

1-23. The company's HQ section embodies the senior leadership of the company and is responsible for leading, training, and caring for all Soldiers assigned to the company. The commander, standardization instructor pilot (SP), safety officer (SO), and tactical operations (TACOPS) officer assigned to the HQ section are part of the company's aircrew structure.

Assault Helicopter Platoon

1-24. The AHC has two assault helicopter platoons, each with five UH-60 helicopters. One platoon has an aircraft survivability equipment/electronic warfare officer (ASE/EWO), while the other platoon has a non-additional skill identifier (ASI) pilot.

AVIATION MAINTENANCE COMPANY

1-25. The aviation maintenance company (figure 1-6) consists of a company HQ; production control and quality assurance (QA) sections; aircraft maintenance platoon with UH-60 repair sections; and an aircraft component repair platoon (CRP) with powerplant, powertrain, structural, pneudraulics, and avionic/electrical sections providing necessary aviation field maintenance and battle damage assessment and repair (BDAR). The aviation maintenance company provides necessary maneuver sustainment to operate autonomously throughout division battlespace. Chapter 4 has additional information.

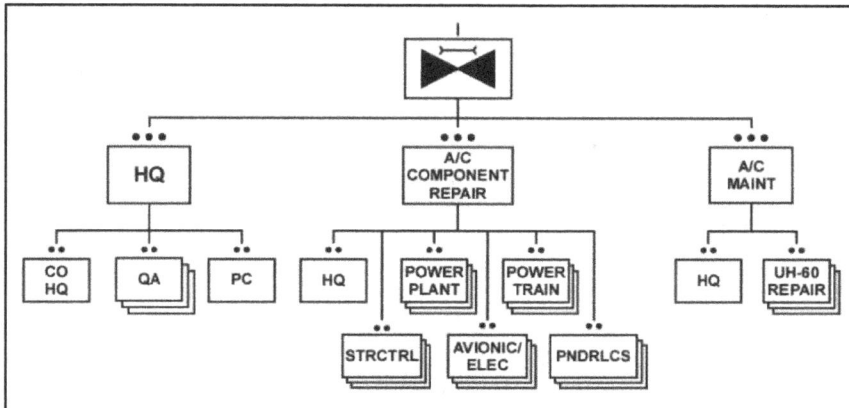

Figure 1-6. Assault helicopter battalion aviation maintenance company organization

PATHFINDER COMPANY

1-26. The pathfinder company (figure 1-7) is organic to the AHB within the medium divisions. It has a company HQ, GS platoon, and direct support (DS) platoon. The HQ section consists of a medical section and communications section. The GS platoon consists of a platoon HQ and two GS pathfinder teams. The DS platoon consists of a platoon HQ and two DS pathfinder teams. The pathfinder company provides the AHB commander with a highly trained, specialized infantry element that conducts landing zone (LZ)/drop zone reconnaissance operations inside enemy held terrain and emplaces navigational aids (NAVAIDs) to assist aircrews on approach into LZ/DZs. The pathfinder company also performs PR team security, downed/isolated personnel extraction and sniper operations.

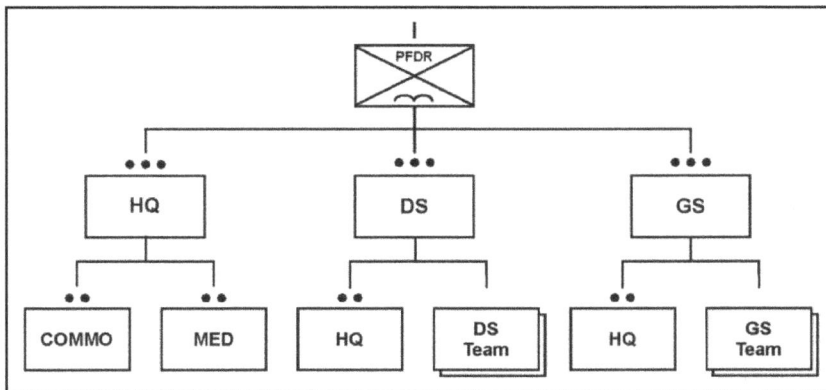

Figure 1-7. Pathfinder Company

GENERAL SUPPORT AVIATION BATTALION

1-27. Division aviation brigades have one GSAB, while theater GS aviation brigades have three GSABs. The air assault division, however, has two aviation brigades, each with its own GSAB. The GSAB (figure

1-8) at all echelons consists of an HHC, FSC, command aviation company (CAC), heavy helicopter company (HvyHC), air ambulance company, ATS company, and aviation maintenance company.

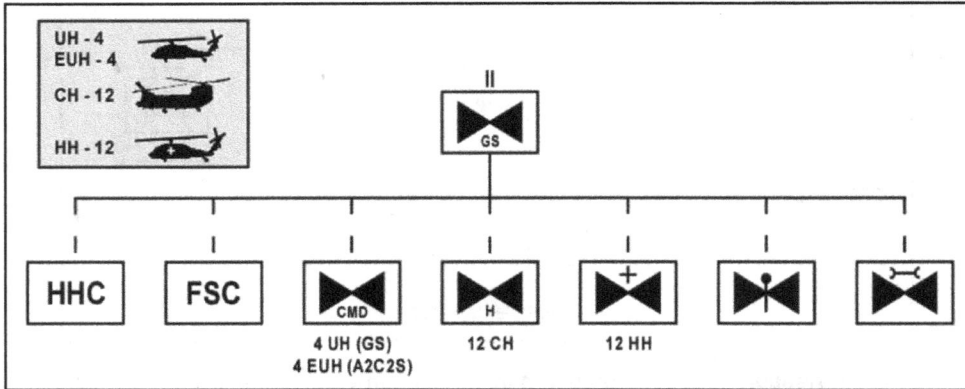

Figure 1-8. General support aviation battalion organization

HEADQUARTERS AND HEADQUARTERS COMPANY

1-28. The GSAB HHC (figure 1-9) consists of the command group, staff, company HQ section, supply section, communications/automation section, medical treatment squad, and UMT. The HHC provides personnel and equipment for C2 functions of the battalion, and security and defense of the CP. The HHC also provides the following types of support: unit-level personnel service, UMT, logistics, medical, and CBRN. Refer to chapter 4 for additional information.

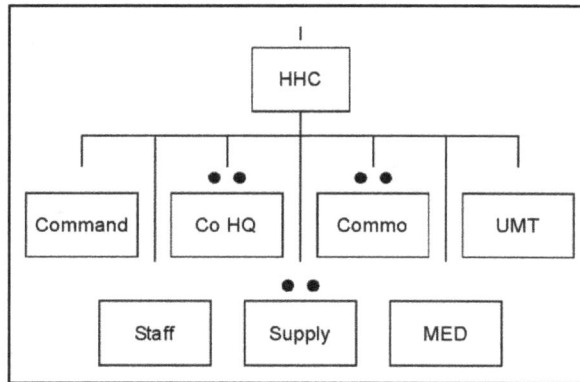

Figure 1-9. General support aviation battalion headquarters and headquarters company organization

FORWARD SUPPORT COMPANY

1-29. The GSAB FSC (figure 1-10) has a company HQ, field feeding section, distribution platoon, and ground maintenance platoon. The FSC provides field feeding, transportation, refueling, ground maintenance support, and coordinates with the ASB for additional support as required. Refer to chapter 4 for additional information.

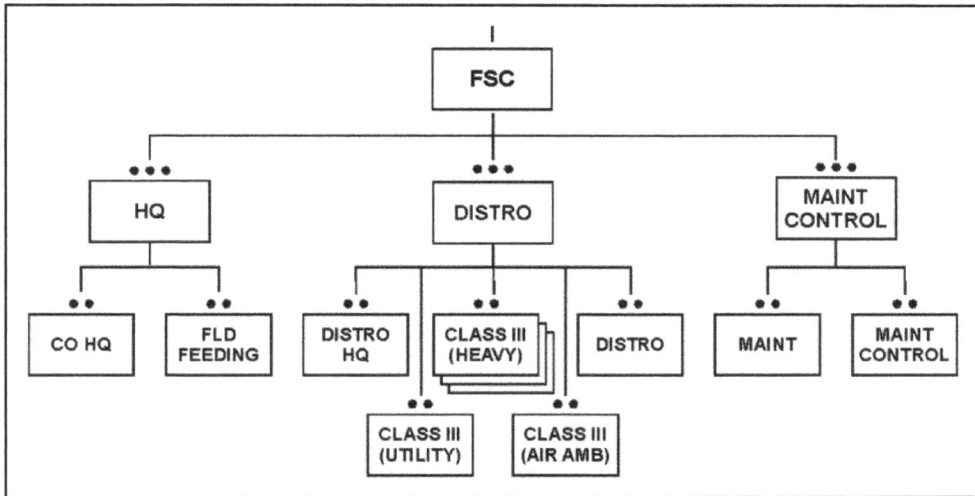

Figure 1-10. General support aviation battalion forward support company organization

COMMAND AVIATION COMPANY

1-30. The CAC (figure 1-11) consists of a HQ section, command, control, and communications (C3) platoon with four EUH-60 aircraft, and GS aviation platoon with four UH-60 aircraft.

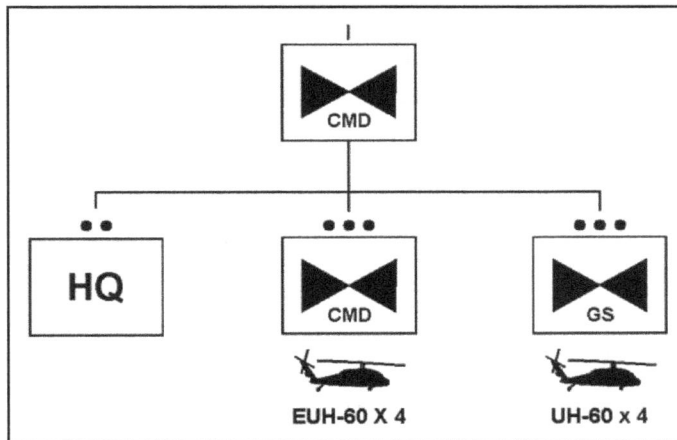

Figure 1-11. Command aviation company organization

Headquarters Section

1-31. The company's HQ section embodies the senior leadership of the company and is responsible for leading, training, and caring for all Soldiers assigned to the company. The commander, SP, SO, and TACOPS officer assigned to the HQ section are part of the company's aircrew structure.

Command, Control, and Communications Platoon

1-32. The C3 platoon's EUH-60s are equipped with A2C2S. A2C2S is the centerpiece of the maneuver commander's ability to maintain airborne BCOTM. A2C2S allows a commander access to the Army battle command system (ABCS) that provides the common operational picture (COP) and means to command maneuver forces. When utilizing A2C2S aircraft, the commander achieves maximum mobility while maintaining access to information and continuity of operations. Refer to chapter 3 for additional information on A2C2S.

General Support Aviation Platoon

1-33. The GS aviation platoon contains four UH-60 aircraft. One UH-60 is modified with a wiring modification work order (MWO) "A Kit" for an A2C2S mission equipment package. These aircraft perform the same mission tasks as the AHC with the exception of Volcano mine dispensing operations.

HEAVY HELICOPTER COMPANY

1-34. The HvyHC (figure 1-12, page 1-12) consists of a company HQ and three flight platoons with four CH-47 aircraft each.

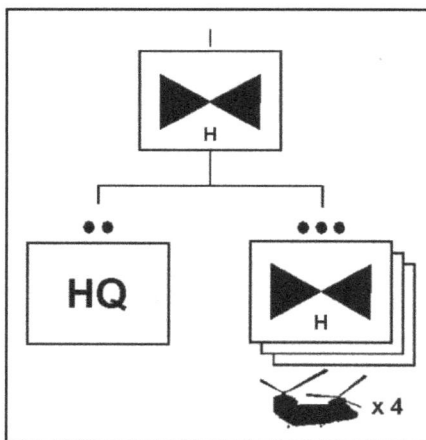

Figure 1-12. Heavy helicopter company organization

AIR AMBULANCE COMPANY

1-35. The air ambulance company (figure 1-13) consists of a company HQ and four forward support medical evacuation (MEDEVAC) teams (FSMTs). Each FSMT consists of three HH-60 aircraft. Each FSMT has its own team leader, instructor pilot (IP), and TACOPS officer to facilitate split based operations.

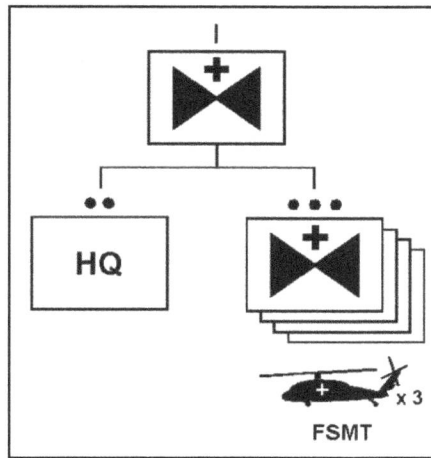

Figure 1-13. Air ambulance company organization

AIR TRAFFIC SERVICES COMPANY

1-36. The ATS company (figure 1-14, page 1-13) consists of a HQ platoon with a communication and navigation maintenance section, terminal control platoon with a tactical tower section and ground controlled approach (GCA) radar section, and an airspace information services platoon with two tactical tower teams and an airspace information center (AIC). ATS companies are not organic to theater aviation brigade GSABs within the theater aviation commands (TACs) .

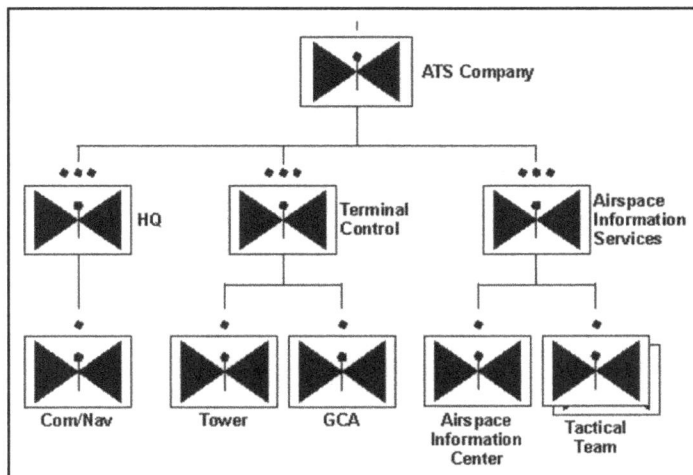

Figure 1-14. Air traffic services company organization

AVIATION MAINTENANCE COMPANY

1-37. The aviation maintenance company (figure 1-15) consists of a company HQ; production control and QA sections; aircraft maintenance platoon with UH-60 and CH-47 repair sections; and an aircraft CRP with powerplant, powertrain, structural, pneudraulics, and avionic/electrical sections providing necessary aviation unit-level field maintenance and BDAR. The aviation maintenance company provides necessary maneuver sustainment to operate autonomously throughout division AO Refer to chapter 4 for additional information.

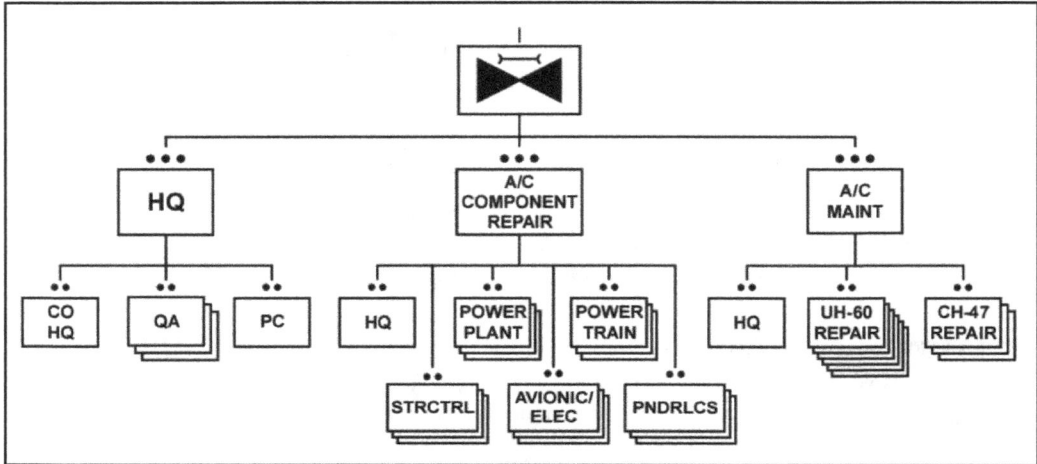

Figure 1-15. General support aviation battalion aviation maintenance company organization

Chapter 2
Command and Control

C2 is the exercise of authority and direction by a properly designated commander of assigned and attached forces. Command includes both the authority and responsibility for effectively using available resources to accomplish missions. Control regulates forces and functions that are necessary when executing the commander's intent. Refer to FM 6-0 and FM I 5-0.1 for additional information on Command and Control.

SECTION I – COMMAND AND CONTROL

COMMAND

2-1. Command at all levels is the art of motivating and directing people and organizations to accomplish missions. Command requires visualizing the current and future states of friendly and enemy forces, and formulating concepts of operations to achieve mission success. Prior to execution, the commander influences the outcome of operations by—

Contents

- Defining his intent.
- Assigning missions.
- Designating priority efforts.
- Prioritizing and allocating support and sustainment.
- Deciding the acceptable risk level.
- Placing reserves.
- Assessing needs of subordinates and seniors.
- Changing task organization.
- Changing allocation of support.
- Changing priority of sustainment.
- Changing boundaries.
- Allocating time.
- Guiding and motivating the organization toward the desired outcome.

CONTROL

2-2. Control of forces and functions aids commanders and staffs in computing requirements, allocating means, and integrating efforts. Control is necessary to determine the status of organizational effectiveness, and identify variance and correct deviations from set standards. Control permits commanders to acquire and apply the means to accomplish intent and develop specific instructions from general guidance. Ultimately, it provides commanders a means to measure, report, and correct performance. Control allows commanders freedom to operate, delegate authority, place themselves in the best position to lead, and synchronize actions throughout the operational area.

2-3. While C2 may be discussed separately for understanding, in practice it is an entity. The commander cannot command effectively without control and cannot exercise control without command. The commander uses C2 to make effective decisions, manage uncertainty of combat, employ forces efficiently, and direct successful execution of military operations. The goal of C2 is mission accomplishment, while the object of C2 is force effectiveness. The staff is the commander's most important resource to exercise C2 when he is unable to exercise it himself. Commanders exercise authority and direction through and with assistance of a C2 system.

COMMAND AND CONTROL SYSTEMS

2-4. The C2 system is defined as the facilities, equipment, communications, procedures, and personnel essential to a commander for planning, directing, and controlling operations of assigned forces.

2-5. ABCS provides unit commanders with the electronic architecture to build SA. Signal planning increases the commander's options by providing the requisite signal support systems for varying operational tempos (OPTEMPOs). These systems pass critical information at decisive times; thus, they leverage and exploit tactical success and make future operations easier. FM 3-04.111 provides additional information on ABCS. The three levels of ABCS are—

- Global Command and Control System-Army.
- Army Tactical Command and Control System (ATCCS).
- Force XXI Battle Command Brigade and Below (FBCB2).

COMMUNICATIONS

2-6. Fundamental to combat operations is accurate and rapid information reporting and the exploitation of that information. This information and the opportunities it presents are of interest to other maneuver units and higher HQ' staffs. Combat information reporting requires wide and rapid dissemination. Battalion elements frequently operate over extended distances from their controlling HQ. Communications must be redundant as well as capable to meet internal and external requirements. Long-range communications can be augmented through signal support. The key is to establish the systems before they are needed.

2-7. Operations at extended distances beyond friendly lines may require cellular, high frequency (HF), tactical satellite (TACSAT), or retransmission to maintain communications. The Aviation Mission Planning System (AMPS) provides a means of transferring information between echelons within the battalion and with the CAB.

COMMUNICATION RESPONSIBILITIES

2-8. All levels of command gain and maintain communications with necessary HQ and personnel. Communications methods and procedures should be established in unit standing operating procedures (SOPs) and practiced during battle drills and flight operations. Regardless of establishment responsibility, all units must take prompt action to restore lost communications. Methods of restoring communications should be established in the unit SOP and practiced during battle drills and daily flight operations.

COMMUNICATIONS DISRUPTION

2-9. Communications, particularly electromagnetic exchanges, are subject to disruption in even the best conditions. Disruption may result from unintentional friendly interference, intentional enemy action, equipment failure, atmospheric conditions, electromagnetic pulse, or terrain interference. To compensate for intermittent communications, the commander should—

- Provide for redundancy in means of communication.
- Ensure subordinates understand the commander's intent so they know what to do during communications interruptions.

- Avoid overloading communications systems.
- Ensure personnel follow signal security and communications security (COMSEC) practices.

OPERATIONS SECURITY

2-10. OPSEC includes measures taken to deny the enemy information about friendly forces and operations. OPSEC consists of physical security, information security, signal security, deception, and countersurveillance. Because these categories are interrelated, the commander normally chooses to employ multiple techniques to counter a threat. Commanders analyze hostile intelligence efforts and vulnerabilities, execute OPSEC countermeasures, and survey the effectiveness of countermeasures. With this information, commanders can then counter specific hostile intelligence efforts.

BATTALION COMMUNICATION NETS

BATTALION INTERNAL RADIO NETS

2-11. The battalion establishes the following internal radio nets (table 2-1) to organize and control information passed via each net:

- **Command net.** A frequency modulated (FM)-secure command net, controlled by the operations staff officer (S-3), is used for battalion C2. As a rule, only commanders, XOs, or S-3s communicate on the net. The command net is used by commanders for sending and receiving critical information on current operations.
- **Operations and intelligence (O&I) net.** The intelligence staff officer (S-2) controls the O&I net. Routine O&I reports are sent using this net; it functions as a surveillance net when required. Brigade or subordinate commanders do not normally monitor the O&I net. This net is used for details and discussion leading to analysis. That analysis, when completed, is relayed to the appropriate commander. The unit XO ensures the analysis is completed and relayed in a timely manner by appropriate means. Subordinate elements may monitor the O&I net to develop SA of critical support requirements and problems.
- **Administrative and logistics (A&L) net.** This net is controlled by the personnel staff officer (S-1) and logistics staff officer (S-4) and is used for A&L traffic. Battalion or subordinate commanders do not normally monitor the A&L net.

Table 2-1. Battalion internal radio networks

Network	Battalion						Artillery	Company
Station	CMD FM	CMD HF (AM)	O&I FM	A&L FM	AVN UHF	FS FM	FS (DIV)	UHF/VHF/ FM
Command Group	X		A	A		X	X	
TAC CP	N		X			X		
Battalion Detachments	X	X		X	X		X	
Co CPs	N		X	O/A		O/A		N
Platoons							A	A
1SG				X				A
FARP	X			X				
N—Network control station X—Enter network A—Enter network as required		O—Monitor 1SG—first sergeant AM—amplitude modulated TAC CP—tactical command post				FS—fire support UHF—ultra high frequency VHF—very high frequency		

2-12. The battalion commander communicates with his company commanders on the battalion command net, typically FM secure; however, VHF and UHF secure radios may be used. The main CP may use the FM-secure radio to communicate with battalion trains and FARP elements through the battalion A&L net. Battalion elements may also communicate with the FARP on the command net; at a minimum, FARPs should monitor the command net. If the A&L net is not active, the O&I net is an alternative to communicate A&L requirements.

BATTALION EXTERNAL RADIO NETS

2-13. The battalion maintains command and O&I networks with the higher HQ main CP. Another net established for mission specific use is the combat aviation net (CAN). The CAN is used when an air assault task force (AATF) is formed. A unique CAN is created allowing commanders from different units to communicate on a common network.

2-14. Ground forces involved in air assault operations use two primary nets to include—

- **Combat aviation net.** Two CAN nets are assigned. The primary CAN is CAN1, the alternate is CAN2. CAN2 is reserved as an air assault operation antijamming net. The primary purpose for the CAN net is providing a common net for communications among the air assault task force commander (AATFC), ground tactical commander (GTC), air mission commander (AMC), and pickup zone control (PZCO). Additionally, terminal guidance may be transmitted from pickup zone (PZ) and LZ control to individual flight leads, when required.
- **PZ control net.** The primary purpose of a PZ control net is to facilitate ground element communications in staging the PZ, executing "bump" or straggler control plan, and disseminating mission-critical changes related to the air assault operation. The battalion A&L will be used for PZ control. On brigade-level operations using a single PZ for multiple battalions, the last lifted infantry battalion's A&L will be used for PZ control. All lifted units must enter the PZ control net 30 minutes prior to the unit's PZ time. Additionally, depending on PZ formation, certain chalks must monitor the PZ control net. For operations with planned radio listening silence, face-to-face coordination between the lifted unit and PZCO is mandatory. Prior to exiting the PZ control net and boarding the aircraft, lifted units will report "PZ clean" to PZ control. PZ control responds with "permission to exit the net."

2-15. The battalion main CP is responsible for maintaining communications with higher, adjacent, and subordinate units. When deployed, the battalion TAC CP may communicate directly with these units. If the situation or terrain prohibits direct contact by the TAC CP, the main CP may act as a communications relay. When airborne, the battalion commander may communicate directly with higher HQ, adjacent units, and subordinate elements via FM-secure radio. The main CP and TAC CP, if deployed, operate the battalion command and O&I nets. These elements also maintain communication with higher HQ on their command O&I and A&L nets.

2-16. Due to distance factors involved, HF radios or satellite communications (SATCOM) are often used to maintain contact with higher HQ. Other external radio nets may be established through supporting elements such as the field artillery (FA) Tactical Fire Direction System (TACFIRE), AC2, and forces participating in air assault operations. Table 2-2, page 2-5, illustrates typical external radio networks for the battalion.

Table 2-2. Battalion external radio networks

Division Control						
Station/Network	*DIV CM FM*	*DIV AO CMD FM*	*DIV CMD AM*	*DIV O&I FM*	*DIV Area Common User*	*DIV A2C2 FM*
Command Group*	X	X^1		X	X^3	
TAC CP*	X^2	X^2	X	X^2	X^3	X^3
Brigade (BDE) Control						
Station/Network	*BDE CMD*	*BDE O&I FM*	*BDE A&L FM*	*DIV Area Common User*	*AVN BDE UHF*	
Command Group*	X	O/A	A	X	X	
TAC CP*	X^2	X				
X—Enter network A—Enter network as required O—Monitor			1—When performing rear operations 2—When deployed; otherwise, main CP 3—Always active *—Enter A2C2 network as required			

SECTION II – BATTALION COMMAND AND CONTROL

2-17. CPs serve the C2 needs of the commander and staff. The dynamics of the operational environment require the highest level of organizational and operational efficiency within every CP. Battalion C2 elements and facilities are positioned according to the situation and include—

- Command group.
- Main CP.
- TAC CP.

BATTALION COMMAND GROUP

2-18. The battalion command group consists of the battalion commander and representatives from battalion staff and supporting units the commander chooses. At a minimum, this includes the S-3, S-2 representative, and air liaison officer (ALO), if available. The command group may operate from ground vehicles or an aircraft. It is not a command facility per se, but a grouping of critical decision makers that may operate separately from the main CP or TAC CP periodically. The command group may deploy when personal observation or presence is necessary to accomplish the mission.

COMMANDER

2-19. The commander's main concerns are accomplishing the mission and taking care of Soldiers. The commander delegates authority and fosters an organizational climate of mutual trust, cooperation, and teamwork. The commander leads the battalion and mentors, guides, trains, and inspires leaders and Soldiers. A commander must also have an in-depth knowledge of enemy forces and how they fight and possess the ability to use terrain to the unit's advantage.

2-20. The battalion commander must understand the impact of the unit's actions and actions of the Soldiers within the operational environment. The battalion commander relies on staff and subordinate commanders to advise and assist in planning and supervising operations. The commander must understand the staff's capabilities and limitations and train them to execute operational concepts during his absence. The commander focuses on key aspects of employing the battalion to include—

- Commanding the organization through the tenants of mission command.
- Positioning to best view and influence the operational environment and gain SA.
- Providing planning guidance and commander's intent in accordance with his operational environment visualization.

- Making recommendations to the supported commander on best employment of the battalion.
- Determining acceptable risk for mission accomplishment and delegating appropriate risk levels to subordinates through the composite risk management (CRM) process.
- Instituting necessary training for Soldiers in media operations; rules of engagement (ROE); rules of interaction (ROI); PR; and survival, evasion, resistance, and escape (SERE).

Commander's Location

2-21. When not in battle, the battalion commander normally operates from the vicinity of the main CP. During battle, the commander operates from a position to best make decisions that are necessary to influence the successful outcome of the mission. The commander must be in a position to affect operations while maintaining communications with higher, lower, and adjacent units. The best location for the commander may be the main CP or TAC CP, or forward with the battle. This decision is based on mission, enemy, terrain and weather, troops and support available, time available, and civil considerations (METT-TC) as well as the commander's assessment of personal presence essential to mission accomplishment. Even as digital linkages improve the ability to see the battle, at times there may be no better option than personal presence.

EXECUTIVE OFFICER

2-22. The XO is second in command and principal assistant to the commander. The scope of XO duties are often tailored by requirements of the commander; however, as a general rule, the XO directs, supervises, and ensures coordination of staff work and logistics except in those specific areas reserved by the battalion commander. During combat operations, the XO is generally positioned in the main CP directing and coordinating the staff. As staff coordinator and supervisor, the XO—

- Is responsible for execution of staff tasks and coordinates staff efforts for the orders process.
- Monitors unit status and mission execution to ensure conformity to commander's intent and scheme of maneuver.
- Assesses/understands timely information updates and disseminates decisions.
- Transmits the commander's decisions to the staff and subordinate commanders, when applicable. Staff members can deal directly with the commander; however, they are obligated to inform the XO of the commander's instructions or requirements.
- Establishes and monitors liaison and liaison activities.
- Directs main CP operations.
- Is responsible for planning and integrating logistics into the operational plan. The XO normally delegates responsibility for planning to the battalion S-4.
- Supervises logistics operations.
- Serves as the materiel readiness officer.

COMMAND SERGEANT MAJOR

2-23. The command sergeant major (CSM) is the commander's primary advisor concerning enlisted Soldiers and acts in the name of the commander in other duties as directed. The CSM focuses attention on functions critical to success of the operation. The CSM assists the commander in the following ways:

- Provides advice to the commander and staff on matters pertaining to enlisted Soldiers.
- Monitors food service and other logistics operations.
- Conducts informal investigations.
- Assists in controlling battalion movements.
- May lead the battalion advance or quartering party during a major movement in coordination with the HHC commander.
- Establishes guidelines and oversees base force protection operations.
- Monitors subordinate unit morale.

- Provides recommendations and expedites procurement and preparation of enlisted replacements for subordinate units.
- Oversees protection measures in fixed-base operations.

STAFF RESPONSIBILITIES

Reduction of Demands on the Commander's Time

2-24. The staff reduces demands on the commander's time by—
- Obtaining, analyzing, and providing information.
- Anticipating the situation.
- Making recommendations. The staff does not ask the commander for solutions; it presents issues, offers courses of action (COAs), and recommends one of those COAs.
- Preparing plans and orders.
- Supervising the execution of orders.
- Coordinating the operation.

Maintains the Common Operational Picture

2-25. The staff provides the commander with an accurate picture of the area of operations (AO). Delays in receiving or disseminating critical information adversely affects the entire operation. The staff must identify key indicators and push for quick and accurate reports from both subordinate and higher HQ. Information flow—both horizontally and vertically—must be on a priority basis. Operational conditions dictate priorities.

Running Estimates

2-26. Running estimates may be informal at battalion level and below; however, they must address operational environment activity, project COAs, and predict results. Careful IPB, important enemy indicator selection, and contingency plan development facilitate estimates and allow for timely response. The XO, who ensures the staff maintains a proper perspective, is the key person in this process.

2-27. A running estimate based on new information is continuously updated as the operation proceeds (see FM 6-0). This staff technique supports the commander's vision and decisionmaking. Staffs continuously update their conclusions and recommendations based on the impact of new facts. Staff sections provide these updated conclusions and recommendations to the commander as required (see FM 5-0). Normally, the coordinating staff provides running estimates during the conduct of operations using personnel, intelligence, operations, and logistics estimates.

Staff Communications with the Commander

2-28. Information flow is critical. For some information, the commander must be informed immediately. It is essential the commander provide the staff with guidance on the types of information he considers critical, typically through the commander's critical intelligence requirements (CCIR). Many commanders emphasize the CCIR by posting them in the main CP and disseminating to all Soldiers.

2-29. Staff members must provide the commander with critical, concise, accurate information and coordinate with higher and lateral units to provide the commander with their running estimates. The XO is key in establishing guidance that ensures briefs do just that and not burden the commander with time-consuming, lengthy, or meandering discussions. Critical information is communicated to the commander on a priority basis set by command guidance. Established briefings to the commander are open and frank but follow a set agenda.

BATTALION SECTIONS

Human Resource Section

Personnel Staff Officer

2-30. The S-1 has coordinating responsibility for finance, religious activities, public affairs, and legal services support for the unit. The S-1 is normally collocated with the S-4 in the main CP. The S-1 and S-4 must cross train enabling them to conduct continuous operations. The S-1 is responsible for all matters concerning human resources including personnel readiness and services. The S-1 also—

- Manages personnel strength and replacement.
- Works with the flight surgeon to plan health services.
- Coordinates morale support activities and legal, financial, and postal services.
- Maintains the awards program.
- Oversees the administration of discipline, law, and order with the provost marshal (if present) and brigade judge advocate.
- Provides casualty operations management.

Personnel Estimate

2-31. The personnel estimate is prepared by the S-1 and focuses on critical personnel aspects including:

- Personnel readiness.
- Leave, school, and temporary duty (TDY) status.
- Casualty status.
- Medical estimate in conjunction with the medical operations officer (including Level I, II, and III locations).
- Personnel replacement status.

Chaplain

2-32. The chaplain provides religious support to all personnel assigned or attached to the battalion. The chaplain advises the commander on religious, morale, and Soldier welfare issues, and establishes liaison with UMTs of higher and adjacent units. The chaplain and chaplain's assistant compose the UMT, which usually operates from the same location as the S-1.

Flight Surgeon

2-33. The flight surgeon advises and assists commanders on matters concerning the medical condition of the command to include preventive, curative, and restorative care. The flight surgeon periodically flies with aircrews to monitor medical and environmental factors affecting crew readiness. The flight surgeon is responsible for conducting flight physicals for unit personnel. The flight surgeon determines requirements for requisition, procurement, storage, maintenance, distribution, management, and documentation of medical equipment and supplies, and operates the battalion aid station (BAS), usually in the assembly area (AA).

Intelligence Section

2-34. The S-2 section provides combat intelligence, which includes collecting and processing information. The S-2 section prepares intelligence collection plans, receives and analyzes operational environment information, disseminates intelligence products, and provides up-to-date intelligence information that assists in planning for and coordinating close and rear battle operations.

2-35. The S-2 staff section also performs the following functions:

- Facilitates the IPB process.
- Participates in development of the decision support template.

- Coordinates intelligence collection activities.
- Maintains classified messages.
- Updates the commander and staff frequently on enemy situation and trends.
- Maintains isolated personnel reports (ISOPREPs).
- Works closely with the commander and S-3 ensuring updated intelligence information is used to plan battalion operations.
- Develops the ISR plan with the S-3.
- Performs terrain analysis.

Intelligence Staff Officer

2-36. The S-2 assists the S-3 in matters concerning ISR. The S-2 provides current information and analyzed intelligence of tactical value concerning terrain, weather, and the enemy. This intelligence helps to facilitate planning and execution of combat operations.

Intelligence Estimate

2-37. The intelligence estimate is prepared by the S-2 and may focus on critical elements including:
- Terrain analysis/hazards map/digital photographs.
- Composition and disposition of enemy forces.
- Enemy capabilities and limitations.
- Incident overlays, significant activities, and/or spot reports (SPOTREPs).
- Pattern analysis of enemy activity to include direct fire engagements, indirect fire engagements, or improvised explosive devices (IEDs).
- Event templates based on enemy patterns.
- Populace and town assessments.
- Key dates and holidays impacting or influencing operations.
- Intelligence requirements.
- Status of collection assets.
- Battle damage assessment (BDA).

Operations Section

2-38. The S-3 section maintains routine reporting, coordinates activities of liaison personnel, and is always planning ahead. The S-3 ensures procedures are in place to resolve complexities posed by different communications systems, ATCCS, and connectivity with aircraft. The S-3 maintains close coordination with the S-4 and S-1 for logistics and personnel statuses.

Operations Staff Officer

2-39. The S-3 is responsible for matters pertaining to operational employment, training, and mission execution of battalion and supporting elements. The S-3 section produces orders for battalion operations including recovery of personnel. The S-3 monitors the battle, ensures necessary assets are in place when and where required, develops the ISR plan, and anticipates developing situations.

Operations Estimate

2-40. The operations estimate focuses on key aspects affecting current or future operations. It is prepared by the S-3 and may include—
- Task organization of internal and supported units.
- Graphic control measures.
- Locations and graphic control measures of supported units.
- Combat power/projections.

- Supported unit's significant activities.
- Future operations of supported units.
- ISR plan.
- Mission statement and commander's intent (two levels up and lateral supported units).
- Battle rhythm/fighter management cycles.
- Synchronization matrix.
- Liaison officer (LNO) status/reports.

Flight Operations Officer

2-41. Although not a TOE position, the commander may designate a battalion flight operations officer. Noncommissioned officers (NCOs) and flight operations specialists assist the flight operations officer. Flight operations officer responsibilities include—

- Monitoring and briefing applicable portions of special instructions (SPINS) and the air tasking order (ATO) relevant to operations.
- Providing relevant AC2 control measures to mission aircrews.
- Maintaining AC2 overlay.
- Establishing and maintaining the flight following net (air traffic control [ATC] network) for unit aircraft, when required.
- Coordinating ATS requirements.
- Maintaining the aircrew information reading file.
- Maintaining the flying hour program and individual flight record folders.

Tactical Operations Officer

2-42. The TACOPS officer is the primary advisor to the commander and staff on the tactical employment of aircraft. He should be included in all aviation mission planning. The TACOPS officer can serve as the other crewmember for the battalion commander or S-3. Other responsibilities include, but are not limited to—

- Conducting the ASE/EW portion of the risk management process.
- Integrating the unit's operational plan into the theater airspace structure.
- Assisting with development of unit tactics, techniques, and procedures (TTP).
- Managing the organization's PR program.
- Assisting in the military decisionmaking process (MDMP), close air support (CAS), and FS planning.

Aviation Liaison Team

2-43. Liaison teams from the S-3's liaison element represent the battalion at the HQ of another unit to facilitate coordination and communication between the two units. Much of the air-ground coordination at BCT level is handled by the brigade aviation element (BAE) at the respective BCT HQ. The liaison team and BAE are not synonymous and perform two unique and different functions. For more information on operations, refer to training circular (TC) 1-400.

2-44. Teams are headed by an experienced LNO who must be well versed in all aspects of aviation operations. The team is expected to act as a cell in planning and battle tracking, so operations can continue in the absence of the LNO. Liaison teams should be certified by the battalion through a standard process before deploying to a supported unit.

2-45. LNOs participate in the supported unit's MDMP to ensure aviation is effectively integrated into planning. LNOs ensure supportability of the COA and relay a clear task and purpose to the parent unit. Battalion commanders must empower LNOs to act on their behalf and ensure liaison teams are fully supported. In return, commanders expect LNOs to maintain positive two-way communication and not commit assets or approve changes to a plan without coordinating with the battalion S-3 or commander.

2-46. LNOs provide the supported unit with the following:

- Capabilities, limitations, and tactical employment of aviation and ATS assets.
- Assistance in preparing aviation estimates, plans, orders, and reports.
- Assistance in planning aviation missions.
- Coordination with airspace users and the higher AC2 element for airspace management.
- Operational status of aviation assets and its effects on the supported unit's mission.
- Informing appropriate aviation units of current and possible future operations.
- Continuous communications with aviation units supporting the ground unit.

2-47. Liaison teams must have access to current battalion status information to provide the most accurate picture of aviation capabilities. Constant communication with the parent unit is essential for updates on aircraft maintenance, aircrew, and FARP status.

2-48. Liaison teams must be properly equipped and manned to support 24-hour operations. Minimum equipment includes—

- Compatible automation equipment to provide connectivity between supported unit and battalion HQ.
- Necessary vehicles and equipment required to operate on the move.
- Two Single Channel Ground and Airborne Radio System (SINCGARS) radios and supporting antennas/equipment to monitor command nets and communicate with aviation units.
- Map of the AO with supporting battle-tracking tools and equipment.
- Aviation FMs, SOPs, charts (equipment weights), and checklists (movement tables) to assist in aviation planning and integration.

Safety Officer

2-49. The SO is the commander's principal assistant during the risk management process and monitors all battalion operations to identify and address potential hazards. Because of the nature of his duties, the SO has a direct line of communication with the commander. The SO recommends actions that permit mission accomplishment in the safest manner possible. The SO is responsible to the flight operations officer for safety contents of the reading files.

Standardization Instructor Pilot

2-50. The SP is a primary advisor to the commander for the standardization program. The SP develops, integrates, implements, monitors, and manages the aircrew training and standardization programs. He also advises, as required, on the crew selection process and employment of aircraft systems, sensors, and weapons. The SP acts as coordinating staff officer for standardization of reading files. He is also a principal trainer and peer leader for subordinate unit IPs.

Chemical Officer

2-51. The chemical officer advises the commander on CBRN operations, decontamination, smoke, obscurants, and flame. The chemical officer works directly for the S-3 and is responsible for integrating CBRN into all aspects of operations. The chemical officer may have other S-3 section responsibilities and can act as an assistant S-3 or battle captain when directed.

Logistics Section

2-52. The S-4 section provides supervision and coordination of food service, supply, transportation, and maintenance support for the battalion. The battalion S-4 is responsible for the logistics estimate. The FSC and aviation maintenance company commander assist the S-4 in development of key information to include—

- Maintenance status (aircraft, vehicles, unmanned aircraft systems [UAS], and equipment).
- Classes of supply status and forecasts.

- Logistics synchronization matrix.
- Resupply schedule.
- FARP status and locations.

Logistics Staff Officer

2-53. The battalion S-4, as the battalion's logistics planner, coordinates with companies concerning the status of maintenance, equipment, and supplies. The S-4 coordinates with supporting units and higher HQ staffs ensuring logistics support is continuous.

Aviation Materiel Officer

2-54. The aviation materiel officer (AMO) works with the S-4 and is an advisor to the battalion commander and staff for aviation materiel issues. The AMO reviews reports and makes recommendations on aviation logistics and maintenance issues. The AMO ensures close coordination with the aviation maintenance company and supporting ASB commanders and is responsible to the flight operations officer for aviation maintenance contents of the reading files.

Command, Control, Communications, and Computer Operations Staff Officer

2-55. The command, control, communications, and computer operations (C4OPS) staff officer (S-6) advises the commander on signal matters, CP location, signal facilities, and best use of signal assets. The S-6 section plans for, coordinates, and oversees employment of communications systems and performs unit-level maintenance on ground radio and field wire communications equipment. This section installs, operates, and maintains the battalion's radio retransmission site. The S-6 monitors the maintenance status of battalion signal equipment, coordinates preparation and distribution of the signal operating instructions (SOI), and supervises COMSEC accounting activities. Included in the above signal responsibilities are supervision of electronic mail on both classified and unclassified nets and the unit local area network (LAN).

HEADQUARTERS AND HEADQUARTERS COMPANY HEADQUARTERS ELEMENT

2-56. The company command section consists of the commander and first sergeant (1SG). They are responsible for providing control and supervision of operations within the support area, and support for battalion staff and organic operational elements.

Commander

2-57. The commander's responsibilities include leadership, discipline, tactical employment training, administration, personnel management, supply, and communications activities. These responsibilities require the commander to understand the capabilities of the unit's Soldiers and equipment and know how to employ them to the best tactical advantage. At the same time, the commander must be well versed in threat organizations and doctrine.

2-58. The commander's mission involves more than company support; he is instrumental in providing support for the entire organization. Ultimately, he must know how to exercise the art and science of battle command effectively and decisively. The commander must be flexible, using sound judgment to make correct decisions quickly and timely based on the higher commander's intent and tactical situation. He must be able to visualize the operational environment, describe situations and operations, and direct subordinate leaders by using clear and complete combat orders.

First Sergeant

2-59. The 1SG is the company senior NCO and usually its most experienced Soldier. He is the commander's primary tactical advisor and an expert in individual and NCO skills. The 1SG enforces unit discipline and is the company's primary sustainment operator. He helps the commander plan, coordinate, and supervise logistics activities supporting the tactical mission. The 1SG operates where the commander directs him or his duties require him. The 1SG also assists the commander in the following ways:

- Executes and supervises routine operations that may include—
    - Enforcing tactical standing operating procedures (TACSOPs).
    - Coordinating and reporting personnel and administrative actions.
    - Supervising supply, maintenance, communications, and field hygiene operations.
- Implements the local security plan.
- Supervises, inspects, and/or observes all matters designated by the commander.
- Plans, rehearses, and supervises key logistics actions supporting the tactical mission. These activities include—
    - Resupplying classes I, III, and V products and materiels.
    - Maintenance and recovery.
    - Medical treatment and evacuation.
    - Processing replacement/return to duty.
- Provides recommendations and expedites procurement and preparation of enlisted replacements for the company.
- Serves as quartering party noncommissioned officer in charge (NCOIC) when necessary.
- Monitors NCO development, promotions, and assignments. This includes assessment of the company's battle focused Soldier and NCO leader training programs.
- Identifies, plans, and assesses Soldier performance on training tasks that support collective (unit) tasks on the mission essential task list (METL).

Supply Sergeant

2-60. The supply sergeant coordinates all supply requirements and actions with the 1SG and S-4. He requests, receives, issues, stores, maintains, and turns in supplies and equipment for the company. Usually, the supply sergeant is located with the HHC CP or near the ASB support area. The supply sergeant communicates with the HHC using the task force (TF) A&L radio net or FBCB2. The supply sergeant's specific responsibilities include—

- Managing the HHC cargo truck(s) and water trailer, and supervising the supply clerk/armorer.
- Monitoring unit activities and/or the tactical situation.
- Anticipating and reporting logistics requirements.
- Coordinating unit logistics requests and monitoring their status.
- Coordinating and supervising organization of the HHC logistics package (LOGPAC).

Human Resources Specialist

2-61. The human resources specialist performs personnel and administrative functions in support of the company. He advises the commander and members of the unit on personnel matters. He also prepares military and nonmilitary correspondence, messages, recurring and special reports, requisition forms, regulations, directives, SOPs, and similar material.

Chemical, Biological, Radiological, and Nuclear Noncommissioned Officer

2-62. The CBRN NCO assists and advises the HHC commander in planning for and conducting operations in a CBRN environment. He is usually located with the HHC CP. The CBRN NCO plans, conducts, and/or supervises CBRN defense training, covering such areas as decontamination procedures and use and maintenance of CBRN-related equipment. The CBRN NCO's specific duties include—

- Assisting the commander in developing HHC operational exposure guidance in accordance with higher HQ guidance.
- Making recommendations to the commander on CBRN surveys and/or monitoring, decontamination, and smoke support requirements.

- Requisitioning CBRN-specific equipment and supply items.
- Assisting the commander in developing and implementing the unit CBRN training program.
- Inspecting HHC elements to ensure CBRN preparedness.
- Processing and disseminating information on threat and friendly CBRN capabilities and activities including attacks.
- Advising the commander on contamination avoidance measures.
- Coordinating, monitoring, and supervising decontamination operations.
- Providing recommendations to the commander on mission-oriented protective posture (MOPP) levels.

Armorer

2-63. The armorer performs organizational maintenance on HHC small arms. He is also responsible for evacuating weapons to the DS maintenance unit as needed. In addition, he usually assists the supply sergeant.

TACTICAL COMMAND POST

2-64. The TAC CP is established as a temporary C2 organization that directly assists the commander in controlling current operations. This CP must be able to communicate with higher HQ, adjacent units, employed subordinate units, and the main CP. The TAC CP is equipped with communications equipment and ABCS that support the WFF, including intelligence, movement and maneuver, and FS. It monitors the battalion command and its O&I nets as well as higher HQ command and its O&I nets. FM 3-04.111 and FMI 5-0.1 provide additional information on CPs. The TAC CP assists the commander in controlling current operations by—

- Maintaining the COP and assisting in developing SU.
- Developing combat intelligence of immediate interest to the commander.
- Maneuvering forces.
- Controlling and coordinating FS.
- Coordinating with adjacent units and forward air defense (AD) elements.
- Serving as the main CP in the event the main CP is destroyed or unable to function.
- Monitoring and communicating sustainment requirements, primarily Classes III and V, to the main CP.

2-65. The TAC CP is small in size and electronic signature to facilitate security and rapid, frequent displacement. Its organization layout, personnel, and equipment must be described in the unit SOP. The TAC CP section must be augmented to operate on a continuous basis.

2-66. The TAC CP is composed of designated personnel from the appropriate staff sections and the responsibility of the S-3 section. TAC CP personnel may also include—

- SP, TACOPS officer, and SO.
- S-2, fire support officer (FSO), ALO, engineer, and civil affairs staff officer (S-9), if available.
- Representatives from the logistics cell.

2-67. METT-TC may dictate an effective TAC CP operate from a C2-equipped UH-60. In this situation, the number of personnel must be reduced.

MAIN COMMAND POST

2-68. The main CP is a C2 facility that contains the portion of the battalion HQ in which the majority of planning, analysis, and coordination occurs (FMI 5-0.1). It serves as the synchronization point for the entire operation. The main CP has a broader and more future-oriented focus than the TAC CP. Led by the XO, the main CP focuses on controlling and synchronizing ongoing shaping operations, assisting the commander and TAC CP in execution of the decisive operation, and planning future operations. The main

CP maintains the COP by receiving information from the TAC CP and higher, lower, and adjacent units. The main CP controls current operations when the TAC CP is not employed. FM 3-04.111 and FMI 5-0.1 provide additional information on CPs.

2-69. Main CP personnel consist of personal, coordinating, and special staff. This workforce may include the S-2, S-3, S-4, and S-6. It may also include the UMT, flight surgeon with medical treatment teams, battalion SO, battalion standardization officer, and HHC HQ elements. Additionally, FSC personnel locate in the main CP as required to facilitate FARP and other logistic requirements.

2-70. The commander operates from the main CP when not operating from the TAC CP, command vehicle, or an aircraft. The main CP is usually organized into the operations cell and plans cell. The operations cell usually functions in shifts ensuring 24-hour ability; the plans cell may or may not operate on a 24-hour cycle.

OPERATIONS CELL

2-71. The operations cell includes the following functional positions.

Battle Captain

2-72. The battle captain is usually the most experienced operations officer other than the S-3. He continuously monitors operations ensuring proper personnel are available for the mission at hand. He does not command the battle but performs battle tracking and makes operational decisions within assigned responsibilities. Each operations cell must have two to three battle captains to maintain 24-hour operations.

Medical Operations Cell

2-73. The MOC provides assistance in planning and coordination for air ambulance employment and utilization. The MOC consists of a medical service corps officer and NCO who provide assistance with synchronization of the air and ground evacuation plan. The medical service corps officer and NCO also manage and distribute information from medical units and surgeon cells of higher echelons regarding medical treatment facility (MTF) locations and status, evacuation routes, casualty collection points (CCPs), and ambulance exchange points. This information assists in developing a medical COP and medical SA. The MOC also performs the following functions:

- Establishes flight procedures specific to MEDEVAC missions including special routes or corridors as well as procedures for escort aircraft link-up.
- Facilitates MEDEVAC briefing and launch procedures ensuring 24-hour access to approval authorities is available for high and extremely high risk missions.
- Provides planning, integration, operational support, communication, and reporting of MEDEVAC assets in the movement of casualties, blood, biologicals, and health care providers in theater.
- Assists in the synchronization of medical logistic support requirements to increase efficiency and effectiveness of the evacuation system.
- Assists with MEDEVAC-related MDMP/IPB and map overlay requirements supporting the aviation brigade/battalion CP operations.
- Coordinates 24-hour MEDEVAC operations support within the main CP.

Noncommissioned Officer In Charge

2-74. The operations NCO is normally the NCOIC and responsible for—
- Moving, setting up, and maintaining the physical functioning of the main CP.
- Shift schedules and organization within the main CP.
- Other functions as assigned.

Operations Noncommissioned Officer

2-75. S-3 NCOs and other assigned personnel assist the NCOIC in support of main CP functions. Other areas of responsibility may include—

- Maintaining unit status.
- Receiving and processing reports.
- Keeping the unit's journal.

Intelligence Personnel

2-76. The S-2, S-2 NCO, and intelligence analysts are responsible for all intelligence functions to include—

- Alerting the commander, XO, or S-3 to situations meeting established CCIR.
- Receiving incoming tactical reports.
- Processing intelligence information.
- Assisting in moving, setting up, and maintaining the physical functioning of the main CP.

Logistics Personnel

2-77. The logistics cell is composed mostly of the S-1 and S-4 sections and representatives from attached sustainment elements. The logistics cell—

- Monitors and assists in C2 of sustainment assets by maintaining contact and coordination with higher and adjacent units, while continuously updating the personnel and logistics situation.
- Maintains SA and SU ensuring sustainment elements are not adversely affected by enemy actions, friendly movements, or ongoing operations.
- Analyzes and disseminates sustainment information, maintains the sustainment situation map, and requests and synchronizes sustainment as required.
- Ensures reports are submitted and received on time.
- Plans for future operations in synchronization with the plans cell to ensure sustainment is integrated into the mission effort.

Radio Telephone Operators

2-78. Radio telephone operators (RTOs) are critical links in the C2 structure. They often use radio headsets, answer telephones, and operate computer consoles. As such, they may be the only people who hear transmissions or see a critical piece of information. They must be well aware of the operation so they can alert the leadership of any situation that might require their attention. RTOs cannot assume all calls, information, and reports they monitor are also monitored or seen by the main CP at large.

PLANS CELL

2-79. The plans cell, due to its personnel-intensive nature, is activated as required. Normally, the plans cell chief is the senior S-3 representative. It consists of the following personnel:

- Primary staff.
- TACOPS officer.
- Attached unit representatives.

MAIN COMMAND POST FUNCTIONS

2-80. The main CP coordinates, directs, and controls operations and accomplishes planning for future operations. The main CP—

- Maintains communications with subordinate, higher, and adjacent units.
- Provides information and assistance to the commander and subordinate commanders.

- Operates on a 24-hour basis.
- Continuously conducts future planning.
- Maintains a continuous estimate of the situation.
- Maintains SA across Army WFF.
- Maintains status of the reserve.
- Receives, evaluates, and processes tactical information from subordinate units and higher HQ.
- Maintains maps graphically depicting friendly, enemy, and noncombatant situations.
- Maintains journals.
- Validates and evaluates intelligence of interest to the commander.
- Coordinates airspace C2 and AD operations.
- Relays instructions to subordinate units.
- Coordinates maneuver, combat support, and sustainment requirements.
- Coordinates terrain management for C2 facilities.
- Maintains aircraft, support, and sustainment capabilities and status.
- Tracks and logs combat losses.
- Submits reports to higher HQ.
- Makes recommendations to the commander.
- Prepares and issues fragmentary orders (FRAGOs), operation orders (OPORDs), operation plans (OPLANs), intelligence summaries, intelligence reports (INTREPs), and situation reports (SITREPs).

MAIN COMMAND POST SITE SELECTION

2-81. The most important considerations for selecting any CP site are security and communications with higher, subordinate, and adjacent HQ. Range of enemy weapon systems, accessibility to adequate entry and departure routes, cover, concealment, drainage, and space for dispersing are other considerations. An adequate LZ should be nearby. The S-3 selects the general location of the CP, while the HHC commander and S-6 normally select the exact location. When selecting the general location of the CP, the S-3 should also select at least one alternate site in the event the primary site proves inadequate.

2-82. The HHC commander, along with his organic assets, must integrate various weapons systems into the security plan based on the task organization. Given the number of personnel and vehicles in an area, the HHC commander must understand command relationships and plan accordingly for their support. It is important for attached elements to understand their relationship to the HHC. The element or staff section may work for the battalion commander or S-3 when DS or attached; however, they also assist the HHC commander in support and defense of the area. Generally, these elements coordinate with the commander for integration into the security plan and positioning and sustainment of the CP. They must keep the HHC 1SG informed of their administrative/personnel status at all times.

2-83. Other important considerations for main CP selection include—

- **During offensive operations,** the main CP should be well forward. In fast-moving operations, the main CP may have to operate on the move. Staff coordination and communications are usually degraded when CPs are moving; thus, CPs must train to operate while moving.
- **During defensive operations,** the main CP normally locates farther to the rear minimizing its vulnerability. The exact location depends on the enemy, terrain, road network, and ability to communicate.
- **During urban operations,** the main CP may set up in built-up areas. Barns, garages, and warehouses minimize the need for detailed camouflage. Basements offer protection from enemy fires. Built-up areas also reduce infrared (IR) and electromagnetic signatures.
- **Reverse slopes** cover and conceal CPs from direct observation and fires. Reverse slopes can degrade the enemy's ability to collect, monitor, and jam electronic transmissions. Electronic profiles reviewed by the S-6 provide information for determining the ability to transmit and

receive. Analysis of those profiles by the S-2 provides information for determining the enemy's ability to degrade CP capabilities or intercept traffic.

- **Avoid establishing CPs on prominent terrain** or major road junctions. Such features are often enemy preplanned artillery and air targets.

MAIN COMMAND POST MOVEMENT

Displacing the Command Post

2-84. The main CP displaces in either a single or phased move. The method selected depends on METT-TC, distance to be moved, and communications requirements. Movement degrades communication on all nets; however, the higher HQ, battalion, and subordinate command nets must be maintained. Maintaining contact with higher HQ may require alternate communications means, such as aircraft or vehicle mounted systems. When operations are ongoing, moving the main CP is accomplished in a phased move requiring displacement of the TAC CP. Critical aspects of C2, such as contact with higher HQ and subordinate units, must be maintained during displacement. Displacements are planned to ensure the main CP is stationary during critical phases of the battle.

2-85. Usually, the main CP hands the battle over to the TAC CP and displaces by echelon using the following technique:

- The main CP conducts a battle update briefing for the TAC CP and transfers the battle.
- The first echelon eavesdrops while moving to the new location.
- The second echelon continues to execute CP responsibilities.
- The first echelon establishes itself at the new location and updates its SU with information received from the second echelon.
- The first echelon assumes responsibility for CP operations and the second echelon displaces.
- During movement, the number of messages to the CP should be minimal. This may require reconfiguration of auto-send and auto-forward functions to route traffic to the TAC CP during main CP displacement.
- Once the second echelon is established, the TAC CP conducts the battle update briefing for the main CP.

Displacement Steps

2-86. The battalion XO/S-3 issues a warning order (WARNO) for movement of the main CP. Leaders usually identify more than one site and route for the new main CP location. The site is not finalized until it has been reconnoitered.

2-87. The S-3 establishes the general area for the new CP. The HHC commander, signal officer, CSM (or senior NCO), and a CBRN team conduct detailed reconnaissance. The following are steps for displacement:

- The reconnaissance party identifies possible routes and sites. Locations must provide effective communications and accommodate all required aircraft, vehicles, and equipment. Several possible site locations must be identified, reconnoitered, and planned to provide flexibility and alternate sites.
- The reconnaissance party makes route and site sketch maps showing the exact element locations within the new CP location.
- The SO surveys the site for aircraft parking suitability.
- The S-3 or commander approves the primary and alternate sites.
- A ground/air movement order is published with decision points (DPs) and a security plan.
- Security personnel and guides are dispatched. The security force ensures the area is clear of enemy and contamination, and the guides prevent wrong turns and assist elements in occupation. Signals are especially important for low visibility and night displacements.

- Reporting and coordinating functions are shifted as required. The shift may be within main CP echelons, to the TAC CP, or to the alternate CP.
- CP and HHC elements prepare and execute movement per SOP. The main CP may displace in one echelon if the TAC CP can provide C2 for the interim. If the TAC CP cannot execute required C2, the main CP displaces in two echelons:
  - The first echelon displaces with enough assets and personnel to establish minimum C2.
  - The second echelon remains in place and provides C2 until the first echelon assumes control, then it displaces.

Planning Considerations

2-88. The HHC commander quickly gains an understanding of the mission requirements. He translates these requirements into a movement order, assembles the convoy, and issues the order. NCOs must be able to organize and assemble the convoy, conduct precombat checks (PCCs)/precombat inspections (PCIs), and ensure personnel complete rehearsals. The convoy commander creates a terrain model, and writes and prepares to issue the order.

2-89. During troop leading procedures (TLP), the HHC commander (and subordinate leaders, as necessary) performs standard tasks prior to a tactical road march that include—

- Conducting an analysis of METT-TC factors. This helps to assess the threat situation and determine probability of air or ground attack.
- Developing a timeline for the preparation and movement of the main CP.
- Designating a marshalling area to organize the march column and conduct final inspections and briefings.
- Establishing detailed security measures.
- Rehearsing actions on contact drills.
- Conducting convoy rehearsal.
- Designating the movement route including the start point, required checkpoints, rally points, and release point (RP). Additional control measures the team might need to identify include critical areas, defiles, choke points, rest and maintenance stops, and danger areas.
- Organizing, briefing, and dispatching the quartering party.
- Specifying the march speed, movement formations, vehicle and serial intervals, catch-up speed, lighting, and times of critical events.
- Establishing the order of march. Key HQ positions in the order of march must enable continuous C2 and maximum protection using available combat assets. Based on its size, the organization divides into multiple serials.
- Planning for indirect FS and contingency actions, and rehearsing actions on contact. Contingency plans should cover vehicle breakdowns, lost vehicles, and accidents.
- Coordinating for sustainment including refueling, mess operations, vehicle recovery, military police assistance, and MEDEVAC.
- Preparing and issuing an order on completion of the planning tasks.

Quartering Party

2-90. The quartering party assists the HHC in moving to and occupying a new AA in a new operations site. The HHC dispatches a quartering party to the prospective site in advance of the main body to—

- Reconnoiter the site and route(s) used to approach and occupy it.
- Secure the area prior to occupation.
- Organize the area prior to the main body's arrival.

2-91. On receipt of the movement WARNO, a reconnaissance team from the quartering party travels to the new area. If either the routes or AAs prove unsatisfactory, the quartering party advises the XO/S-3 of their findings and recommends changes, if possible. The HHC TACSOP should designate members of the reconnaissance team to assist reconnaissance in special ways, such as:

- Determining if the new area can support HHC operations and C2.
- Determining if the location selected can support the main CP.
- Identifying sites able to support communications and retransmission.
- Conducting CBRN reconnaissance of the new site as METT-TC dictates.
- Providing additional security, as available.

2-92. Time available for the reconnaissance team to complete its mission varies depending on the situation. The reconnaissance team reconnoiters routes the main body will use, and identifies built-up areas, grades, fords, obstacles, and defiles affecting the move. The team also identifies alternate routes to the new site and rally points. Once the quartering party selects a site, it conducts CBRN reconnaissance of the site. The reconnaissance team leader then compiles graphics for the routes and area, and sends them to the quartering party via FBCB2, if available. When possible, the team leader directs a security element to observe the new site. The remainder of the team returns to the main CP as some members of the reconnaissance team may also be part of the quartering party.

2-93. While the reconnaissance team is at work, the HHC 1SG assembles and conducts PCIs of the quartering party. The quartering party should be ready to move 2 hours prior to actual movement of the main body. The HHC TACSOP should include quartering party task organization and operation. Elements in the quartering party should include representatives from each element comprising the main CP, namely:

- HHC section.
- S-3 representative.
- S-6 representative.
- Signal team.
- Chemical reconnaissance team.
- Security team, if available.
- Additional vehicles as required.

2-94. The HHC commander prepares and issues a movement order. During the move from the start point through the RP to the site, the quartering party verifies whether the route selected by the reconnaissance party is still able to support the unit's operations. When the quartering party reaches the new site, it verifies whether the site will support the main CP, and begins to prepare the site for occupation by the main body. The quartering party first establishes security and communications. The quartering party identifies and marks vehicle and crew-served weapons positions, and routes from the RP to the AA and positions. Guides from specific sections help position vehicles when they arrive.

Main Body Actions

2-95. On arrival of the first main CP convoy serial at the RP, quartering party guides meet the main body and guide it into position. Once all vehicles are in position, each platoon/section establishes 100 percent local security. Platoon/section sergeants walk the perimeter with a quartering party guide, making adjustments to crew-served weapons or individual fighting positions, if needed. Platoon/section sergeants ensure all positions tie into the CP perimeter and coordinate fires with left and right positions.

2-96. Once the last serial arrives, the HHC commander inspects the main CP perimeter. If satisfied with the defensive layout, he can reduce security to a level appropriate to the threat condition. All sections begin the occupation timeline (table 2-3), and each vehicle deploys concertina wire on the perimeter.

Table 2-3. Example of main command post occupation timeline

Within 5 minutes	Clear RP without stopping and pick up quartering party guides. Move directly to marked positions. Account for personnel, equipment, and sensitive items. Report sent to HHC commander.
Within 30 minutes	Maintain security and air guard. Digital and FM communications established. Vehicles in final positions. Main CP vehicles connected. Crew-served weapons in hasty fighting positions. Hasty defensive and survivability positions designated. Entry point gate established with barriers and communications to the main CP. Sector sketches started. CBRN-detection equipment emplaced. Initiate set-up of main CP.
Within 60 minutes	Platoons/sections establish land line communications to each crew-served weapon position. Logistics support areas (LSAs) finalized. Complete security plan and set-up of TAC CP. Establish CCPs. Emplace inner concertina wire.
Within 90 minutes	Begin emplacement of outer ring of wire or berm. Land line communications checks completed. LSAs established. Establish security defense level. Vehicle/tent camouflage started.
Within 2 hours	Guard and patrol rotation started. Continued improvement of machine gun and individual fighting positions. Helicopter LZ identified and marked. Sector sketches to HHC commander.
Within 4 hours	Refuel and resupply basic load. Update maintenance status. Perimeter wire continued until triple strand is emplaced. Quick reaction force (QRF) rehearsal. Camouflage complete. Continue to improve machine gun and individual fighting positions. Implement CP shifts and sleep plan. Check load plans.

BATTALION PLANNING CONSIDERATIONS

2-97. The battalion develops its operational plans parallel with both higher and subordinate HQ. In addition to planning for the operational mission, battalion and companies ensure aviation operation details are accomplished. Units plan, coordinate, and rehearse concurrently while the operational plan is in development. Examples of ongoing preparation include—

- Fighter management cycles.
- Task organization.
- Aircraft designation and configuration.
- Auxiliary fuel tank distribution and management (if applicable).
- Communications planning.
- ASE requirements and settings.
- Identification friend or foe (IFF) procedures and Mode 4 settings.
- Airspace C2 coordination.

- Review of the current air control order (ACO), ATO, and SPINS.
- Crew selection.
- Tasks and responsibilities (company, platoon, team, aircrew).
- En route formations and security.
- Formation actions on contact and break-up procedures.
- Selected rehearsals and training.
- FARP movement, composition, and emplacement.
- Maintenance support movement, composition, and emplacement.
- Plans and procedures for recovery of personnel and equipment, specifically downed aviator pickup points (DAPPs), in-stride/immediate aircrew recovery, and downed aircraft recovery teams (DARTs).
- Weather (to include inadvertent instrument meteorological conditions [IIMC] recovery procedures).
- Creation of emergency global positioning system (GPS) recovery procedure if required.
- Passage of lines planning.
- AD status.
- AA departure procedures.
- Bump plan.

2-98. Operations beyond friendly lines feature extended distances and require tremendous speeds in execution. These operations may involve deep penetrations and wide sweeps, while bypassing enemy forces and terrain obstacles, almost always at night. To react quickly to intelligence on hostile forces, planning and execution must keep pace with the accelerated attack tempo, maximizing surprise to ensure effective execution at the decisive place and time.

MILITARY DECISIONMAKING PROCESS

2-99. To plan and coordinate missions effectively, the commander and staff follow MDMP (figure 2-1). Staff planners must focus on previously listed aviation planning considerations to formulate a complete plan. Due to the complexity inherent in the process, battalions should practice the process regularly prior to deployment. FM 5-0 covers the MDMP process in detail.

MDMP Steps

Step 1: Receipt of Mission

← WARNO

Step 2: Mission Analysis

← WARNO

Step 3: COA Development

Step 4: COA Analysis (Wargame)

Step 5: COA Comparison

Step 6: COA Approval

← WARNO

Step 7: Orders Production

Rehearsals and backbriefs occur during preparation and ensure an orderly transition between planning and execution.

If an AVN TF is conducting an air assault, the air mission brief (AMB) becomes part of the orders brief at the supported maneuver headquarters followed by a combined arms rehearsal.

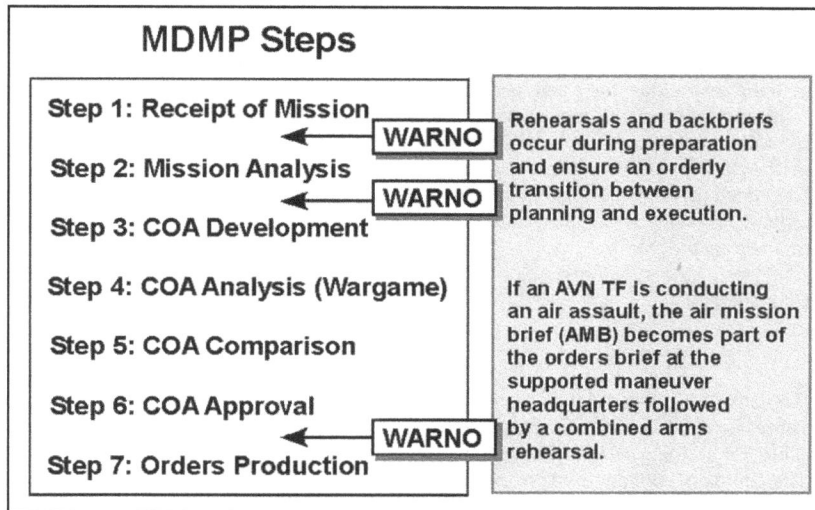

Figure 2-1. Military decisionmaking process

2-100. The dynamic battlefield often does not allow a complete MDMP due to time constraints. The commander and staff must know current aircraft and crew availability to immediately assess feasibility of mission requests.

2-101. The steps of an abbreviated MDMP are the same as those of the full process; however, the commander performs many of them mentally or with less staff involvement. The commander may direct a COA based on experience to expedite planning. The products developed during an abbreviated MDMP may be the same as those developed using the full process; however, they are usually less detailed and some may be omitted altogether. Unit SOPs should address how to abbreviate MDMP based on commander's preferences.

SECTION III – COMPANY COMMAND AND CONTROL

COMPANY COMMAND POST

2-102. The company CP is an austere setup and not specifically designed to be a staff-level planning and tracking environment. The bulk of the company's mission information comes from the battalion, BCT, or AATF. The company CP is for company specific mission planning, briefings, and rehearsals. Often, the company CP is collocated within the same shelter grouping as the company's maintenance and supply personnel, offering limited designated mission planning space. The company CP operates under the same principles as the main CP.

SPLIT-BASED OPERATIONS

2-103. Operations of platoons/sections independent from the company HQ is referred to as split-based operations. Modularity of forces supporting BCTs requires companies to operate while geographically separated and with a decentralized command. Company HQ may be collocated with their platoons, or the platoons may be deployed forward in support of a BCT, ABTF, or TF. Companies must be able to deploy, sustain combat operations, and fight wholly or as independent platoons or sections. The duration depends on mission requirements and will require sufficient logistics support. Additional augmentation of personnel and/or equipment may be required to fill essential mission support roles.

CAPABILITIES

2-104. Aviation company capabilities are a combat multiplier for the GTC. Modularity of companies allows a "plug and play" capability for BCTs, ABTFs, and TFs. Aviation companies are capable of 24-hour continuous operations for short periods of time. Sustained operations involving surges, such as offensive operations, drain the unit causing a reduced capability following the operation. This permits required aircraft maintenance to be accomplished and allows for management of fighter endurance for aircrews. The aviation modular design also allows assets of the corps and theater to reinforce the brigade, providing an added capability to BCTs, ABTFs, and TFs during surge operations. This design also supplies aviation support following surge operations, while BCT-, ABTF-, and TF-organic aviation unit companies are in a reduced capability time frame.

COMPANY ELEMENTS

Commander

2-105. The company commander is a warfighter, responsible for the integration of his company into the combined arms fight. He leads, mentors, guides, and inspires the Soldiers of the company. The commander is responsible for training platoon leaders and evaluating crews and individuals as well as assessing training. The company commander is responsible for ensuring aircraft and crews are available to meet the battalion commander's intent. He determines crew selections as well as composition of flight teams. The 1SG, platoon leaders, IPs, TACOPS, and pilots in command (PCs) assist the commander in ensuring combat crew readiness.

First Sergeant

2-106. The 1SG is the senior NCO and senior enlisted aviation maintainer at company level. The 1SG is the commander's primary advisor concerning enlisted Soldiers and performs other duties directed by the commander. The 1SG focuses attention on functions critical to success of the operation. The 1SG assists the commander in the following ways:
- Provides recommendations and expedites procurement and preparation of enlisted replacements for the company.
- Supervises daily maintenance operations.
- Oversees protection measures in fixed-base operations.
- Organizes, deploys, and supervises all support elements assigned, attached, or under operational control (OPCON) to the company. This includes food service, transportation, maintenance, and other support personnel.
- Coordinates medical, mess, supply, administrative, and other logistics support.
- Receives, consolidates, and forwards all administrative, personnel, and casualty reports to the battalion CP via radio, hard copy, or digital format.
- Establishes and organizes the company resupply point.
- Leads company ground movements when required and establishes AAs.
- Monitors NCO development, promotions, and assignments. This includes assessment of the company's battle-focused Soldier and NCO leader training programs.
- Identifies, plans, and assesses Soldier performance on training tasks that support collective (unit) tasks on the METL.

Platoon Leader

2-107. The platoon leader leads his platoon and is responsible for the conduct of crew training, selection to ensure mission accomplishment. Unit IPs assist the platoon leader in ensuring crews are properly selected and trained. The platoon leader is responsible for all maintenance operations of the platoon to include—
- Updating the commander on all aircraft status changes.

- Developing and implementing a tracking system to monitor critical maintenance services, such as scheduled, unscheduled, and deferred maintenance; phases; the flow chart and status chart; and parts and work order requests.
- Supervising daily maintenance operations.

Platoon Sergeant

2-108.   The platoon sergeant is the primary adviser to the platoon leader. He is responsible for soldier and equipment readiness. The platoon sergeant assesses Soldier training proficiency with input from section leaders, identifying Soldier and collective tasks needing training. The platoon sergeant assists the platoon leader, as the 1SG assists the commander, by—

- Ensuring the platoon has aircraft available to accomplish assigned missions.
- Providing recommendations and requests for procurement and preparation of enlisted replacements for the company through the platoon leader to the commander.
- Coordinating medical, mess, supply, administrative, and other logistics support for the platoon.
- Reviewing maintenance forms ensuring crew chiefs verify deficiencies and completing additional forms as necessary.
- Ensuring submittal of maintenance forms and appropriate tracking is initiated.
- Monitoring status of replacement parts, including parts on order and valid parts requisition numbers.
- Ensuring all recoverable parts are turned in.
- Leading platoon ground movements and conducting pre-execution checks when required.
- Providing input to platoon leader's collective task assessment.
- Ensuring Soldiers are prepared for and attend training.
- Monitoring NCO development and promotions.
- Identifying, planning, and assessing Soldier performance on training tasks that support individual and collective (unit) tasks on the METL (to include maintenance tasks).

Standardization Instructor Pilot

2-109.   SPs assist the commander in developing and implementing the unit aircrew training program (ATP). He also assists the commander in crew selection, normally performs as a member of the company operations planning cell, and may serve as an AMC during combat operations. SPs provide quality control for the ATP via the commander's standardization program. Along with their primary responsibilities, they mentor and professionally educate all unit crewmembers. SPs are tasked to provide expertise on unit, individual, crew, and collective training to the commander, and perform the following functions:

- Serves as member of the battalion standardization committee.
- Advises commander on development of commander's task list (CTL).
- Monitors unit standardization and ATPs.
- Maintains unit individual aircrew training folders (IATFs).
- Monitors unit no-notice programs.
- Assists the battalion SP in
- development and execution of realistic company gunnery tables. This may include ammunition forecasts, helicopter gunnery skills tests, engagement scenarios, simulator situational training exercises (STXs), and computer-based ASE training (CBAT) requirements.
- Develops company STXs accurately reflecting current combat operations and the full spectrum of aircraft capabilities.
- Attends training meetings.

Instructor Pilot

2-110. IPs are responsible for assisting the platoon leader in properly training combat ready crews. IPs provide quality control for the ATP via the commander's standardization program. Although IPs work directly for the platoon leader, they receive guidance and delegated tasks from the company SP. This ensures training is standardized throughout the company, provides for an economy of effort in the company, and contributes to professional development of the IP. IPs also mentor and professionally educate all unit crewmembers and are responsible for—

- Performing as designated IP and/or instrument examiner.
- Conducting no-notice evaluations.
- Assisting the company standardization officer in maintaining IATFs.
- Assisting in development of company STXs.
- Assisting in development and execution of company gunnery tables.

Unit Trainer

2-111. Unit trainers are aviators designated to instruct in areas of specialized training (refer to TC 1-210). They assist IPs in unit training programs and the achievement of established training goals. Areas in which they instruct are—

- Night vision goggles (NVGs).
- Instrument flight.
- Tactics.
- Border and corridor qualifications.
- Local area qualifications.

Maintenance Test Pilot

2-112. Maintenance test pilots (MPs) work with the Platoon Sergeant in developing and managing the unit maintenance program. The MP is involved in all aspects of aircraft maintenance within the company. They interface with the Production Control Officer to maintain coordinated efforts across the battalion to ensure the efficient use of resources and establish priority of effort. The MP's goal is to provide maximum availability of aircraft. The MP also—

- Conducts maintenance test flights and maintenance operational checks.
- Advises the commander and platoon leader on maintenance operations
- Serves as an operational mission pilot.
- Conducts pilot training on maintenance-related tasks.

Safety Officer

2-113. SOs assist the commander in developing and implementing all unit safety programs. The SO is not just an observer; he is expected to be tactically and technically proficient, and an active participant in the ATP. Commanders rely on their SOs to monitor all safety aspects of the unit, and provide feedback and advice from a different perspective than that of the commander. The SO serves as the commander's advisor on risk management during flight mission planning. SOs are the commander's primary trainer for annual safety training requirements and CRM including—

- Individual risk assessment.
- Crew risk assessment and mitigation.
- FARP and AA site surveys.
- Convoy risk assessment and safety briefs.

Tactical Operations Officer

2-114.   TACOPS officers are subject matter experts related to threat, aviation survivability measures, and the organic AMPS and its associated products. Additional responsibilities include—

- Conducting the ASE/EW portion of the risk management process.
- Assisting in development of unit TTP.
- Assisting the battalion TACOPS in managing the organization's PR program.
- Determining ASE settings and countermeasures.
- Advising the commander and company leaders on appropriate ASE techniques and procedures, and if necessary, coordinating for integration of joint assets for each major mission.
- Integrating FS and CAS into company mission planning.
- Managing/tracking company ASE systems.
- Assisting in development of company STXs and gunnery tables.
- Advising the commander on development of CTL.

Standardization Flight Instructor

2-115.   Standardization flight instructors (SIs) are nonrated crewmembers (NCMs) responsible for training NCM flight instructors (FIs) and nonrated Soldiers within the command. SIs provide quality control for the NCM ATP via the commander's standardization program. They also train NCMs to perform FI duties aboard aircraft and monitor/evaluate the instructor's performance while training NCMs essential to operation of the aircraft. SIs work with aviators in-flight using the team concept. Their duties are included in the corresponding aircrew training manual (ATM).

2-116.   For CH-47/UH-60 equipped units, the commander designates a NCM standardization instructor to help administer the door gunnery program. The master gunner/door gunnery NCM standardization instructor duties are described in FM 3-04.140.

Flight Instructor

2-117.   FIs are NCMs who have been trained by the SP/SI and certified by the commander to train other NCMs for operational flight duties. FIs are responsible for the training of NCMs in flight operations of the unit's assigned aircraft. The SP and SI monitor/evaluate FIs.

Aviation Life Support Officer

2-118.   Aviation life support officers (ALSOs) assist, advise, and represent commanders in all matters pertaining to the aviation life support systems (ALSSs). ALSOs—

- Review, analyze, and develop procedures ensuring planning, budgeting, and maintenance of ALSS.
- Ensure training of aircrew personnel in proper operation, use, and operator maintenance of survival equipment and techniques of survival.
- Supervise the life support section and ensure qualified personnel are available to conduct life support and survival training and maintenance of organizational-level aviation life support equipment (ALSE).
- Maintain a current file of regulations, procedures, and technical manuals (TMs) pertaining to inspection, maintenance, and use of assigned life support equipment.
- Ensure units have adequate information and training before using new equipment or system changes.
- Ensure materiel deficiency reports are submitted on life support equipment failing to operate as designed.

2-119. Additionally, the commander appoints ALSE technicians and specialists to assist, advise, and represent the ALSO in all matters pertaining to ALSE. Technicians—

- Establish a library of ALSE publications and ensure the unit's pinpoint distribution account is updated to include ALSE publications and necessary forms.
- Ensure all ALSE is maintained in a high state of readiness by inspecting, cleaning, fitting, testing, adjusting, and repairing equipment.
- Maintain files on inspection, maintenance, expiration dates, and supply pertaining to ALSE.
- Inspect all controlled drugs used in survival kits and vests.

COMPANY PLANNING CONSIDERATIONS

TROOP LEADING PROCEDURES

2-120. Although MDMP is essential to accomplish the mission, effective TLP are equally important. Commanders with a coordinating staff use MDMP. Company-level and smaller units do not have formal staffs and use TLP to plan and prepare for operations. Figure 2-2 depicts TLP along with key planning tasks. The box on the left shows the steps of TLP. The box in the middle (METT-TC) represents the initial METT-TC analysis leader's conduct to develop an initial assessment. This occurs in TLP steps 1 and 2 and is refined in plan development. The box on the right depicts plan development tasks. Plan development occurs in TLP steps 3 through 6. These tasks are similar to the MDMP steps (refer to FM 5-0).

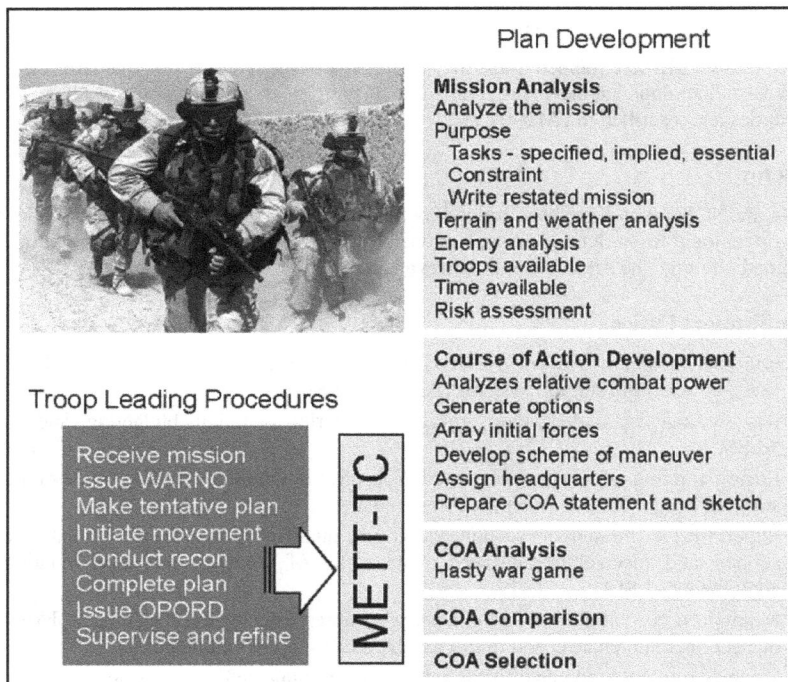

Figure 2-2. Troop leading procedures and key planning tasks

2-121. TLP must be a part of the SOP and its checklists. Although quick directives can accomplish much in certain circumstances, a missed step can easily lead to mission shortfalls or failure. Written TLP steps provide a guide the leader applies in ways consistent with the situation, leader's experience, and experience of subordinate leaders.

2-122. Leaders use TLP when working alone to solve tactical problems or with a small group. A company commander may use the 1SG, platoon leaders, SP, and SO for assistance during TLP. Additionally, aviation company commanders utilize planning cells to perform much of the TLP process.

PLANNING CELLS

2-123. Company planning cells are utilized by the commander to plan, organize, and effectively execute the mission. This section defines a method for planning conducted at company level, and the process a company follows to ensure completion of required tasks for mission planning.

2-124. The company commander or senior officer acts as the AMC. He selects crews and assigns them to planning cells. The AMC assigns suspenses for planning cells providing products to the reproduction/distribution cell.

Process

2-125. The following process establishes information requirements necessary to successfully plan and execute company missions. Cells conduct planning concurrently. The information required for planning and execution is located in the WARNO. To begin planning, the following is needed from a WARNO: (Some of this information can be generated into AMPS.)

- Threat and friendly situation along routes and AOs.
- Mission, objective, or target time, and any alternate missions.
- Weather and light data for time of operation.
- Number of aircraft required.
- Location of specified passage points or corridors with occupying unit designation, call sign, and frequency.
- Specific tasks for planning cells.
- Time and place of OPORD.
- AMPS integration.
- Cell assignments matrix (table 2-4. page 2-29).

Table 2-4. Sample cell assignments matrix

Route Planning Cell
Operate AMPS: • Select air control points (ACPs), altitudes, airspeeds, and formations using friendly situation graphics. Coordinate with other units as necessary. • Calculate/confirm time/distance/heading data. These data and grid coordinates will be checked by another cell member. • Identify obstacles and hazards. Coordinate with weather/hazards cell. • Obtain FARP layout data and post on unit FARP sketch. • Coordinate with ASE/EW cell to avoid known enemy hazards. • Coordinate with operations cell concerning mission timeline. • Produce/update AMPS graphics (such as flight plan, control measures, battlefield graphics, and mission essential data. • Provide reproduction/distribution cell with kneeboard products. • Load mission from AMPS to data transfer cartridges and provide to all copilots at briefing.

Table 2-4. Sample cell assignments matrix

Communications Cell
Develop communication sets for the mission.
Ensure COMSEC equipment in all mission aircraft (including spares) is keyed and operational (such as KY-58, KIT 1C, SINCGARS and Have Quick).
Collect frequency and selective identification feature/IFF data from the OPORD, ACO, Aviation Planning Guide, automated network control device (ANCD), SOP, and Flight Information Publication covering all mission aspects from communications check to completion.
Prepare the unit communications card.
Provide the reproduction/distribution cell with all data in a timely manner.

Performance Planning Cell
Obtain mission load data.
Obtain planning weather data (temperature and pressure altitude).
Prepare a generic performance planning card (PPC).
Calculate fuel-planning data for all phases of the mission. If unit aircraft are equipped with internal tanks, perform planning for those aircraft allowing for two contingencies:
(1) Auxiliary tanks are operational
(2) Tanks are full of fuel but do not transfer fuel.
Calculate minimum fuel including return to FARP/AA (commonly code worded as "bingo") and visual flight rules reserve.
Place all calculations and data on the unit PPC/fuel planning card and provide timely data to the route planning cell and reproduction/distribution cell.

Operational Planning Cell (usually composed of commander and team leader/leaders)
Selection of LZs, PZs, and holding areas (HAs).
Control measures for routes.
Selection of target reference points (TRPs) if required.
Team employment procedures.
Integration into ground tactical plan (GTP).
Provide the reproduction/distribution cell with all data in a timely manner.
Brief actions on the objective at the unit mission briefing.

Weather, Notices to Airman (NOTAMs), Hazards Cell
Compare forecasted weather and mission requirements. Consider illumination, sunrise/sunset times.
Review NOTAMs, airmen's advisories, and ACO for items that may influence the mission including IIMC recovery airfields.
Update wire hazards map.
Provide the reproduction/distribution cell with all data in a timely manner.
Conduct contingency planning for follow-on missions if necessary.
Brief weather, NOTAMs, and hazards at the unit mission briefing.

Flight Plan/Mission Brief/Risk Assessment Cell
Complete mission brief and risk assessment sheets. Make available to mission crews prior to briefing.
Inform the AMC if initial risk assessment warrants any amendments to the mission profile.
Complete the flight plan or collect data for flight operations log.
Obtain squawk codes, prior permission requests, and diplomatic clearances as required by mission.
Provide the reproduction/distribution cell with all data in a timely manner.

Table 2-4. Sample cell assignments matrix

IIMC Cell
Develop a IIMC recovery plan. For long en route portions, more than one recovery airfield may be required.
Select appropriate instrument approach procedures at each recovery airfield.
Create emergency GPS recovery procedure if required.
Prepare an IIMC plan and post on unit IIMC card.
Provide the reproduction/distribution cell with all data in a timely manner.

Threat Cell/ASE/EW
Analyze threat composition, disposition, order of battle, array, and numbers.
Using AMPS inter-visibility plots, analyze threat weapons systems that may influence the mission.
Coordinate with the route planning cell concerning threats that may influence the en route phase.
Coordinate with the operations cell concerning any threats in the vicinity of the objective.
Prepare the threat risk assessment. Much of the data for this form may be obtained from the Air Force technical training publication (AFTTP). The AFTTP is a classified document and may be obtained from the TACOPS/battalion EWO/S-2.
Provide the reproduction/distribution cell with all data in a timely manner.
Brief the threat risk assessment at the unit mission briefing.

Reproduction/Distribution Cell
Actively collect and safeguard all data provided by planning cells.
If possible, photcopy uniform packets for all crewmembers. Arrange in the same order and clip together.
Post the mission briefing boards as soon as possible to allow aircrews to post their own mission packets if reproduced packets are not available.
Distribute packets prior to start of mission briefing.
Assist AMC with mission briefing preparation. This includes posting graphics/overlays to briefing maps.
Products that are reproduced and distributed:
• Route cards.
• FARP, objective, and PZ/LZ sketches.
• Communication card.
• PPC.
• Weather, NOTAMs, and hazards briefs.
• Flight plan/mission brief/risk assessment.
• IIMC recovery plan.
• Threat risk assessment.
• Mission execution matrix (if not provided from battalion).

SECTION IV – MEETINGS AND BRIEFINGS

INITIAL PLANNING CONFERENCE

2-126.   Although not required, an initial planning conference (IPC) may be conducted by the unit. The IPC is the first meeting between the ground maneuver unit and aviation unit or TF. The IPC takes place when the AATFC has a general idea of his intent and GTP scheme of maneuver. During the IPC, each unit involved in the air assault backbriefs task and purpose, general scheme of maneuver, and task organization. The information gained in the IPC is used to develop the aviation OPORD and air mission brief (AMB). The unit personnel attending the IPC should have the following:

- An air mission coordination meeting (AMCM) checklist (refer to appendix D).
- Maps.
- An execution matrix template.
- An ANCD for receiving mission frequency set.

2-127. Briefing products produced may include—

- A staging plan.
- PZ and LZ plans.
- An air movement plan.
- Routes.
- LZs and landing plans.
- HA/restricted operations zone (ROZ) plans.
- A CASEVAC plan.

AIR MISSION COORDINATION MEETING

2-128. The purpose of the AMCM is to complete coordination between ground and aviation units. The AMCM is a critical event in synchronizing air-ground integration. The AMCM coordinates operational information between ground and aviation operations officers, and key members of the BCT staff. The AMCM takes place immediately after the backbrief to the BCT. The end result of the AMCM is a finalized air movement plan, landing plan, air routes, PZs, and LZs. See chapter 3 for more information.

OPERATION ORDER BRIEF

2-129. The OPORD briefing provides information, specific instructions, and a thorough overview of the mission. The briefing should be organized to follow the written order's format and presented by a single briefing officer, who may be the commander, an assistant, staff officer, or special representative depending on the nature of the mission or HQ level. Refer to FM 5-0 for more information on orders production and briefings.

2-130. In an operational situation or when the mission is of a critical nature, individuals or smaller units may need more specific data, which may be provided by a mission briefing. The mission briefing reinforces orders, provides more detailed requirements and instructions for each individual, and explains the significance of each individual role.

AIR MISSION BRIEF

2-131. The AMB is a focused adjunct to the OPORD and where the battalion commander approves the plan. The term AMB is used to mean both the written product and the briefing itself. The AMB should not be a working meeting; an OPORD should have already been published. Therefore, the AMB is essentially a backbrief to the commander. All units involved in the operation should attend and receive a copy of the order.

2-132. The AMB should focus on concepts, sequence of events, and reasons the staff developed the sequence for the mission. The slightest change in route selection, LZs/PZs, or other elements of the mission can significantly affect the rest of the plan.

2-133. Changes to the mission after the AMB must be approved by the commander. It is very difficult to resynchronize the different combat systems in the short time remaining between the AMB and mission execution. Unit personnel attending should bring—

- An AMB checklist (refer to appendix D for an example checklist).
- Maps.
- An execution matrix.
- An ANCD for receiving frequency set changes/updates.
- An AMPS data transfer cartridge for receiving changes/updates to routes.

2-134. Briefing products produced may include—
- Mission.
- Friendly graphics.
- AC2 procedures.
- A communication card (frequencies/call signs).
- An execution matrix.
- Routes (AMPS cartridge).
- An ANCD frequency set load.
- A risk assessment/mission brief/mission schedule.

TEAM BRIEF

2-135. Team briefings can occur at different levels. The team can be briefed by the battalion or company for specific missions or missions that are part of larger operations. An example of a team brief is teams being briefed by battalion for missions supporting battalion PR or QRF operations. Information and products reviewed during the brief include—
- PPC.
- FS card.
- Actions on contact.
- Contingency planning.
- Scheme of maneuver.
- Weather, NOTAMs, and hazards briefs.
- Flight plan/mission brief/risk assessment.
- IIMC recovery plan.
- Threat risk assessment.

CREW MISSION BRIEF

2-136. The PC briefs the mission and flight requirements that demand effective communication, proper sequencing, and timing of actions according to a unit-approved crew mission briefing checklist. The appropriate aircraft type ATM contains an example of a detailed crew mission briefing checklist and instructions for completing this task. Unit SOPs should also address crew briefing checklists.

SECTION V – REHEARSALS

2-137. A rehearsal is essential for success in operations. FM 6-0 contains a discussion of rehearsal types, techniques, responsibilities, and conduct. Following is a discussion of items critical to aviation operations.

2-138. Once commanders are satisfied and personnel understand the concept of operation, they must rehearse the plan. The rehearsal cannot become the brief to commanders. The purpose is to validate synchronization of subordinate units' tasks to execute the commander's intent.

2-139. Rehearsal types include—
- Confirmation brief.
- Backbrief.
- Combined arms rehearsal.
- Support rehearsal.
- Battle drill or SOP rehearsal

2-140. Rehearsal techniques include—
- Full dress rehearsal.
- Reduced force rehearsal.

- Terrain model rehearsal.
- Sketch map rehearsal.
- Map rehearsal.
- Network rehearsal.

2-141.   Although a full dress rehearsal is preferred, a terrain model rehearsal is most common. The terrain model must represent the unit's area of influence and be large enough for participants to easily traverse. An effective rehearsal is dependent on an accurate terrain model, complete with key terrain features, reliefs, obstacles, and unit positions (friendly and enemy) correctly portrayed. Additionally, an effective technique for utilizing terrain models is to increase the scale of the objective area for better visualization by rehearsal participants. A standardized terrain model kit is an effective tool to reduce setup time.

2-142.   Rehearsals are accomplished at all levels. They may be conducted separately at each echelon, in one large rehearsal, or using a combination of the two. An appropriate large rehearsal would be a cross-forward line of own troops (FLOT) air assault. Rehearsals are as detailed as time and resources permit. They may be a series of full-up, live-fire rehearsals or as simple as a quick review on the map. All rehearsals must include reviewing or conducting the following:

- Actions on the objective.
- Maneuver, movement, and fires.
- Critical event rehearsals (such as FARP and PZ/LZ).
- Contact drills en route.
- Contingencies.

REHEARSAL SEQUENCE AND ATTENDANCE

2-143.   Rehearsals follow a script and proceed in action, reaction, and counteraction sequence. Elements of the script include—

- Agenda.
- Attendee response sequence to actions.
- Unit actions response checklist (standardized format).
- Sequence of events.

2-144.   If time becomes critical during the rehearsal, then the most critical part of the mission must be given adequate attention. Rehearsals must include a representation of the enemy and should cover—

- Actions at the objective.
- Actions at the PZ, en route, and LZ.
- Enemy positions and disposition.
- Friendly scheme of maneuver/GTP.
- Integration of fires/suppression of enemy air defenses (SEAD).
- Actions on contact.
- Occupation of reconnaissance or security positions, battle positions (BPs), and landing plans.
- Passage of lines.
- Flight plans including primary/alternate routes, PZ/LZ ingress/egress procedures, maneuver formations, flight techniques, and altitudes.
- Actions in the AA (communication checks, line up for takeoff, takeoff, and landing on return).
- FARP information.
- Loading plan (troops, equipment, and supplies).
- CASEVAC procedures.
- IIMC procedures.
- In stride/immediate downed aircrew recovery procedures.
- Contingency plan TTP (such as change of mission, aircraft equipment malfunction, or hot LZ).

All critical members of units should attend the rehearsal. Critical members are those who have key parts in the operation and whose failure to accomplish a task could cause mission failures.

REHEARSAL QUESTION RESOLUTION

2-145.   The battalion commander and staff may conduct or observe the rehearsal. Detailed questions ensure units thoroughly understand the mission. The following questions are examples of critical questions that should be answered during the rehearsal:

- Who provides security?
- Who collects and sends SPOTREPs, whom do they call, and on which net?
- Who initiates communications checks?
- Who coordinates with the ground force commander?
- Who confirms call signs, nets, and authenticators?
- What radio calls (digital and voice) are required during the conduct of the operation?
- What are the success criteria, and how do we know if they have been met?
- What are the mission criteria and who selects the mission criteria?
- What are the divert criteria and who makes that decision?
- What are the mission abort criteria?
- What are the in-stride downed aircrew procedures?
- What are the CASEVAC procedures?
- What are the ROE?
- What are the ASE requirements and settings?
- What are the critical times (PZ, start point, rally point, and LZ)?
- What is the entry/exit plan?
- What is the bump and spare aircraft plan?
- What Pathfinder support is available?
- What are the hot LZ procedures and alternate LZ divert criteria?
- What is the plan to sequence serials through the FARP?
- What are the contingencies at the objective or LZ for various enemy actions?
- Where do crews get the time sequence for Have Quick (unless automatic)?
- Where are the FARPs and what are their procedures?
- Where is the AATFC, GTC, AMC, and air battle captain (ABC) during each phase of the mission, and who uses/monitors the CAN for coordination between air and ground forces?
- How are PZs and LZs marked?

CONFLICT RESOLUTION AT THE REHEARSAL

2-146.   Conflicts may arise during a rehearsal. The commander must ensure conflicts are resolved, and the rehearsal does not become a war game. Wargaming should have been accomplished during the planning process. The rehearsal ensures all members of the unit understand their roles and how they contribute to success. It is not the time to develop a new plan, but if required, refinements may be made.

ADDITIONAL REHEARSALS

2-147.   Additional rehearsals include—

- **The ground tactical rehearsal** includes the air movement plan, landing plan, GTP, and extraction plan. Designed to ensure synchronization of all efforts, this full, detailed rehearsal has all key personnel in attendance. A terrain model of the AO is required.
- **The communications exercise (COMMEX)** should mirror the signal requirements of the mission. The COMMEX ensures assignment of nets, equipment capabilities, range,

retransmission requirements, and COMSEC requirements. All elements participating in the mission participate in the COMMEX. The use of a common communications card is highly recommended and allows for a quick reference guide to frequencies and call signs.

- **The PZ rehearsal** is run by the battalion XO. All pilots flying the mission, the PZ NCOIC, and supported unit commander(s) attend. The staging, loading, and air movement plans are rehearsed in detail as well as the pilots' actions in and around the PZ. A terrain model of the PZs with a depiction of the aircraft and loads is recommended.
- **Company rehearsals** are required to cover key company events not portrayed at the battalion rehearsal, such as formation, bump plan, departure sequence, radio calls, and actions on the objective. Attendees include all aircrews and key leaders.

REHEARSAL COMPLETION

2-148. At the end of any rehearsal the commander should receive correct responses from every member present concerning—

- Mission/actions at the objective.
- Commander's intent.
- Timetable for mission execution.

2-149. Following rehearsal and prior to executing the mission, commanders conduct PCI ensuring PCC on aircraft and mission equipment are complete.

PRECOMBAT CHECKS

2-150. Aircrews and vehicle operators conduct PCC. Checks include—

- Posting graphics on maps.
- Completing aircraft performance planning.
- Completing preflight/before operations preventive maintenance checks and services (PMCS).
- Ensuring proper configuration of vehicles, aircraft, and weapons systems.
- Ensuring data transfer cartridge upload.
- Ensuring IFF and COMSEC are loaded.
- Verifying communications checks.
- Test firing of weapons systems, if possible.

SECTION VI – END OF MISSION DEBRIEFING AND AFTER ACTION REVIEW

DEBRIEFS

MISSION DEBRIEF

2-151. Units should address mission debrief procedures in their SOP and conduct mission debriefs as soon as practical on completion of the mission. All mission personnel should attend. Mission debriefs cover mission planning, preparation, and execution phases. The purpose is to capture what happened during a mission to ensure all requirements were achieved. The intent is to capture better SA/SU and intelligence of the area. Table 2-5, page 2-37, shows an example mission debrief format.

Table 2-5. Sample mission debrief

Date:
Time:
Mission:
Location:
AMC:
Aircraft #1: Call sign and crew
Aircraft #2: Call sign and crew
Takeoff time
Route
Actions on objective
Significant events
SPOTREPs
BDA
PIR answered
FARP/team rotations
Battle handover/end of mission time
Maintenance: Hours flown and thorough postflight analysis of the aircraft
SAFIRE Incidents:
Aircraft (A/C) location
A/C heading, altitude, and airspeed
Evasive maneuvers performed
Enemy
Weapon system/# of rounds
Enemy location
Number of personnel
Subsequent actions

CREW

2-152. Commanders must emphasize the critical importance of crew debriefs and crew coordination, not only during flight mission execution but in the crew internal debrief. Unit SPs/IPs must ensure crews are trained and execute crew coordination before, during, and after flight.

2-153. The crew debrief provides information that assists the crew in enhancing mission execution, safer operations, and reduction of errors. The commander should institute and promote the posting of crew coordination lessons learned to a forum. The forum also allows other crews to learn through an aircrew's experience as not all problems encountered are associated only with the aircraft and crews. This event becomes a mission enhancer for future flight operations.

2-154. Many errors occur in the interaction between aircraft crews and supported ground units. Aviation units will habitually work with the same ground units. The sharing of learned errors from past experience with all flight crews allows them to be aware and prepared and adjust risk as necessary. This same learned information is forwarded to the ground unit commander so corrections can be made to reduce risk.

TEAM

2-155. Platoons and sections operating independently from company HQ (in support of a BCT for example) conduct the same debriefs and are responsible for submitting information to the S-2/S-3 and platoon's/section's respective commander.

COMPANY

2-156. Commanders ensure unit personnel conduct mission debriefs as soon as practical on completion of the mission with all mission personnel attending. Mission debriefs cover mission planning, preparation, and execution phases with a focus on how to improve the operation. Additionally, the commander ensures the higher HQ S-2/S-3 receives debrief information and is afforded the opportunity to debrief the crew if warranted.

BATTALION INTELLIGENCE

2-157. The front line Soldier is a valuable intelligence source. Commanders instill in crewmembers they are reconnaissance Soldiers fighting for and confirming intelligence. Their sightings and reporting of any activity (or lack thereof) may make the difference between victory and defeat. The S-2 debriefs aircrews as an essential part of gathering information. The crews provide the S-2 with all sketches, checklists, and video imagery collected during the mission.

AFTER ACTION REVIEW

PURPOSE

2-158. An after action review (AAR) is a structured review process of an event, focused on performance standards, enabling Soldiers to discover for themselves what happened, why it happened, and how to sustain strengths and improve on weaknesses. It is a tool units and leaders can use to obtain maximum benefit from every mission or task. The AAR consists of four parts:

- Review what was supposed to happen (training plan).
- Establish what happened.
- Determine what was right or wrong with what happened.
- Determine how the task should be done differently next time.

2-159. Unit AARs focus on individual and collective task performance, identifying shortcomings and training required to correct any deficiencies. AARs with leaders focus on tactical judgment. These AARs contribute to leader learning and provide opportunities for leader development. AARs with trainers, evaluators, observer controllers, and opposing forces provide additional opportunities for leader development. If applicable, AARs are forwarded to the next higher HQ S-3. Commanders should emphasize what they believe to be key critical elements within the AAR. Refer to FM 7-1 for more information.

Application to Future Missions Training

2-160. Each AAR has a direct impact on the next mission or training event. Commanders review and annotate recommendations from AARs. The commander can then implement recommendations he feels are necessary to enhance mission execution and safety. The commander ensures all leaders (officer and NCO) review the AAR with his comments posted. These include improvements to the SOP, TTP, battle drills and, at a minimum, include mission critical elements. This allows officers and NCOs to learn from the AAR and understand the commander's guidance on recommendations.

2-161. Following the reviews and commander's guidance, the recommendations are highlighted in planning the next mission or training event. Following the mission or training, the debrief covers the results of an implemented recommendation. The commander reviews the outcome and determines if he wants to continue as recommended or modify the recommendation for a better outcome.

Chapter 3

Employment

This chapter addresses employment aspects for the AHB and GSAB. The AHB provides the means to extend the tactical reach of the maneuver commander, negate the effects of terrain, seize key nodes, achieve surprise, and isolate or dislocate enemy forces. The unique makeup of the GSAB provides the commander with a wide variety of capabilities. Both the AHB and GSAB allocate resources based on METT-TC, scheme of maneuver, available assets, and commander's priorities.

SECTION I – FUNDAMENTALS

3-1. Principles for employment of aviation assets follow these general guidelines:

- Fight as an integral part of the combined arms team.
- Capitalize on intelligence-gathering capabilities.
- Destroy or suppress threat weapons and logistics capabilities.
- Exploit firepower, mobility, and surprise.
- Mass forces.
- Maintain flexibility.

Contents

3-2. The primary missions of assault and GS aviation units are air assault, air movement, C2 support (GSAB), aeromedical evacuation, CASEVAC, ATS (GSAB), and PR. Each company must be prepared to fight as a part of the battalion as a whole, as part of an ABTF, or independently in support of a BCT.

MANEUVERING FORMATIONS

3-3. When different types of aircraft operate in a formation, the operating procedures, characteristics, and limitation of each type must be evaluated. Additionally, when aircraft are mixed at night, differences between NVGs, thermal imaging systems (TISs), and external lighting must be identified and considered in planning. Inconspicuous use of IR chemical lights or tape, IR strobes, and/or IR position lights, and IR anticollision lights enhances identification and improves spatial reference.

3-4. Maneuverability is the prime consideration for formations flying in tactical situations. These formations allow lead to maintain formation integrity, yet maneuver the formation with few restrictions. Wingmen must maintain a position that will not hamper the preceding aircraft's ability to maneuver. Due to their authority to maneuver, wingmen must understand that lead is free to maneuver near terrain and will expect wingmen to provide their own horizontal and vertical clearance.

3-5. Over open terrain or during high illumination, greater spacing is used to increase survivability and flexibility. Formation spacing becomes tighter in rough terrain or reduced illumination/visibility. It is important to avoid flying over the same spot on the ground; variations in flight path between aircraft/flights should be the norm. Aircraft and flight separation may range from 3 to 5 rotor disks to 1 kilometer or more (see figure 3-1).

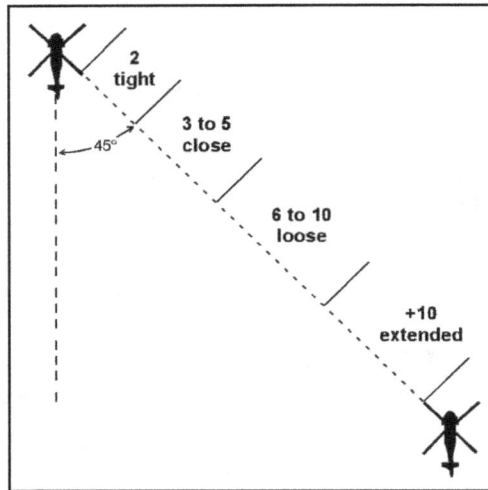

Figure 3-1. Formation separation

3-6. Primary concerns when establishing separation are METT-TC and the ability to provide mutual support. The basic flight formations are combat cruise, combat cruise left/right, combat trail, and combat spread. These formations serve as the basic building blocks to create larger formations and may be interchanged throughout a mission. Refer to FM 3-04-203 for more information.

COMBAT CRUISE

3-7. Combat cruise is used when teams wish to move quickly and maximize use of terrain for masking. Combat cruise allows the wingman flexibility in maneuvering the aircraft left or right of the lead aircraft's centerline. The wingman is allowed to vary separation and angle anywhere in the maneuver area from approximately 3 to 9 o'clock (see figure 3-2). The wingman should never track in straight trail as it limits forward observation and the ability to provide suppressive fires for lead. It also increases the possibility of alerting the enemy to the wingman's flight path due to the lead's presence. Separation should be 150 meters or more depending on terrain and threat.

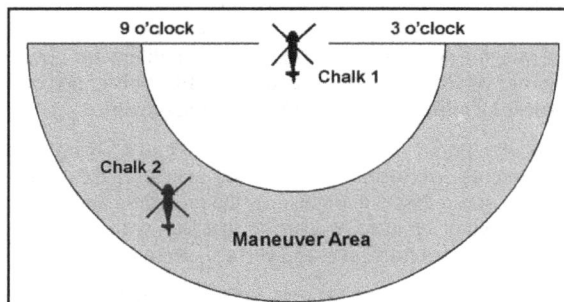

Figure 3-2. Combat cruise formation

3-8. Combat cruise formation is preferable—

- At very low altitudes for long flights to break up the predictability of the formation and permit optimal terrain flight using masking terrain.
- During day and high-visibility weather when small arms fire threat is substantial.

COMBAT CRUISE LEFT/RIGHT

3-9. Unlike combat cruise, combat cruise left/right requires the wingman remain in either left or right cruise and change sides only after coordinating with the lead aircraft (figure 3-3). Using combat cruise left/right, the wingman remains in an arc 0 degrees aft to 90 degrees abeam of lead to the left or right side. Optimum position is 45 degrees. Observation sectors are divided between lead and wing providing overlapping observation and fire.

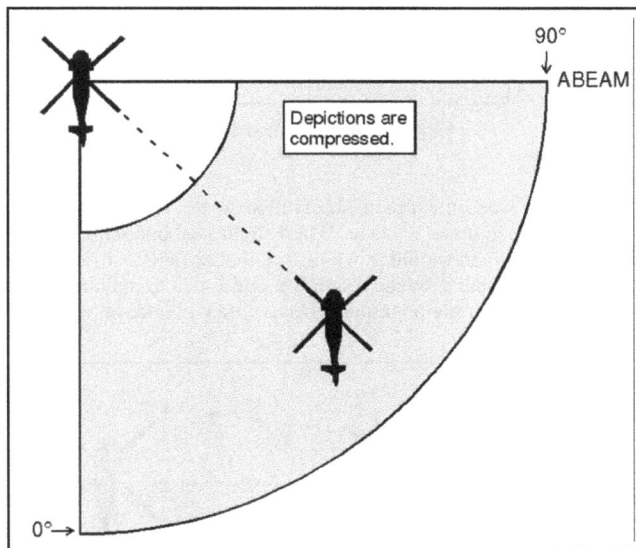

Figure 3-3. Combat cruise right

3-10. Combat cruise left/right formation—

- Is preferable at very low altitudes for long flights breaking up predictability of formation and permitting optimal terrain flight using masking terrain.
- Is preferable to combat cruise when weather and night vision systems are marginal, but threat is still high.
- Can be used at night for larger formations as an alternative to echelon when NVGs are used.

COMBAT TRAIL

3-11. While combat cruise allows wingmen maximum flexibility, there may be instances where flight lead requires more control of the flight and must restrict some maneuverability. Combat trail can be used to limit wingmen's movement to plus or minus 30 degrees from the proceeding aircraft (figure 3-4, page 3-4). This formation is useful for negotiating narrow terrain or LZs. It should not be flown for extended periods of time or at night due to the difficulty of determining rates of closure for proceeding aircraft.

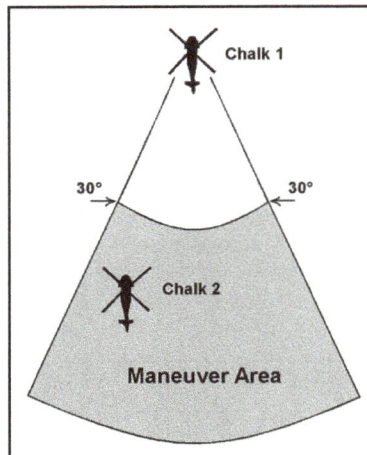

Figure 3-4. Combat trail

COMBAT SPREAD

3-12. Combat spread is used when maximum observation to the front is desired or an attempt to limit package exposure time over open areas is made. When flight lead announces combat spread, he includes the command right or left. Wingmen should move toward that abeam position, either lead's 3 or 9 o'clock position (figure 3-5). Flying in combat spread requires a rapid scan to maintain SA on the other aircraft as well as approaching terrain. This formation requires even more vigilance at night.

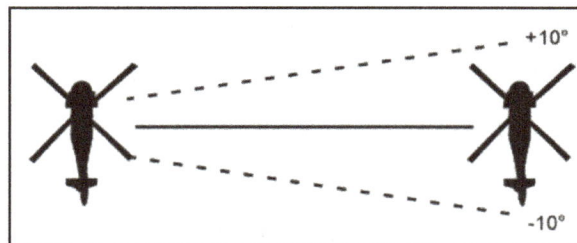

Figure 3-5. Combat spread

3-13. Combat spread formations—

- Can be used when maximum observation to the front is desirable or when attempting to limit exposure of the flight when crossing open areas.
- May be used en route to minimize vulnerability of trail aircraft.
- Is not advised for use in the objective area when constant maneuvering is required.
- Increases pilot workload to maintain formation, especially under night vision systems.

PLANNING CONSIDERATIONS

3-14. The factors considered in determining the best formation, or sequence of formations, are—

- Mission of supported and aviation units.
- Current enemy situation, enemy AD capability and placement, and vulnerability to enemy visual or electronic surveillance.

- Weather and environmental conditions such as ceiling and visibility, wind and turbulence, ambient light levels, and IR crossover throughout the mission.
- Artillery support available, naval surface fire support (NSFS), planned types of ordnance, and en route J-SEAD.
- Possible changes in mission or situation and evasive tactics to be used.
- Type of night vision devices (NVDs) used.
- Level of crew training and experience.
- Aircraft capabilities.

FLIGHT MODES AND MOVEMENT TECHNIQUES

3-15. Flight modes include low-level, contour, and nap-of-the-earth (NOE). They are often referred to as terrain flight. Based on METT-TC, all three modes of flight can be combined during execution of missions.

3-16. Movement techniques include traveling, traveling overwatch, and bounding overwatch. Movement techniques are designed to exploit mobility of helicopters while employing fire and maneuver concepts.

3-17. Security is established and maintained by adapting the flight to specific flight modes and movement techniques according to METT-TC. Flight modes and movement techniques incorporate principles of overwatch that include—

- Locating the enemy with a minimum of forces.
- Using all available cover and concealment.
- Overwatching lead elements and preparing to fire and maneuver.
- Adjusting movement technique and type of terrain flight to factors of METT-TC.

3-18. Flight modes and movement techniques are determined by available terrain and probability of enemy contact. Battalion or TF S-3s recommend terrain flight modes and movement techniques based on IPB; however, companies refine this information during TLP by choosing the appropriate scheme of maneuver for the assigned mission(s).

TERRAIN FLIGHT

Terrain Flight Mission Planning and Preparation

3-19. Using elements of METT-TC is essential to the safe and successful accomplishment of missions at terrain flight altitudes. Flight routes, LZs, and PZs are determined and planned according to commander's intent. Contingency planning is also a critical element during this stage of the operation and includes alternate flight routes, alternate LZs and PZs, and suspected enemy positions. The entire planning sequence is a methodical and thorough effort, eliminating confusion and clarifying each step in the planned execution phase. This intensive level of preparation also better prepares each aircrew to react to changes, unexpected events, and emergencies. This planning phase must include appropriate personnel from the next lower level of operation ensuring adequate dissemination of information and mission accomplishment.

3-20. The rapid dissemination of information allows maximum planning and familiarization time for aircrews. It also permits maximum time to brief the mission and address the questions and inquiries that inevitably result. There must be a sense of urgency in expediting the flow of information to aircrews as quickly as possible. Essential planning for terrain flight may include—

- Analyzing the mission using the factors of METT-TC.
- Performing a map/photo reconnaissance using available map media, an AMPS video map terminal, or photographs (ensure all known hazards to terrain flight are plotted on the map or into AMPS).
- Selecting appropriate terrain flight modes.
- Selecting appropriate primary and alternate routes and entering them on the map or route sketch, or into AMPS.

- Determining distance, ground speed, and estimated time en route (ETE) for each leg of the flight.
- Obtaining and evaluating weather briefing.

3-21. Terrain flight planning and preparation also include aircraft preparation to ensure aircraft are configured, preflighted, and readied for the ensuing mission. This is most effectively accomplished with a timely and continuous information flow from higher HQ, such as through the battalion S-3.

Terrain Flight Limitations

3-22. Terrain flight imposes additional factors on aircrews and units not encountered on missions flown at higher altitudes. The following are considerations for missions at terrain flight altitudes:

- Mountainous or uneven terrain restricting use of line of sight (LOS) radios, making it difficult or sometimes impossible to conduct normal communications.
- In terrain flight operations, control may be delegated to a lower level due to inherent problems. Aircrews and platoon or section leaders must be knowledgeable enough to execute the mission using sound tactical judgment. This is a result of training and experience.
- IED/vehicle borne IEDs can have effects on aircraft flying over or too close to roads.

3-23. Such missions should be coordinated with higher HQ to ensure appropriate airspace management and acquire the latest intelligence updates. Even in a training scenario, the plan to conduct terrain flight operations must be disseminated ensuring safe use of the training area.

3-24. The unit anticipates increased maintenance as a result of increased demands placed on aircraft and components.

3-25. Demands on aircrews increase dramatically when terrain flight operations increase, especially NVD terrain flight. Specifically, fighter management becomes a larger issue with an increase in psychological and physiological stress. The factors increasing stress include—

- Increased workloads (physical dexterity and mental processes).
- Limited field of view when using NVD.
- Reduced visual acuity, viewing distances, and depth perception.
- More complex aircrew coordination.

Modes of Terrain Flight

3-26. Terrain flying includes appropriate tactical application of low-level, contour, and NOE flight techniques, as appropriate, to diminish the enemy's capability to acquire, track, and engage aircraft. Terrain flight requires aircrew proficiency in map reading, preparation, and terrain interpretation. It also requires constant vigilance in identifying terrain features and hazards, and understanding effects of surrounding terrain, ambient light, and seasonal changes in vegetation. Continuous NOE or contour flight is unusual as terrain and vegetation vary. Normally, there is a transition from one mode to another as the situation dictates. Modes of terrain flight are defined as—

- **Nap-of-the-earth flight.** NOE flight is conducted at varying airspeeds as close to the earth's surface as vegetation and obstacles permit. Aviators should decrease airspeed if weather and ambient light restrict visibility.
- **Contour flight.** Contour flight is conducted at low altitudes conforming to the earth's contours. It is characterized by varying airspeeds and altitude and dictated by terrain and obstacles. Aviators should decrease airspeed if weather and ambient light restrict visibility.
- **Low-level flight.** Aviators perform low-level flight at constant altitude and airspeed dictated by threat avoidance. Aviators should decrease airspeed if weather and ambient light restrict visibility.

Selection of Terrain Flight Modes

3-27. Companies must determine which terrain flight mode to use in each segment of the planned route during the mission planning sequence (see table 3-1). This determination is based on METT-TC.

Table 3-1. Mission, enemy, terrain and weather, troops and support available, time available, and civil considerations and terrain flight modes

Mission
The mission influences selection of terrain flight techniques. This is especially true if the company performs night missions. Factors such as light levels and moon illumination complicate NVD flight at terrain flight altitudes. Lack of visual acuity may demand a lower airspeed and higher altitude.
Enemy
Threat weapons can detect and engage aircraft at low altitudes. To avoid or minimize detection, the company must select the appropriate terrain flight mode.
Terrain and Weather
Vegetation and terrain features masking an aircraft from visual and electronic detection significantly degrade the capability of threat weapons to detect an aircraft. The company determines a maximum safe flight altitude by availability of terrain features and vegetation to mask the aircraft. Companies use the highest terrain flight altitude for a specific condition. A higher flight altitude reduces difficulty in navigation, permits a higher airspeed, reduces hazards to terrain flight, and minimizes fatigue.
Troops and Support
Periods of deteriorating weather with low ceilings/restricted visibility may make any terrain flight mode extremely difficult or impossible. These weather conditions make navigation more difficult and increase potential for IIMC, especially when flying in formation or operating in an unfamiliar environment.
Time
Personnel factors may affect selection of terrain flight techniques. These may include aircrew availability, experience level, and effects of the fighter management program. Time also influences selection of the terrain flight mode. Whenever possible, the route should be flown at the highest flight mode to permit the shortest completion time.
Civilian Considerations
Selection of a particular mode must consider the safety of and potential threat from any civilian AO.

MOVEMENT TECHNIQUES

Traveling

3-28. Company elements employ the traveling technique to move rapidly over the battlefield when enemy contact is unlikely or the situation requires speed for evading the enemy. In this technique, all aircraft move at the same speed. Although this technique is the fastest method for aircraft formation movement, it provides the least amount of security. Units often employ low-level and contour flight at high airspeeds using the traveling movement technique.

Traveling Overwatch

3-29. Company elements employ traveling overwatch when speed is essential and enemy contact is possible. This technique is normally associated with reconnaissance, security, and attack missions when threat and/or environmental conditions preclude use of bounding overwatch. Lead aircraft or teams move constantly and trail aircraft or teams move as necessary maintaining overwatch of lead. Overwatching aircraft key their movement to terrain and their distance from the main element, and remain ready to fire or maneuver, or both, to provide support to main elements. Units often employ contour or NOE flight with the traveling overwatch technique using high and varying airspeeds depending on weather, ambient light, and threat.

Bounding Overwatch

3-30. Company elements employ bounding overwatch when enemy contact is expected and the greatest degree of concealment is required. It is the slowest movement technique; too slow for high tempo operations and too vulnerable for nonlinear and/or urban operations. Individual aircraft or aircraft teams employ alternate or successive bounds.

3-31. One element remains in position to observe, fire, or maneuver before the other element moves. Overwatching elements cover the progress of bounding elements from a covered and concealed position, that offers observation and fields of fire against potential enemy positions.

3-32. The length of the bound depends on terrain, visibility, and effective range of the overwatching weapon system. Units normally employ contour and NOE flight with the bounding overwatch technique. Airspeed during each bound is varied depending on availability of vegetation and terrain for concealment.

MANEUVERING FLIGHT

3-33. In addition to terrain flight, NOE tasks, and hovering engagements, aviators must be well versed in maneuvering weapons-employment techniques such as running fire and diving fire. These TTP require Army aviators to be intimately familiar with aircraft aerodynamics and the maneuvers associated with high-energy weapons platform employment. These skills are required to support engagement of a distributed enemy in complex terrain.

3-34. Combat maneuvers should only be used as required to accomplish the mission. Units should incorporate training programs to develop combat maneuvering skill sets as well as define factors of METT-TC that precipitate the need for transition to high-energy tactics. AMCs or flight leads identify and brief changes in the flight profile based on threat and mission changes. FM 3-04-203 has more information.

LANDING ZONES AND PICKUP ZONES

LANDING ZONE

3-35. The LZ is the site where aircraft approach to touchdown or hover to unload passengers or cargo. It is the location where ground forces consolidate, establish security, account for personnel and equipment, and reorganize/reorient to execute the GTP or other ground operations. The AATFC may use single or multiple LZs. LZ ground time is minimal; however, some aircraft may be redirected to PZs in or near the LZ for immediate backhaul of casualties and slings/cargo nets.

PICKUP ZONE

3-36. The PZ is the location where aviation forces meet and load AATF or supported ground elements, equipment, or cargo. It may be in friendly or enemy territory. The AATF or supported commander uses ground force HAs to avoid massing forces near loading points in the PZ until the last possible moment. Air assault planning is discussed in section II of this chapter.

SECTION II – AIR ASSAULT

3-37. Air assault operations are the movement of assault forces using the firepower, mobility, and total integration of helicopter assets to engage and destroy enemy forces or seize and hold key terrain. Air assaults allow friendly forces to strike over extended distances and terrain to attack the enemy when and where it is most vulnerable.

3-38. Army aviation integrates with other combat teams to form an AATF to rapidly project combat power. Air assaults require detailed, centralized planning and precise synchronization. FM 90-4 covers air assault operations in detail.

FUNDAMENTALS

3-39. Both assault and GS helicopter units perform air assault operations, normally lifting company to brigade-size TFs. Light and medium divisions rely extensively on heliborne assault for battle insertion and extraction. Heavy force assaults may involve the assistance of dismounted infantry or reserve light infantry elements in gap-crossing security and in seizing key terrain and chokepoints before arrival of armored and mechanized forces.

3-40. Air assaults routinely involve night operations, false insertions, and multiple LZs and PZs. J-SEAD and route planning are extensive with attack reconnaissance aircraft and CAS often providing assault force security en route and at the objective.

3-41. The directing or establishing HQ allocates assets, defines authority, and assigns responsibility by designating command and support relationships. The HQ forms the AATF early in the planning stage. If divisional aviation assets are inadequate, additional resources must be requested from the TAC.

3-42. The complexity of air assault operations emphasizes the need for close coordination and communication between participating units. Regularly scheduled training events, familiarity with unit SOPs, and the operating environment will inherently reduce planning time requirements.

CAPABILITIES AND LIMITATIONS OF AIR ASSAULT FORCES

3-43. AATFs provide the unique capability to extend the battlefield and concentrate combat power rapidly. An AATF can—

- Attack enemy positions from any direction.
- Bypass obstacles and strike objectives in otherwise inaccessible areas.
- React rapidly to tactical opportunities.
- Exploit success to complete the enemy's destruction.
- Secure and defend key terrain rapidly.
- Achieve surprise.
- Reinforce committed units rapidly.

3-44. The AATF also has limitations that include—

- Adverse weather that hinders helicopter operations.
- Near total reliance on air LOCs for deep assaults.
- Reduced ground mobility once inserted, especially for artillery.
- Dependence on availability of LZs and PZs.
- Susceptibility to battlefield smoke and obstacles, especially at night.
- Significant logistics requirements.
- Detailed planning requirements.

AIR ASSAULT ELEMENTS ROLES AND RESPONSIBILITIES

ASSAULT HELICOPTERS

3-45. The primary mission of the utility helicopter in air assault operations is to move troops. With seats installed, the allowable combat load (ACL) for the UH-60 is 11 combat-loaded soldiers. Refer to appendix C for more information on aircraft characteristics.

3-46. Assault and GS helicopters also perform a wide range of missions to support air assaults to include—

- Providing airborne C2 systems for the AATFC and staff.
- Supplying Volcano-emplaced mines to slow enemy forces attempting to react to assaults.
- Performing artillery raids.
- Transporting light vehicles and equipment to support the ground force.

- Providing air movement of supplies to sustain ground force operations (including FARP emplacement and support).
- Performing CASEVAC.
- Performing DART operations.

HEAVY HELICOPTERS

3-47. The CH-47 can carry up to 33 seated combat-loaded troops. The CH-47 is the only Army aircraft capable of transporting the 155-mm towed howitzer. Heavier high-mobility multipurpose wheeled vehicle (HMMWV) variants also require CH-47 transport. The aircraft also has extensive internal and external cargo carrying capability to carry bulky and heavier items. In the Fat Cow configuration, the aircraft can carry four 600-gallon fuel pods to support FARP operations. It can carry up to 24 litter patients for CASEVAC. The helicopter internal cargo handling system (HICHS) allows internal transport of 3 463L pallets or 10 standard warehouse pallets for ease of loading and unloading ammunition and other supplies. Refer to appendix C for more information on aircraft characteristics.

KEY PERSONNEL

Air Assault Task Force Commander

3-48. The AATFC normally is the infantry brigade or battalion commander whose subordinate echelon constitutes the main combat force. In some instances, higher level commanders may designate an aviation battalion commander as the AATFC. In a light or medium division movement to contact, the aviation brigade commander may be the AATFC.

3-49. The AATFC commands assault elements and is responsible for assault planning and execution. The AATFC usually locates in a C2 aircraft to maintain positive control.

Air Assault Task Force Operations Officer

3-50. Normally from AATFC staff, the AATF operations officer serves as the AATFC in the commander's absence and positions himself in either the main CP or TAC CP along with the aviation S-3.

Air Assault Task Force Staff

3-51. The AATF staff plans air assaults. The AATFC's staff must divide and coordinate planning tasks between the infantry staff and aviation unit staff. The staff must resource and synchronize all elements of the combined arms AATF.

Air Mission Commander

3-52. The AMC is designated from the supporting aviation unit and responsible for all aviation operations. He performs much of the attack, FS, and CAS coordination and assumes control over aviation assets during the mission. For major assaults involving multiple aviation elements, the aviation brigade commander is the AMC. The AHB commander is the AMC when his battalion is the primary assault force with limited attack security. For smaller assaults, the AHB commander may designate a company commander or platoon leader as the AMC, but the battalion staff still plans most assaults. The AMC—

- Receives and executes AATFC guidance and intent.
- Ensures all participating aviation units conduct operations according to the AMB.
- Coordinates actions during the assault and synchronizes attack reconnaissance, EW, CAS, and artillery assets as required. (The attack reconnaissance helicopter ABC may be designated to coordinate much of the attack, FS, and CAS coordination.)
- Advises the AATFC on any situation that might require adjusting the air assault scheme of maneuver and recommends changes that fully exploit aircraft capabilities.

- Designates a flight lead, serial commanders (if required), LNO, and planning cell to the AATF HQ.
- Usually collocates with the AATFC.

Ground Tactical Commander

3-53. The GTC is the commander of the ground maneuver force in the air assault. He plans and briefs the GTP, loading plan, and staging plan, and ensures the AMC's landing plan reflects the requirements of the GTP. The GTC staff assists the AATFC staff in air assault planning.

Brigade Aviation Officer

3-54. The primary duty of the brigade aviation officer (BAO) is to integrate aviation into the ground scheme of maneuver. The BAO accomplishes this by close coordination with the BCT S-3, commander, and BCT staff. He is responsible for advising the BCT commander and staff on status and availability of aviation assets and their capabilities and limitations. The BAO recommends and assists in coordinating the allocation of aviation assets, and helps determine priorities for their employment.

3-55. The BAO works for the BCT commander and is an integral part of the BCT commander's staff. The BAO must also maintain a relationship with the aviation brigade commander/aviation TF commander and staff. The BAO must ensure appropriate information is exchanged between the aviation brigade, BCT, and the rest of the BAE to facilitate smooth and timely aviation support.

Aviation Liaison Officer

3-56. The aviation LNO is the AMC's representative to the AATFC. He advises the AATFC and staff on matters relating to aviation's mission in the air assault. The LNO assists the AATF staff and AMC in—

- Selecting PZs, LZs, and the primary/alternate flight axis.
- Developing the air movement table (AMT).
- Developing an ingress/egress security plan.
- AC2 coordination.
- PZ operations.

3-57. The LNO does not replace the AMC during the planning phase of the air assault but acts according to AMC guidance in his absence. The LNO must understand the AMC's intent and coordinate with the AMC to receive guidance and update him on planning status, changes, and adjustments. The LNO should not make decisions for the AMC unless delegated such authority. To function, the LNO and aviation planning staff require transportation, AMPS, and communications equipment.

Flight Lead

3-58. The flight lead is responsible for assisting the AMC in selecting flight routes (primary and alternate) within the flight axis, developing timing for the routes, and submitting route card data to the aviation staff for production of route navigation cards. During the mission, the flight lead navigates the flight routes and ensures air assault times are met according to the AMT.

Serial Commander

3-59. Serial commanders are responsible for two or more aircraft separated from other tactical groupings within a lift by time or space. He is also the flight lead.

Pickup Zone Control Officer

3-60. The AATFC designates a PZCO (generally from his staff) for each PZ to organize, control, and coordinate PZ operations. The PZCO operates on a designated PZ control frequency and executes mission changes according to the AATFC's orders and aircraft availability.

3-61. The PZCO executes the bump plan as necessary and keeps the AATFC informed of any PZ situation requiring adjustment of the air assault scheme of maneuver. The PZCO ensures the PZ is clear of obstacles, marks landing areas, plans PZ security and FS, and communicates with aircraft on the PZ control net. The aviation LNO assists the PZCO in all aviation-related PZ functions.

Aviation Unit Staff

3-62. The staff of the aviation battalion performing the air assault conducts mission-specific planning and execution. During the IPC, the aviation battalion S-2 and S-3 are on hand to assist the AMC and LNO coordinate the aviation scheme of maneuver, flight routes, and mission timing for the air mission table; plan security against threats to assault aircraft; discuss ISR assets to monitor those threats; coordinate airspace and passage of lines; and develop J-SEAD plans. The brigade S-2 and S-3 may also participate. The aviation unit staff ultimately develops the aviation OPORD for all aviation elements involved in the assault.

3-63. The S-4 coordinates necessary FARP requirements for the assault and works with the S-3 to determine the need for auxiliary tanks.

Attack Reconnaissance Helicopter Commander/Air Battle Captain

3-64. The ABC is responsible for coordinating, integrating, and controlling all aviation attack reconnaissance and supporting fires (ground and air). He understands the AATFC's FS plan and places himself where he can maintain positive control of all air and ground FS assets.

3-65. Attack reconnaissance aircraft provide security en route and support the GTP. If air reconnaissance assets are available, they generally precede the assault force to reconnoiter the flight route, LZ, and objective areas. Attack reconnaissance aircraft may initiate preplanned fires according to the AATF's J-SEAD and preparatory FS plan. The AATFC may designate an ABC to control attack reconnaissance employment if employing extensive security and objective-support attack reconnaissance aircraft assets.

3-66. Attack reconnaissance assets often accompany the assault force providing security while flying at the front, rear, or sides. Generally, an AATF has no more than an attack reconnaissance company providing air assault security; however, METT-TC and support for the GTP may require more.

3-67. At some point in the mission, the AATFC diverts some or all attack reconnaissance assets from the assault force security mission to support at the objective as part of the GTP. The AMB covers all aspects of attack reconnaissance support planned by the AATF staff, executed by the AATFC, and under AMC/ABC control.

COMMAND AND CONTROL (KEY PERSONNEL LOCATIONS)

3-68. The AATFC, assisted by the AMC, addresses C2 requirements early in the assault planning phase. Controlling diverse and dispersed air and ground elements between the LZ and PZ requires effective C2 networks functioning at NOE altitudes and over the horizon. Planning must include digital data transfer and preplanned voice brevity codes to minimize radio traffic.

Command Posts

3-69. The AATF CP may be a ground C2 node of the AATFC HQ or an airborne C2 aircraft. If the AATF CP is on the ground, the AHB should collocate a TAC CP with the AATF CP. Typical AATF CPs are staffed by the AATFC, AATF S-2, AATF FSO, AMC (aviation brigade or battalion commander), aviation S-3, and ALO if joint FS is planned.

Radio Nets

3-70. A mix of air-to-air, air-to-ground, and ground-to-ground nets supports assault C2. The number of nets involved often exceeds the ability of a single aircrew to monitor. This requires task splitting among several aircraft. The following nets support a typical air assault:

- **AATF command net.** The AATFC and subordinate ground commanders use this FM net to execute the GTP (an HF or TACSAT command link may exist to communicate to the infantry brigade main CP).
- **CAN.** The AMC, AATFC, ground commanders, and PZCO use this secure FM net for air-ground communication at the PZ/LZ and to transmit SITREPs and mission changes (all aviation units monitor this net, especially in the vicinity of the PZ/LZ).
- **Air battle net (ABN).** The AMC uses secure Have Quick for air-to-air communication to include joint air assets (all aviation units monitor the net).
- **FS net.** The AATF FSO and designated aviation unit use this secure FM-relayed net to initiate preplanned and on-call fires.
- **Aviation internal nets.** Flight lead and serial leaders use VHF for internal communications.
- **PZ control net.** The PZCO uses this FM net to control the flow of personnel/vehicles in and around the PZ.
- **AHB command net.** The AMC or aviation S-3 use this secure FM-relayed, HF, or SATCOM net to communicate with battalion and brigade main CPs.

If CH-47 assets are available, the AATFC may opt to use assault mobile subscriber equipment (MSE) HMMWV assets and relays to facilitate integration into the division and corps MSE network.

AIR ASSAULT PLANNING

3-71. Air assault planning begins immediately on receipt of a mission involving an air assault. All personnel involved with air assault planning conduct continuous coordination under the AATF S-3 during COA development to ensure air assault considerations are factored into COA development. The BAE is critical to the AATF staff planning process during mission analysis and COA development. The BAE must anticipate requirements of the aviation brigade and disseminate these requirements as soon as possible.

DELIBERATE PLANNING

3-72. Due to their complexity, air assault operations are deliberate. Ideally, the AATF receives 96 hours or more, after issue of the order, to complete planning for a BCT-sized air assault. When time is available, units should use the timeline outlined in figure 3-6, page 3-14, to develop the best possible plan.

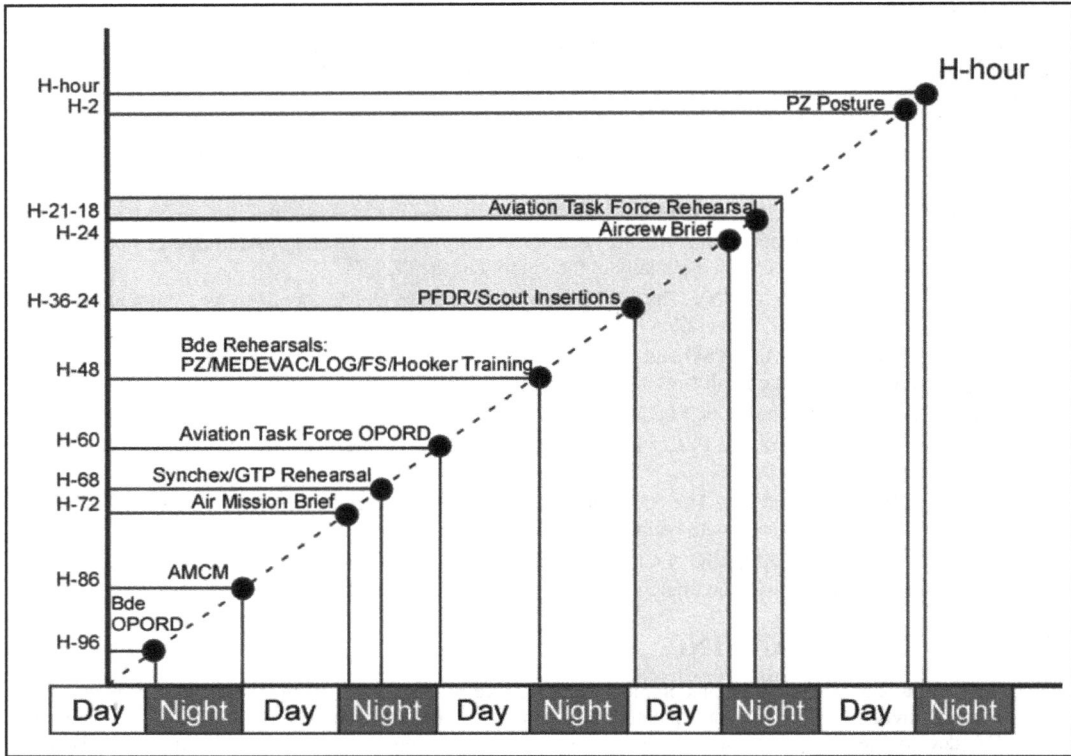

Figure 3-6. Deliberate air assault planning timeline

3-73. The air assault planning process (figure 3-7, page 3-15) mirrors the steps in MDMP and incorporates parallel actions necessary to provide the additional time and detailed planning required for successful air mission execution.

MDMP Steps | Planning Steps | Key Attendees

Step 1: Receipt of Mission

WARNO ←

Step 2: Mission Analysis

Step 3: COA Development

Step 4: COA Analysis

Step 5: COA Comparison ← IPC

BCT S-2, S-3	Avn LNO	Atk Recon CDRs
AHB S-2, S-3	Co CDRs	BAO
GSAB S-3	TACOPS	Others as required
Inf Bn S-2, S-3, S-3 Air		

Step 6: COA Approval ← AMCM

BCT S-2, S-3, S-6, S-3 Air		Assault LNO
AHB S-3	Pathfinder Co CDR	Atk Recon LNO
GSAB S-3	FSC CDR	HSSO
BAO	FSCOORD	Flight Leads
TACOPS	Weather Officer	

← Orders Development

Step 7: Orders Production
OPORD Brief

← AMB

AATFC	AATF XO, S-2, S-3, S-3 Air, S-4, S-6	
FSCOORD	Aslt S-3, S-4, S-6	Atk Recon S-3/CDR
TACOPS	Flight Leads	HSSO/Air Amb Co CDR
AMC	GSAB S-3	FSC CDR

AATF Rehearsal

← Aircrew Brief

AMC
BCT S-3
BAO
Aircrews

← Avn TF Rehearsal

AMC	Aircrews
BCT S-3	Others as required
BAO	If available BCT CDR
FSCOORD	and subordinate leaders

H-hour

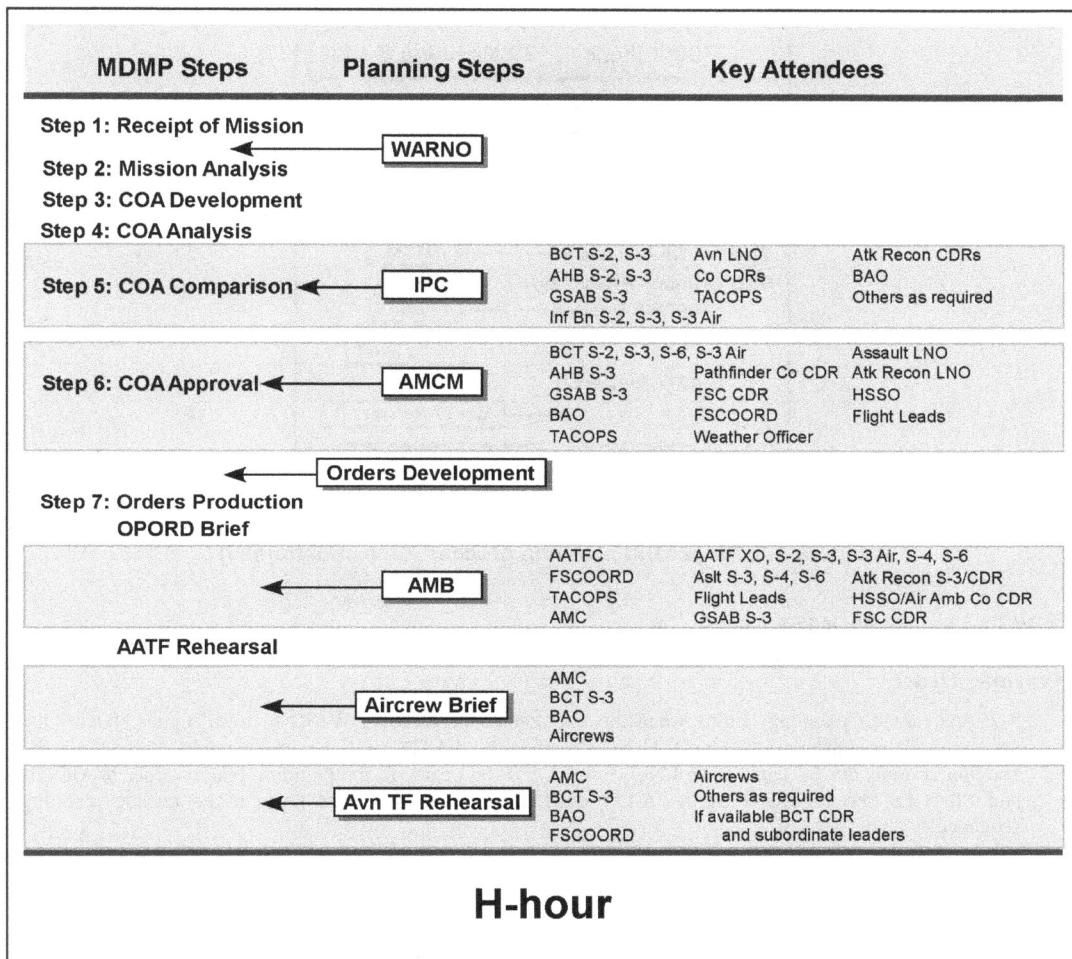

Figure 3-7. Air assault planning process

TIME CONSTRAINED PLANNING

3-74. Recent combat experience has shown that due to the fluid nature of operations, units are required to execute air assaults with less than 96 hours from the time of the OPORD. Successful execution of an air assault under time constrained planning requires parallel planning by all levels of command and units that are habitually aligned. Figure 3-8, page 3-16, provides a method to reduce the time involved in the planning process.

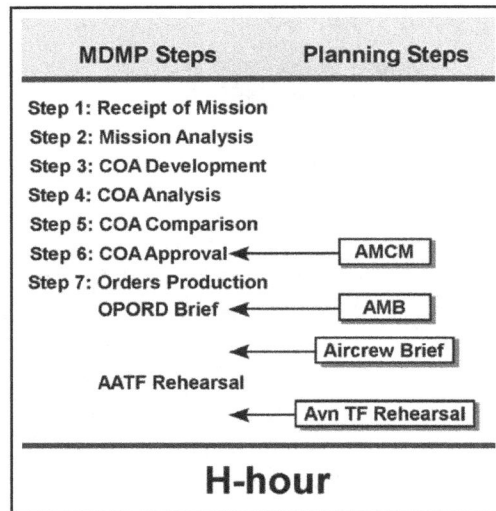

Figure 3-8. Air assault planning process (time constrained)

THE PLANNING PROCESS

Warning Order

3-75. Air assault planning begins when the aviation unit receives a WARNO from higher HQ for the upcoming air assault mission. The WARNO specifies the AATFC and task organization. This allows the aviation commander to dispatch an LNO to the AATF HQ early in the planning phase. Other WARNOs and FRAGOs should follow as the AATF staff and commander work through the reverse planning sequence.

Aviation Orders Development

3-76. Throughout the air assault mission planning process, the aviation HQ produces its OPORD, conducts aircrew briefs at company and serial level, and rehearses the aviation portion of the mission. The OPORD covers all aviation elements including attack reconnaissance, MEDEVAC, and heavy helicopters. The AMC and his staff brief other aviation unit commanders at the main CP. Planners comply with the one-third/two-third rule during the orders process to give subordinate leaders time to prepare. WARNOs and AMPS maximize preparation time for subordinate echelons.

Initial Planning Conference

3-77. The IPC is the first meeting between the AATF staff and aviation unit. The AMC, LNO, AHB S-2 and S-3, flight leads, ABC, attack reconnaissance security commander, and select aviation brigade staff personnel should represent the aviation unit. The IPC generally is held at the AATF HQ.

3-78. The AATF staff should have hastily wargamed the concept for the GTP before the IPC, so assembled planners can discuss and determine LZs, routes, and PZs. If more planning time exists, units may conduct a subsequent AMCM (similar to the IPC), but this occurs after the GTP and other mission details are finalized.

3-79. Following the IPC, both ground and aviation staffs should understand the distance and general time involved for each lift. The staffs should know what forces are planned to be in the first lift and in each serial of the first lift, and which first-lift serials are going to which LZs and by which route. Subsequent lifts and follow-on echelon lifts, while discussed at the IPC, can be planned in detail at a later AMCM if time permits.

Air Movement Table

3-80. The AATF S-3 Air and aviation LNO begin work on the AMT after the IPC. This preparation gives them an early idea of the challenges involved in relocating units to the LZ with the accurate number of aircraft available and distance and number of lifts involved. Table 3-2 provides AMT planning guidelines for light, airborne, or assault divisions with two assault helicopter companies.

Table 3-2. Lift scenarios with two assault companies

One-Way Distance Number of lifts	150 km 2 lifts	100 km 4 lifts	50 km 6 lifts
Mission Duration (at 120 kts - actual lift time only)	2 hr, 9 min	3 hr, 23 min	2 hr, 56 min
Aircraft per Lift (80% availability)	16 UH-60 loads; 32 total	16 UH-60 loads; 64 total	16 UH-60 loads; 96 total
Transportable Troops 11 fully loaded troops/aircraft[1] 16 fully loaded troops/aircraft[2] 20 partially loaded troops/aircraft[2]	342 (171 per lift)[1] 512 (256 per lift)[2] 640 (320 per lift)[2]	684 (171 per lift)[1] 1,012 (256 per lift)[2] 1,280 (320 per lift)[2]	1,026 (171 per lift)[1] 1,536 (256 per lift)[2] 1,920 (320 per lift)[2]
Notes. 1. With seats 2. Without seats Times indicate en route times only and not times associated with loading/unloading, FARPs, false insertions.			

Air Mission Coordination Meeting

3-81. The AMCM provides the conduit for coordination of operational information between ground and aviation operations officers and key members of the BCT staff. The AMCM is the true "good idea cut-off point". All changes must be approved by the BCT S-3, XO, or commander after the AMCM.

3-82. The AMCM is an S-3 level meeting that follows GTP development. The BAE plans the AMCM with the aviation TF S-3 present. The BCT S-3 chairs the AMCM and is also the final arbitrator. The AMCM is scheduled to allow sufficient time for maneuver units to establish a specific ground COA, based on the WARNO and standard planning factors. The AATFC should have already approved the maneuver COA.

3-83. At the AMCM, battalion S-3s brief the concept of their GTP including composition of combat power required, by echelon, to be delivered to each LZ. It is imperative subordinate S-3s attend this meeting with an approximate 80 to 90 percent solution on their requirements.

3-84. The meeting is not complete until the AHB LNOs understand the loads each LZ will receive and in what sequence. Attack reconnaissance LNOs must know which air routes and attack by fire (ABF)/support by fire positions to utilize, and all must understand the LZs as well as agree on a tentative AMT (with the start and end times of the first and last serial on the LZ). The BAE is the central figure in coordinating this information. The brigade S-3, XO, or commander must approve changes after the AMCM. It is critical that the supported infantry unit and assault planners come to the AMCM with their required information for an effective meeting to occur. Refer to table 3-3 for a sample AMCM agenda. See appendix D for a sample AMCM checklist. The end result of the AMCM is a finalized air movement plan, landing plan, air routes, PZs, and LZs.

Table 3-3. Air mission coordination meeting agenda

Roll call	BAO/S-3 Air
Intelligence update (aviation focused)	BCT S-2
Weather (aviation focused)	Squadron weather officer
GTP and FS (air assault specific)	BCT S-3
Air movement plan (routes)	Assault LNO
Attack reconnaissance aviation concept (en route and LZ)	Attack reconnaissance LNO
Fires (PZ, SEAD, LZ prep)	Fire support coordinator (FSCOORD)
C2 plan	BCT S-6
MEDEVAC/CASEVAC plan	Health service support officer (HSSO)
FARP plan	Assault LNO
Load plan (detailed)	BAO/S-3 Air
Review decisions	BCT S-3
S-3 closing comments	BCT S-3
If scout or pathfinder insertions are conducted, also cover the following: emergency extraction plan/trigger, alternate communications plan and rehearsals, communications check, and final coordination. For an artillery raid, include the following: Laager time/location and trigger for extraction.	

Air Mission Brief

3-85. The AMB is the final coordination meeting where key air assault personnel brief the plan to the AATFC for approval. The AMC, aviation S-3, TACOPS officer, aviation S-2, flight lead, serial commanders, all PCs, essential NCMs, and LNO should attend. If the air assault is planned on a time-constrained timeline, the S-4 and S-6 should also attend to ensure aviation logistics and signal needs are coordinated with the AATF staff in a timely manner. The AMC or his S-3 briefs the aviation portion of the AMB. FM 90-4 contains other information about the AMB. Table 3-4 contains the AMB agenda. Refer to appendix D for an example of an AMB checklist.

Table 3-4. Air mission brief agenda

Agenda Item	Individual Responsible
Task organization and roll call	AATF S-3
Time hack	AATF S-6
Enemy forces	AATF S-2
Friendly forces	AATF S-3
TF mission	AATF S-3
BCT/battalion commander's intent	AATFC
Ground scheme of maneuver	AATF S-3
Concept of fires (SEAD and ground tactical)	AATF FSO
Aviation mission	Assault AVN S-3
Staging plan	BCT XO
Loading plan	AATF S-3 Air
Air movement plan	Assault S-3/Mission Lead
Landing plan	Assault S-3/Mission Lead
Laager plan	Assault S-3/Mission Lead
Attack reconnaissance aviation mission/concept	ATK Recon S-3/commander (CDR)
Tasks to subordinate units	AATF S-3
Coordinating instructions	AATF S-3
Service support (FARP plan)	Assault AVN S-4

Table 3-4. Air mission brief agenda

Agenda Item	Individual Responsible
MEDEVAC/CASEVAC plan	HSSO/Air Ambulance Co CDR
Command	AATF S-3
Signal	AATF S-6
Operational risk assessment	AATF S-3
AATFC comments	AATFC

3-86. Seven basic documents should be available at the AMB to assist air-ground integration:

- AMT, regulating sequence of flights from PZ to LZ (AATF S-3 Air/aviation LNO).
- Tadpole diagram describing each lift's composition (AATF S-3 Air).
- Kneeboard-sized communications cards (AATF signal officer).
- Kneeboard PZ diagram (AATF PZCO).
- Kneeboard LZ diagram for each primary and alternate LZ (AATF S-3).
- Kneeboard sketch of the GTP scheme of maneuver for attack reconnaissance crews (AATF S-3).
- Route cards for all ingress/egress routes (AMC/flight lead).

3-87. Additional air assault planning products include—

- Air assault execution checklist.
- Checklist with codewords permitting communication brevity.
- Sequential list of events to ease battle tracking.
- FARP sketch(s).
- FS graphics.
- GTP overlay.

Aircrew Brief

3-88. Subordinate aviation unit and serial commanders brief flight crews. The aircrew brief covers essential aircrew actions and aviation planning necessary to successfully accomplish the mission.

Rehearsal

3-89. Aviation elements rehearse to synchronize elements. Representatives from the supported unit, AATF, and supporting units should participate. Aviation units can also conduct rehearsals without supported ground elements but must include key aviation personnel and start with the GTP/actions on the objective. AMPS can be a good rehearsal tool. Actual flight rehearsal on similar terrain is another possibility, given time and resources. For most air assaults, a full-dress rehearsal is desired.

Pickup Zone Update Brief

3-90. The PZ update brief is the final assembly of key leaders prior to conducting the air assault. The purpose of the brief is to disseminate the most current operational and intelligence information. It is conducted on the PZ after aircraft arrive so pilots can attend. The following components are reviewed: enemy situation update, operations update (target location), communications update, time hack, and commander's comments. At the conclusion of the brief, higher HQ is contacted for the final decision to proceed or terminate the mission.

Abort Criteria

3-91. Abort criteria are a change of one or more conditions that seriously threatens mission success. As such, they are CCIR relating to any ongoing air assault operation and require command consideration regarding mission continuation. It is important the AMB clearly defines abort criteria and the AATFC monitor the criteria throughout conduct of the operation.

3-92. Planners establish proposed abort criteria to assist commanders in deciding when success of the operation is no longer probable. The AATFC retains authority for abort decisions. Six factors considered to determine abort criteria for air assault missions are—

- **Weather.** Adverse weather conditions may reduce visibility and degrade effectiveness of helicopter weapon systems.
- **Aircraft available.** The GTP for an air assault operation depends on the rapid massing of combat power at the critical place. The number of aircraft available determines how rapid the AATF can build its combat power on the objective.
- **Time.** Times are set so the AATF operates during periods that will ensure mission success to include required time on the objective, time of day, and crew endurance.
- **Mission essential combat power.** Abort criteria are used to ensure friendly forces have the required combat ratio for the operation.
- **Mission criticality.** The success of other units and future operations may depend on the seizing of the air assault objective. Therefore, some air assault operations may proceed despite the presence of circumstances that would normally abort the mission.
- **Enemy.** Changes in enemy situation on or en route to the objective can cause the mission to be aborted.

Condition Setting

3-93. Conditions are set for all air assault operations. Condition setting includes both lethal and nonlethal systems against enemy forces and systems that can affect the assaulting force. Normally, 3 days are allocated for condition setting. The threat and ability to assess the impact of condition setting determines the duration. The purpose of condition setting is to limit and/or mitigate risk to an acceptable level. The same criteria and process apply to most aviation missions, thus they can be adapted for use with other missions.

3-94. Condition setting follows the decide, detect, deliver, and assess (D3A) targeting process. In this iterative process of setting conditions, unacceptable risks can be negated until final conditions are acceptable to launch the air assault.

Air Assault Security

3-95. Reconnaissance and security elements may precede the AATF and protect it en route using lethal and nonlethal means. J-SEAD fires, attack reconnaissance helicopters, Pathfinders, ground scouts, LRS teams, the Joint Surveillance Target Attack Radar System (JSTARS), UAS, and EW are among the assets that can disrupt enemy communications, radars, and air support.

3-96. Attack reconnaissance assets can provide LZ and PZ reconnaissance and security as well as en route security based on METT-TC. Refer to FM 3-04.126 for additional information on attack reconnaissance air assault security.

Backhaul of Casualties During Air Assault Operations

3-97. During air assault planning, the AATF staff and AMC plan the combined use of aeromedical evacuation (see section V) and aerial CASEVAC (see section VI). While assaulting aircraft may evacuate wounded from the PZ, the time required to load and unload casualties could desynchronize the AMT. If possible, separate CASEVAC aircraft should be used.

3-98. The AATF plans a means of marking the CCP for aircrew identification. Preferred signaling methods include smoke or panel markers during the day and strobe or chemical lights (not blue-green) at night. If air assault crews evacuate casualties, they must know where to take them and how to rejoin remaining lift aircraft for subsequent lifts. Using a backhaul LZ within the normal assault PZ, FARP, or both can minimize disruption of the loading plan while helping maintain serial integrity.

3-99. The backhaul of casualties on an air assault is a critical mission for assault helicopters, and one requiring detailed planning to execute successfully. During the planning stages of the air assault, the AATF S-3, S-3 Air, AMC, aviation S-3, and LNO must be involved. If the AATF commander's intent is to backhaul casualties, then planning must include the considerations discussed in the following paragraphs.

Note. CASEVAC aircraft and crews do not include medical personnel, are not able to provide en route medical care, and are not protected under the Geneva Convention.

Air Assault Task Force Commander's Intent

3-100. The AATFC must clearly state his intent for casualty backhaul during the air assault. The AMC must inform the commander of the tradeoff between using assault helicopters for backhaul and continuing with the air assault. If the AATF takes casualties early in an air assault operation, it may become necessary to reduce the amount of assault helicopters to accomplish backhaul of casualties. The AATFC should determine the number of aircraft he can bump from the air assault to pick up casualties. He may decide not to bump any and conduct all MEDEVAC or CASEVAC after completion of the air assault, or he may designate aircraft in each lift (such as the last two aircraft) for backhaul of casualties from the LZ. It is imperative the AMC understands the AATFC's intent on casualty backhaul and advises him on COAs.

Signaling

3-101. Night operations provide a significant challenge for casualty backhaul operations. Light signals should be planned so aircraft arriving at the LZ can be prepared to accept casualties. For example, a flashlight or chemical light (not blue-green) coming from the designated LZ casualty location may indicate there are casualties to be backhauled. Through this signal, the aircrews know they must remain on the LZ and be prepared to accept casualties.

Communications

3-102. Once established in the LZ, communications on the CAN or predesignated radio net can alert the flight of the necessity to backhaul casualties from the LZ.

Designated Area for Casualty Drop Off

3-103. The AATF should designate a specific area in the LZ for casualties. This designation will facilitate rapid movement and minimize ground time in the LZ for the aircraft. Since most air assaults occur at night, it is critical the CCP be designated and all members of the AATF know its location. The aircrews, as they arrive at the LZ, will be able to focus on the CCP and prepared to accept casualties.

3-104. The AATF commander must decide where to transport casualties if they occur during the air assault. During the planning process, the AATFC should develop a plan for the use of MEDEVAC helicopters. As assault aircraft drop off casualties, they can be loaded onto a MEDEVAC aircraft for transportation to higher level care facilities. Options include the PZ, forward support medical company at the brigade support area (BSA), or another designated area. Considerations for selecting a CCP include—

- **Casualty status.** A site should be selected that is secure and has medical personnel ready to accept casualties.
- **Aircraft availability**. Aircraft conducting casualty backhaul will separate from the serial at some point. The AATF commander must be prepared to affect the bump plan if aircraft carrying casualties do not return to the PZ for the next lift.
- **Confusion.** A CCP should be selected so it does not interfere with the air assault still in progress. Aircraft arriving at the PZ full of casualties may cause confusion on the PZ as troops are trying to load and casualties are being unloaded from the aircraft.

- **Aircraft rejoin.** A site should be selected permitting the assault helicopters to quickly drop off casualties and return to the PZ to continue the tempo of the air assault operation.

THE PLANNING SEQUENCE

3-105. Successful air assault execution requires METT-TC analysis and the reverse planning sequence. The five basic plans composing an air assault operation are: GTP, landing plan, air movement plan, loading plan, and staging plan (figure 3-9, page 3-22). Air assaults are planned in reverse sequence to ensure timing and synchronization.

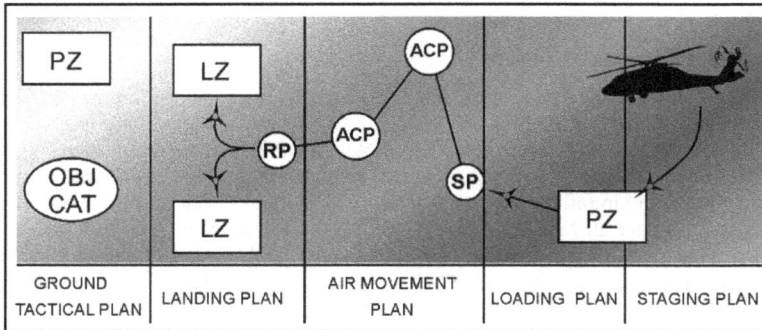

Figure 3-9. Air assault planning stages

3-106. These plans are not developed independently. They are coordinated, developed, and refined concurrently by both the AATF and aviation brigade staffs making the best use of available time. The GTP is normally developed first and the basis from which the other four plans are derived.

Ground Tactical Plan

3-107. The GTP is the focal point of planning and foundation for a successful air assault. All other operations support this plan. It specifies actions in the objective area to accomplish the mission and sets the stage for subsequent operations. It also indicates actions from exiting the LZ to attacking the objective area. The GTP addresses the following factors:

- **Task organization for combat.** This identifies the number and type of maneuver, support, and sustainment elements essential to mission accomplishment.
- **FS** identifies systems available and within range to strike the LZ and objective area, such as:
  - FA assets.
  - CAS or close combat attack (CCA) assets.
  - EW assets.
- **Scheme of maneuver** defines how the commander intends to maneuver the ground force from the LZ to accomplish the mission and seize assigned objectives.
- **Commander's intent** describes the method of execution and end state that initiates subsequent plans including:
  - Location of the force (land on the objective or near it and maneuver to it).
  - The value of surprise versus J-SEAD and preparatory fires.
  - Supporting fires guidance.
  - Observation plan guidance.
  - Other factors based on METT-TC and CCIR.
  - Use of attack reconnaissance helicopters including when and which units will transition from assault force security under AMC control to support the GTP under the AATFC/GTC.

■ Laager sites in support of PZ operations during extraction.

Landing Plan

3-108. The scheme of maneuver and GTP directly impact the selection of LZs, landing formations, and the amount of combat power entering the LZs. The landing plan outlines the distribution, timing, and sequencing of aircraft into the LZs.

3-109. After coordinating with the AMC and LNO, the AATFC selects primary, alternate, tertiary, and false insertion LZs (if applicable and METT-TC dependent) based on the following factors:

- **Location.** The LZ may be on the objective, nearby, or some distance from the objective.
- **Capacity.** LZs must accomodate for TF aircraft without excessive slope or uneven terrain.
- **Enemy disposition and capabilities.** The location of potential enemy reinforcements, AD, and other weapon locations and ranges influence LZ location.
- **Unit tactical integrity.** Squads must land intact with platoons and companies in the same serial to ensure unit integrity.
- **Supporting fires.** LZs should be within range of supporting fires.
- **Obstacles.** LZs should be free of large rocks, debris, mud, ice, fine dust/snow, and brush, unless executing special patrol infiltration/exfiltration system (SPIES)/fast rope insertion/extraction system (FRIES) operations or allowing troops to safely jump to the ground from a low hover.
- **Identifiable from the air.** LZs should be identifiable by aircrews at night and from low altitude yet should be shielded from enemy direct fires and observation.
- **Orientation.** Prevailing winds, illumination, and sun direction at landing time affect elements in the LZ.

3-110. The AATFC's intent and GTP influence the decision to use single or multiple LZs. Using a single LZ has the following advantages:

- Simplifies C2.
- Requires less planning and rehearsal time.
- Centralizes resupply operations.
- Concentrates supporting fires on one location.
- Provides better security on subsequent lifts.
- Masses more combat power in a single location.
- Reduces fratricide risk.
- May make enemy detection more difficult due to confinement in a smaller area of the battlefield.

3-111. Using multiple LZs has the following advantages:

- Reduces the risk of concentrating the entire assaulting force in one location the enemy could mine or target with fires.
- Forces the enemy to fight in multiple directions.
- Allows rapid dispersal of ground elements to accomplish tasks in separate areas.
- Makes it more difficult for the enemy to determine the size and main effort of the assault force.

3-112. During the landing phase, attack reconnaissance helicopters provide overwatch of the LZs, reconnoiter egress routes, call for fire (if designated), and screen to warn the AATFC and ground force commander of any enemy counterattack during the ground tactical phase.

3-113. The plan must address door gunner fires to reduce the risk of hitting other aircraft in the formation or troops on the ground. Dependent on landing formation, door gunners are usually free to fire. As Soldiers exit the aircraft, fires must shift or cease. On subsequent lifts, units limit door gunner fires with controlled or restrictive fire lines.

3-114. The unit may plan single door exits away from a potential enemy position. This technique allows the door gunner closest to the enemy position to continue firing while Soldiers exit from the other side of the aircraft. In this scenario, rucksacks may hamper rapid exit from the aircraft. The same applies to other cross-leveled equipment belonging to Javelin and mortar sections.

Air Movement Plan

3-115. The AATF staff develops the air movement plan and corresponding AMT with the AMC, LNO, and flight lead. This plan schedules movement of troops, equipment, and supplies from the PZ to the LZ. It also provides a plan of action for serial and lift routes, start points, ACPs, RPs, aircraft speeds, altitudes, en route formations, actions on enemy contact, FS en route, and egress.

3-116. Factors of METT-TC determine flight route selection. Higher HQ may recommend general flight axes or designate flight corridors from which to plan exact flight routes. The AATF staff and flight lead develop primary and alternate flight routes while considering the following:

- **Airspace management.** Coordinate flight corridors, axes, and PPs with ground maneuver, artillery, AD, joint, UAS, aeromedical evacuation, and other potential airspace users to reduce fratricide risks (a ground and/or aviation brigade usually coordinates airspace management).
- **Support of the landing plan.** Develop flight routes and LZ formations that conceal and facilitate rapid aircraft approach and departure into the LZ and exact landing/take-off locations.
- **Enemy capabilities.** Avoid known or suspected enemy positions en route; choose routes providing maximum terrain masking at contour speeds and altitudes.
- **FS.** Select routes friendly artillery can range; plan to lift towed artillery to support en route and objective fires. Deconflict routes with position areas for artillery (PAAs) and gun-target lines.
- **Distance.** Minimize flight route distance to decrease aircraft exposure time and increase speed of turnaround.

3-117. Table 3-5 provides an example of how to calculate en route time. Add 2 to 5 minutes of flight time to an LZ 3 to 8 kilometers from the RP, 2 to 5 minutes of flight time for a PZ 3 to 8 kilometers from the start point, and one minute for acceleration/deceleration time.

Table 3-5. Computing en route time

Flight time computation	
T = $\dfrac{D \times 60}{S \times 1.85}$ (60 converts hr to min) (1.85 converts kt to km/hr) **Note:** Round up fractions of a minute to the next whole minute.	T = Time in minutes D = Distance in kilometers S = Groundspeed in knots Aviation planners convert airspeed to groundspeed.
Example: Given 80 km distance from start point to RP at an average groundspeed of 100 kt.	
T = $\dfrac{80 \text{ km} \times 60}{100 \text{ kt} \times 1.85}$ T = $\dfrac{4800}{185}$ T = 25.9	(Round up to 26 minutes one-way from the start point to RP.)
Note: Sample groundspeeds in kts converted to rounded off km/hour and km/minute 80 kt = 148.2 km/hr = 2.5 km/min = 110 kt = 203.7 km/hr = 3.4 km/min 90 kt = 166.7 km/hr = 2.8 km/min = 120 kt = 222.2 km/hr = 3.7 km/min 100 kt = 185.2 km/hr = 3.1 km/min = 130 kt = 240.8 km/hr = 4.0 km/min	

3-118. The RP should be chosen so flights cross it within a 30-degree arc of the final approach path to the LZ. This allows more precision in timing and simplifies transition from the en route formation to the landing formation.

3-119. If the AATF employs J-SEAD, en route fires, or CAS/air interdiction, it may request designated flight corridors for portions of the flight route. The aviation brigade or AATF staff coordinates the corridor through airspace management channels. A flight corridor has a maximum width and altitude restricting navigation within the corridor.

3-120. Air corridors may exist only within the vicinity of the PP and at en route locations deemed potentially dangerous and requiring long-range indirect fires or air interdiction. The AATF may designate the remainder of the planned route as a wide flight axis, giving the AMC and flight leads greater latitude in choosing a route.

3-121. The aviation brigade or AATF should request a high-density airspace control zone (HIDACZ) around the vicinity of the LZ/objective. The inner and outer HIDACZ boundaries should not restrict CAS and aviation reconnaissance. Units request the HIDACZ within the ACO cycle.

Loading Plan

3-122. The loading plan establishes PZ operations including appointment of the PZCO and air loading table. The air loading table designates the troops, equipment, and supplies load for each aircraft in a manifest along with the priority of loads, frustrated load plan, bump plan, and cross-loading of equipment and personnel.

3-123. Although ultimate responsibility for aircraft loading rests with the aviator and aviation unit, SOPs and loading plans must be coordinated between the aviation and supported unit. At the least, SOPs must address the following:

- PZ markings.
- Hand and arm signals.
- Hookup procedures.
- Troop entry/exit sequence and direction.
- Securing equipment.
- Assigned seating (if applicable).
- Individual to open/close the door (if applicable).
- Contingencies (hot PZ, lost communications, aircraft malfunction, broken loads).

3-124. The loading plan and PZ selection should aim to maintain ground unit integrity. Just as a squad should not be divided between chalks, a platoon should remain in one serial and a company should not be divided into different lifts or PZs.

3-125. The AATF staff selects primary and alternate PZs with the AMC and LNO. Multiple PZs can speed the assault. Units often designate multiple PZs to separate internal and external loads, troops and equipment, or UH-60 and CH-47 operations.

3-126. The AATF staff bases PZ selection on METT-TC, AATFC's intent, assault force's location in relation to the PZ, and capacity of available terrain. Each PZ should be—

- Large enough to accommodate all supporting aircraft at one time.
- Close to the troops being lifted so they do not have to travel a long distance.
- Accessible to vehicles supporting PZ operations but away from unrelated traffic.
- Free of excessive slope; blowing dust, sand, or snow; rocks; mud; ice; brush; and other obstacles.
- Masked by terrain from enemy observation.
- Outside the range of enemy medium artillery.

3-127. The AATFC appoints a PZCO for each PZ. The PZCO forms a PZ control party with troop control teams, rigging-support, ATS, and security personnel. PZ communications occur using wire and a secure FM PZ control net. Units minimize radio communications using preplanned brevity codes.

3-128. To avoid confusion at night, the PZCO establishes marking procedures and lighting controls. The PZ control party may employ blue flashlight filters and chemical lights to designate active ground staging areas as these lights do not interfere with aircraft night vision systems. Table 3-6 illustrates examples of marking techniques units may employ to mark PZs.

Table 3-6. Marking techniques for day and night pickup zones

Position In PZ	Daylight Marking	Night Marking
PZ entry	Guide and sign	Guide with 2 blue chemical lights
PZ control	M998 and VS-17 panel	2 green chemical lights on antenna
Aid station	M997	Steiner device
Chalk stage points	PZ control party guides/signs	Guide/blue chemical light per chalk
Lead touchdown point	VS-17 panel, smoke	Inverted Y, IR flashlight
Chalk touchdown points	Soldier on knees with raised rifle	IR chemical light per aircraft
Obstacles	Notify pilots on radio	Red chemical ring around obstacle
Loads to be picked up	Hookup team on loads	Swinging IR chemical light per load

3-129. The PZCO directs the marking of the PZ to simplify night identification. Beanbag or chemical lights in a shallow trench forming an inverted "Y" form a reliable marker for inbound aircrews. Chemical lights placed near each chalk can mark touchdown points. Other night marking mechanisms include glint tape; strobe lights with IR filters; meal, ready to eat (MRE) heaters; flares; and reverse polarity tape. VS-17 panels and smoke are good daylight markers.

3-130. PZ sketches promote understanding of the loading plan. The PZCO or LNO should provide the flight leader with kneeboard PZ sketches at the rehearsal or AMB. There should be space on the sketch where aircrews can enter new information and changes. The landing formation corresponds to the PZ sketch to simplify chalk staging and expedite loading. See appendix D for a sample PZ/LZ kneeboard diagram.

3-131. The AATF may have spare aircraft to offset mechanical problems or combat losses during the air assault. The bump plan indicates how spares join serials in the PZ and fit into the bump plan. One technique is to employ all available aircraft during the first critical lift, and park one or two aircraft to serve as spares during less critical subsequent lifts. The bump plan also addresses the elements or cargo to be delayed or left behind if aircraft numbers fall short.

3-132. During the loading phase, attack reconnaissance aircraft can overwatch the PZ and conduct route reconnaissance of the air assault flight routes.

Staging Plan

3-133. The staging plan prescribes arrival times and order of aircraft, ground personnel, and equipment movement to the PZ. Loads must be ready (inspected and certified) prior to aircraft arrival. The PZCO and PZ control party have primary roles in the efficient transition from the staging plan to loading plan.

3-134. During the staging phase, the aviation unit conducts mission planning, orders, and checks to ensure mission times are met during the air assault. Other preparation includes—

- Coordination between the AATF and AMC.
- Load preparation and inspection.
- Aircrew briefings, mission planning, and rehearsals.
- Aircraft preparation, reconfiguration, and spacing.
- Preflight inspections and PCC.
- Emplacement of FARPs to sustain the mission.
- Selection of flight routes to the PZ.
- Selection of routes to and from refueling points.
- Confirmation of communications card and frequency/COMSEC fill accuracy.

INSERTION AND EXTRACTION OPERATIONS

3-135. Team insertion/extraction missions can be conducted at any time during TACOPS. These operations usually occur prior to offensive operations such as air assaults or movements to contact. Teams may consist of long-range surveillance detachment (LRSD) troops, special operations forces (SOF), combat observation laser teams (COLTs), reconnaissance scouts, or retransmission elements. Teams may be inserted by fast-rope, single-point, or landing to an LZ.

FUNDAMENTALS

3-136. Assault and GS helicopter units perform team insertions and extractions of LRSDs, rangers, special operations teams, infantry patrols, forward observers and COLTs, combat engineer demolition teams, and Pathfinders. Missions may also require SPIES or FRIES equipment, rappelling ropes, hoists, auxiliary fuel tanks, and additional training or rehearsals.

3-137. The inserting or extracting aviation element commonly consists of two UH-60s and two AH-64s. UH-60s conduct multiple false insertions before and after actual insertion and enable immediate downed aircrew recovery. AH-64s provide security and may conduct feints or demonstrations to help cover the operation.

3-138. The unit may have as few as 6 hours to plan a team insertion due to the need to gather intelligence early in the planning process of a larger mission. A major mission may involve multiple team insertions/extractions. For example, the mission may require insertion of—

- LRSD and/or Pathfinders 72 to 96 hours prior to H-hour.
- Scouts 48 hours before H-hour.
- Advance elements and forward observers/COLT teams several hours or less before H-hour.

3-139. Aviation elements should expect the inserted element to choose insertion/extraction points 5 to 10 kilometers or more from planned mission objectives. They should also plan different ingress/egress routes. Insertion mission orders must include—

- Planned extraction points.
- Emergency extraction rally points.
- Lost communications extraction points.

3-140. Planned extraction points and emergency extraction rally points require communications to verify the preplanned pickup time or coordinate an emergency pickup time window. The lost communications extraction point involves ground teams moving to the emergency extraction point after two consecutive missed communication windows and waiting up to 24 hours for pickup.

3-141. Battalions must plan team insertions/extractions as companies lack the resources to both plan and prepare for the mission. Unit SOPs should outline an abbreviated planning process for these missions.

3-142. On short-notice missions, it may be impossible to coordinate J-SEAD or units may elect to avoid using lethal J-SEAD depending on threat and stealth requirements. Escorting armed helicopters and artillery can provide some protection.

PLANNING CONSIDERATIONS

3-143. Although insertions and extractions follow the same five-stage planning process, the primary difference between air assaults and team insertions is that a formal AATF may not exist. A command structure must be established to plan, organize, and execute the operation. Assault, GS, and attack reconnaissance units may internally task-organize for habitual insertion/extraction missions. Alternatively, the TF may be temporarily OPCON or under tactical control for these missions. Other planning considerations include—

- Coordinating with the supported unit and verifying mission requirements with higher HQ (battalion/brigade staff). Normally, the order is sent from the higher HQ to the company, platoon, or section conducting the insertion/extraction.

- Planning and rehearsing with the team members to be inserted prior to the mission if possible. If armed escort accompanies the operation, the assault or GS aviation unit should ensure the attack reconnaissance aircrews are included in the planning and rehearsal.
- Leaders gathering as much information as possible (such as enemy situation) in preparation for the mission and ensuring J-SEAD coordination as appropriate.
- Ensuring mission fuel requirements can be met and coordinating for FARPs.

SPECIAL PATROL INFILTRATION/EXFILTRATION SYSTEM OPERATIONS

3-144. SPIES was designed for use in inserting and extracting patrol personnel where a helicopter landing is impractical. The system provides a means of exfiltrating up to 14 Soldiers over short distances. It is not recommended for infiltration as team members are exposed the entire time. Due to the nature of SPIES operations, a thorough briefing is required for all participants before the operation. Careful coordination is crucial when additional assets (attack reconnaissance helicopters, aerial observers, or artillery support) are employed with the extraction helicopter.

3-145. Soldiers must have SPIES harnesses as part of their individual equipment. The commander and SP must ensure unit rated members and NCMs are trained and complete rehearsals prior to conducting SPIES. For detailed information on SPIES, refer to FM 3-05.210, FM 7-93, and the applicable ATM.

FAST ROPE INSERTION/EXTRACTION SYSTEM OPERATIONS

3-146. FRIES provides the capability to insert troops and equipment into areas not suitable for helicopter landing. FRIES is also the fastest method of deploying troops from a helicopter unable to land. The UH-60 has provisions for two fast ropes, one on either side of the cargo door area. The CH-47 has provisions for up to three fast ropes, one out the forward right door and two out the ramp. The fast rope consists of a polyester rope, which is 1¾ inches in diameter, olive drab in color, and various lengths (20, 40, 60, 90, and 120 feet).

3-147. Fast rope serves to insert troops without the aircraft contacting the ground or an obstacle. FRIES is used for team insertion or extraction in various settings:

- DART in mountainous terrain.
- Urban settings with no room to land.
- Pinnacles and ridgelines.
- Decks of ships.

3-148. The commander and SP must ensure crewmembers are trained, thoroughly briefed, and complete rehearsals prior to conducting FRIES. For detailed information on FRIES refer to FM 3-05.210, FM 7-93, and the applicable ATM.

HELICOPTER CAST AND RECOVERY OPERATIONS

3-149. A helicopter cast and recovery (HELOCAST) operation involves inserting/extracting troops and/or equipment from a helicopter overwater. HELOCAST is a very effective means of inserting and/or extracting combat swimmers, combat divers, LRS teams, SOF, snipers, and combat rubber raiding crafts. A HELOCAST operation is planned and conducted much the same as an air movement operation, except the LZ is in the water. Refer to the following FMs for detailed information on HELOCAST operations:

- FM 3-05.210 for SOF.
- FM 7-93 for LRS units.
- FM 23-10 for sniper training.

SECTION III – AIR MOVEMENT

FUNDAMENTALS

3-150. Air movement operations involve the use of Army airlift assets for other than air assaults. These operations are used to move troops, equipment, and supplies. The same planning sequence and phases used for air assault operations apply to air movement operations. In these operations, aviation is not necessarily task-organized with other members of the combined arms team.

3-151. Assault and GS helicopter units perform air movement on a DS or GS basis. Air movements are especially effective in moving forces and their equipment when—

- Ground routes are nonexistent, limited, congested, damaged, or blocked by enemy activity or obstacles.
- The supported unit does not have adequate available vehicles.
- Time is critical.

EXTERNAL LOADS

3-152. Typical external loads include bulk supplies, fuel or water drums, vehicles, trailers, materiel handling equipment, towed artillery and other weapons systems, and ribbon bridges. The supported unit is responsible for preparing, weighing, and rigging external loads. FM 10-450-4 and FM 10-450-5 contain information on typical loads and their weights. FM 4-20.197 contains additional detail related to required rigging equipment and methodology for preparation and transport. Appendix C of this manual contains information on UH-60 and CH-47 characteristics, capabilities, and limitations.

3-153. High altitudes and temperatures degrade aircraft performance, reducing the weight they can carry and/or the amount of fuel onboard. Reduced fuel restricts the distance items can be carried and causes more frequent refueling during missions with multiple lifts. Ground units operating in hot weather and performing missions with PZs, LZs, or flight routes in areas of high elevation must consider these factors when planning for heavier loads. Available aircraft power is higher during the cooler night, early morning, and late afternoon hours.

3-154. Supported units must avoid loading vehicles, trailers, pallets, and other containers beyond maximum weights that have been coordinated with the aviation unit. If the aircraft is unable to lift the load or transport it the required distance, the supported unit must reduce the weight by removing items. This could involve partial derigging, rerigging, and reinspection delays. These unexpected delays could cause the ground unit to lose aviation support if the aircraft are scheduled for other missions.

AIR MOVEMENT RESPONSIBILITIES

Supported Unit at the Pickup Zone

3-155. In the PZ, the sending unit must provide rigging equipment and complete the sling-load inspection checklist according to FM 4-20.197. It is the responsibility of the aviation LNO to verify that the supported unit is aware of the sending unit's duties in this area. If the sending unit desires backhaul of slings and rigging equipment, this must be precoordinated. The sending unit also prepares loads for air movement that includes marking, prioritizing, rigging, inspecting, weighing, and tracking loads. The sending unit is also responsible for PZ marking and operations, including ground guides and radio communication. For external loads, the ground unit performs the static discharge and hooks the load.

Aviation Unit

3-156. The aviation unit makes the final determination of the load's worthiness to fly and determines in advance what portion of the load to carry internally or externally. The aviation unit also transports the loads and notifies the receiving unit of any changes it makes in the precoordinated plan.

Supported Unit at the Landing Zone

3-157. The supported unit is responsible for LZ markings and operations, including ground guides and radio communications. The supported unit guides the aircraft to the desired point for landing or external load release. It prepares the LZ, unrigs the load, and loads rigging materiel for backhaul for subsequent lifts, if coordinated.

AVIATION STAFF RESPONSIBILITIES

3-158. The S-2 section identifies threats to air movement operations and disseminates reports. CH-47 aircraft are particularly at risk due to their large signatures, especially when transporting external loads. The S-2 section provides assessments of the safest routes if the mission is cross-FLOT or nonlinear.

3-159. The S-3 section provides mission, PZ, route, and LZ information including grid locations, frequency, call signs, markings, and landing direction. The S-3 provides critical mission times and a supported unit point of contact (POC). The S-3 section specifies the means of flight following and periodic situation reporting of activities and locations by precoordinating modes of communication. The S-3 section ensures compliance with the AC2 structure and advises aircrews of other potential airspace users along projected flight routes. If a threat is anticipated, the S-3 coordinates for preplanned or on-call fires available to support operations. The S-3 will also coordinate for attack reconnaissance helicopter security as needed. The S-3 section ensures aircrews are aware of downed aircraft procedures. A detailed mission brief can suffice instead of an OPORD for most air movement operations.

3-160. The S-4 section arranges refuel and maintenance coverage to support extended distance missions. When in DS of a particularly large air movement mission, the S-4 section may plan throughput of fuel supplies directly to the supported unit's trains where class III sections can link up their FARP equipment with supplies.

DOWNED AIRCRAFT RECOVERY TEAM

3-161. The DART's mission is recovering an aircraft damaged on the battlefield. Although downed aircarft recovery is an aviation enabling mission, it is a specific and detailed form of air movement. Considerations include extent of damage, location on battlefield, proximity to enemy and friendly forces, and recovery resources available.

3-162. Assault and GS helicopter units transport maintenance contact teams along with a security element (if required) to repair or evacuate downed aircraft. UH-60 aircraft can recover the OH-58D by sling-load. The CH-47 can externally transport all types of Army helicopters including another CH-47 (when properly prepared). The maintenance team provides recovery equipment but typically requires augmentation from the owning unit. Refer to chapter 4 for more information.

FAT HAWK OPERATIONS

3-163. A Fat Hawk is a UH-60 that provides fuel and/or ammunition. The UH-60 provides fuel to another aircraft from its internal or external fuel tanks via a micro-forward area refueling equipment (FARE) system. A Fat Hawk crew can refuel and rearm four OH-58D aircraft in less than 15 minutes without sling-loading fuel or ammunition. The absence of an external load increases UH-60 survivability, reduces emplacement time, and limits enemy capability to target the FARP. Normal operation consists of two external stores support system (ESSS)-equipped UH-60 aircraft with full crew; three to four petroleum, oils, and lubricants (POL) personnel; a combat lifesaver/medic; security personnel; armament personnel; and armament and refuel equipment to support the mission. See FM 3-04.104 for additional information.

UNIQUE HEAVY HELICOPTER OPERATIONS

3-164. Heavy helicopters have a few unique missions they predominantly perform rather than assault helicopter units.

Air Movement of Special Munitions

3-165. Nuclear, chemical, and other special munitions require transport in some battlefield scenarios; heavy helicopters provide the requisite lift and onboard security capability. Due to the sensitivity of this mission, a backup CH-47 and UH-60s with additional reaction forces normally accompany the flight. In hostile environments, armed aircraft provide en route security.

Air Movement of Oversize, Tandem, Side-by-Side, and Internal Equipment

3-166. Some equipment cannot be externally or internally transported by assault aircraft due to size, weight, or a high-altitude and/or high-temperature environment. Loads too heavy for the UH-60 include critical items such as the M198 155-millimeter towed howitzer and several HMMWV variants.

3-167. The CH-47's triple cargo hook system enables transport of vehicles and trailers or towed howitzers in tandem (vehicle and towed equipment are externally transported together). Likewise, some HMMWVs and other equipment can be lifted side by side. FM 10-450-5 details procedures and required equipment.

3-168. The helicopter HICHS gives the CH-47 unique abilities to load and offload palletized cargo. In addition, the rear ramp permits some drive-on/drive-off capability. Units also internally transport some trailers and M119 towed howitzers.

Fat Cow Operations

3-169. CH-47 aircraft carry the extended range fuel system (ERFS) or ERFS II and FARE or advanced aviation forward area refueling system (AAFARS) equipment to provide a mobile FARP supporting deep shaping operations and other special missions. One CH-47 can carry up to four 800-gallon fuel tanks, FARP personnel, and equipment, while other aircraft transport internal and external ammunition loads. See FM 3-04.104 for additional information.

High Altitude Operations

3-170. Some regions and mountainous areas have such high altitudes above mean sea level (MSL) that only the CH-47 can safely operate with adequate range and payload. High-altitude rescue of lost and/or injured civilian and military personnel is also a CH-47 mission. CH-47s can also insert combat teams and observers in high-altitude areas. Higher HQ may task units to externally transport communications equipment, AD systems, and towed artillery to higher altitude positions for optimal ranging.

PLANNING CONSIDERATIONS

AIR MOVEMENT PLANNING AND DECENTRALIZED CONTROL

3-171. Large air movements require planning and C2 similar to air assaults but usually without the associated task organization. Most air movements are smaller and highly decentralized. On a typical mission, one or two mission aircraft may operate at distances that often outstrip maintenance support and normal radio communications ranges. These missions may require extensive premission planning to coordinate—

- Maintenance support from other units.
- Alternate communication means (SATCOM, aerial retransmission, HF radio, or message relay by the supported unit).
- Threat data along the route and an alternate means for obtaining intelligence updates.

- PZs and LZs.
- POCs at supported and supporting units.

3-172. AC2 for air movement may include having the mission published in the airspace tasking order and coordinated by the ATS Tactical Airspace Integration System. Unit aircrews still have the responsibility of exercising caution and being aware of and not overflying artillery units, UAS launch/recovery locations, AD sites, and other airspace users. Battalions must coordinate with the brigade to ensure flight standards across the FLOT, or forward in nonlinear theaters, are published in the ACO to reduce potential for fratricide. Flight following or procedural control is normal for air movement operations with altitude restrictions often in place.

SECTION IV – COMMAND AND CONTROL SUPPORT

3-173. C2 aircraft allow commanders to maintain communications with their forces and provide timely information supporting critical decisions without sacrificing mobility and efficiency. There are currently two types of C2 platforms supported by the UH-60. The first is an aircraft with a C2 console. The second is an aircraft modified with the A2C2S console.

FUNDAMENTALS

3-174. C2-mission aircraft may employ ERFSs to extend station time up to four to 6 hours. Although C2 missions are normally flown in C2-system aircraft, other UH-60s may be required to perform this role.

3-175. Since C2 aircraft may need to fly at higher altitudes to maintain LOS communications, the supported unit S-3 section should request a ROZ or airspace control area. The aviation battalion and supported unit S-2 must analyze the threat to operating at higher altitudes. C2 aircraft supporting a ground operation must maintain awareness of friendly locations so as not to overfly and reveal locations to the enemy.

PLANNING CONSIDERATIONS

AIRSPACE COMMAND AND CONTROL

3-176. C2 aircraft must operate within a designed airspace structure. Normally, a ROZ or airspace control authority will be established for C2 aircraft. Selection of a suitable ROZ must consider several factors to include scheme of maneuver, threat, communications, and routes to/from the ROZ.

Scheme of Maneuver

3-177. The ROZ must be located in an area that supports the maneuver commander's plan and does not conflict with the current operations of the supported unit. The S-3, or S-3 Air, of the supported unit should request the ROZ. It may be necessary to plan for multiple ROZs. In offensive operations, on order ROZs must be planned, so as the battle moves, C2 aircraft can move forward and continue to provide effective C2.

Threat

3-178. Aviation battalion S-2s, S-3s, and TACOPS officers must carefully analyze the threat and the impact potential threats can have on aircraft working in a ROZ. ROZ operations can be high risk. Often aircraft will be operating in a ROZ for an extended period of time and may go above the coordinating altitude. A careful analysis of the ROZ by the aviation unit will ensure the ROZ can support the ground maneuver commander's concept and remain clear of high threat areas.

Communications

3-179. The ROZ must be selected so LOS communications are capable of being maintained with all elements of the unit. Altitude is a factor in ROZ selection. Higher altitudes allow for better communications but increase risk from threat systems. A careful analysis of the factors of METT-TC allows the ROZ to be selected in an area providing security and uninterrupted communications.

Routes to/from the Restricted Operations Zone

3-180. Flight routes must be developed supporting the aircraft's transition to the ROZ. These flight routes must be planned carefully, should avoid overflight of friendly artillery units, and should be opened and closed as needed by C2 aircraft.

COMMAND AND CONTROL CONSOLE OPERATOR

3-181. A console operator must be available to run console operations while the commander and staff are controlling the battle. The operator may or may not be from the supporting aviation unit. There are no special requirements needed to operate the console, just an understanding of the system's OPCONs. The aviation unit may not have personnel available to operate the system. The supported unit commander must be prepared to provide an additional Soldier to operate the console during missions.

ARMY AIRBORNE COMMAND AND CONTROL SYSTEM OPERATOR

3-182. A master operator manages the software/hardware, while the commander and staff control the battle. The operator must be trained to initialize and troubleshoot the system, use each of the component systems, and provide immediate work-around solutions in case of malfunctions. The aviation unit may not have personnel available to operate the system; therefore, the supported unit commander must be prepared to provide a systems operator.

ARMY AIRBORNE COMMAND AND CONTROL SYSTEM INITIALIZATION

3-183. Initialization is an important step in preparing A2C2S automated systems. To achieve maximum use of the system's capabilities, initialization must be accomplished prior to conducting airborne operations. If A2C2S begins a mission without proper initialization, it may be difficult to transfer the necessary volume of initial information while en route (in a timely manner) to exploit the capabilities of the automated workstations and data communications. The steps for A2C2S initialization include—

- Initializing radios.
- Initializing ABCSs.
- Loading the supported unit's maneuver data and graphics.
- Conducting a communications rehearsal.

COMMUNICATIONS FILLS

3-184. Some consoles require a fill from a modified ANCD existing at brigade level and higher. Coordination must be made as soon as possible after receipt of the mission for the supported unit to provide the necessary ANCD fills. To ensure the COMSEC fills are compatible, the console operator should conduct communications checks with the supported unit prior to mission execution. If the communications check proves unsuccessful, the aircrew should try loading the COMSEC fills from the secure loading device (KYK-13 or ANCD) at the supported unit.

COMMAND RELATIONSHIPS

3-185. Aircraft conducting C2 missions will be OPCON to the maneuver commander. The aviation unit providing the aircraft must coordinate with the supported unit early to integrate the C2 aircraft during the planning process. The aircrew of the C2 aircraft should attend OPORD briefings and rehearsals of the supported unit to fully understand the operational scheme of maneuver and concept for the C2 aircraft.

ROLES AND MISSIONS

3-186.   The airborne C2 mission often requires independent operations by aircrews and aircraft OPCON to commanders and staffs down to brigade and battalion level. A2C2S provides the maneuver commander with a highly mobile, self-contained, and reliable airborne digital CP with the C2 systems needed to C2 in JIM environments. A2C2S allows the commander and his staff to maintain voice and digital connectivity with required C2 elements. A2C2S will roughly replicate the systems and capabilities of a digitized maneuver brigade commander's TAC CP.

3-187.   A2C2S provides the maneuver commander a rapidly deployable means of C2 that can support any mission. The commander and staff can perform all battle command and coordination functions from the A2C2S. A2C2S provides tactical internet access to manipulate, store, manage, and analyze SA information, intelligence data, mission plans, and mission progress data to support the C2 decisionmaking process. A2C2S provides the commander the ability to "see" his portion of the AO, exercise C2 regardless of location, control his part of the battle, and rapidly respond to fluid situations.

COMMAND AND CONTROL AIRCRAFT CONFIGURATIONS

3-188.   UH-60 aircraft can be configured with a C2 console or EUH-60 with A2C2S mission kit to provide maneuver commanders with an aerial C2 platform.

> *Note.* For an aircraft to operate a console system or A2C2S, the airframe must undergo modification. Not all UH-60s are modified to operate as a C2 platform.

COMMAND AND CONTROL CONSOLE CONFIGURATION

3-189.   UH-60 C2 aircraft contain a command console and map board that functions as an airborne or ground CP and provides communications in both secure and nonsecure modes. The C2 aircraft provides the commander with—

- VHF/AM or FM-secure communications.
- FM SINCGARS frequency hopping/secure communications.
- HF secure with Have Quick I and II communications.
- SATCOM.
- HF-nonsecure communications.

3-190.   The C2 aircraft is configured with a C2 console in the front of the aircraft (figure 3-10, page 3-35). The C2 console contains radio sets, console controls, and six internal communications system (ICS) boxes for internal aircraft communications and receiving/transmitting on the console radio systems. The back row of the UH-60 contains a map board with four additional ICS boxes allowing 10 personnel to be hooked up to the console's radio systems. The C2 console is NVG-compatible allowing the commander to conduct C2 operations at night. The C2 console runs off aircraft power and internal aircraft antennas.

3-191.   The C2 console has the capability to operate in a ground mode. In this configuration, the console can either remain mounted on the aircraft or be dismounted and operated away from the aircraft. Using the C2 console in a ground mode requires a generator for power and external antennas. Figure 3-11, page 3-36, depicts the ground configuration for the C2 console.

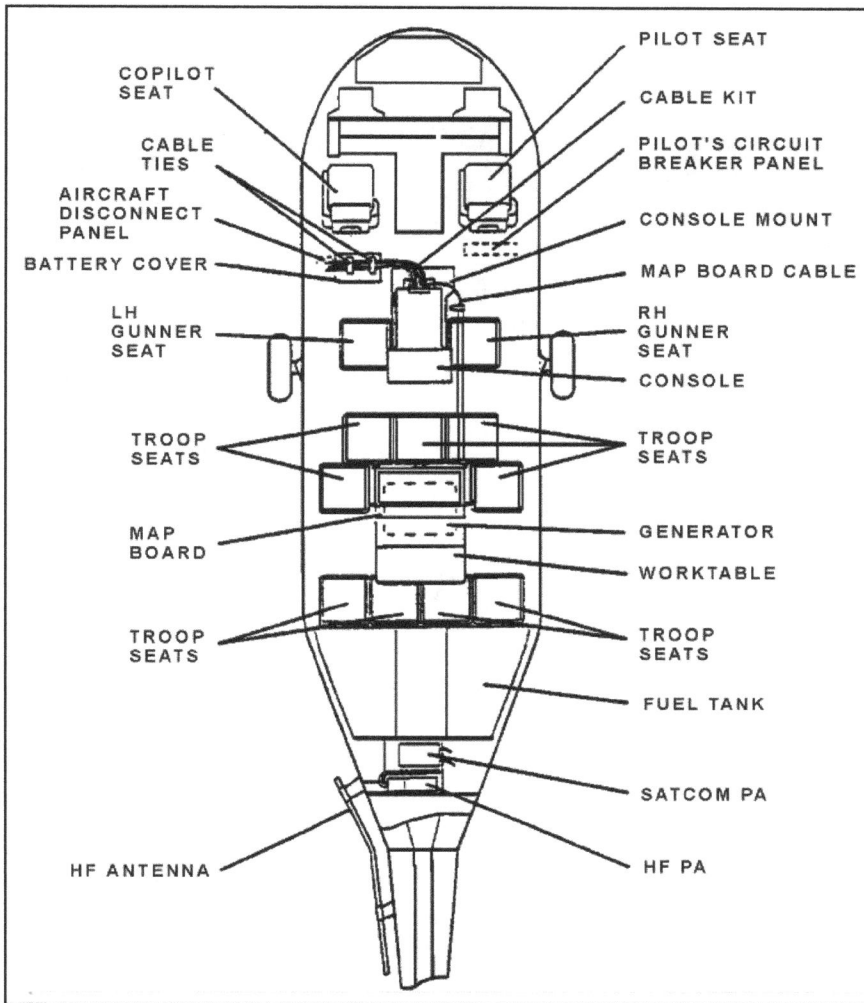

Figure 3-10. Aircraft command and control console configuration

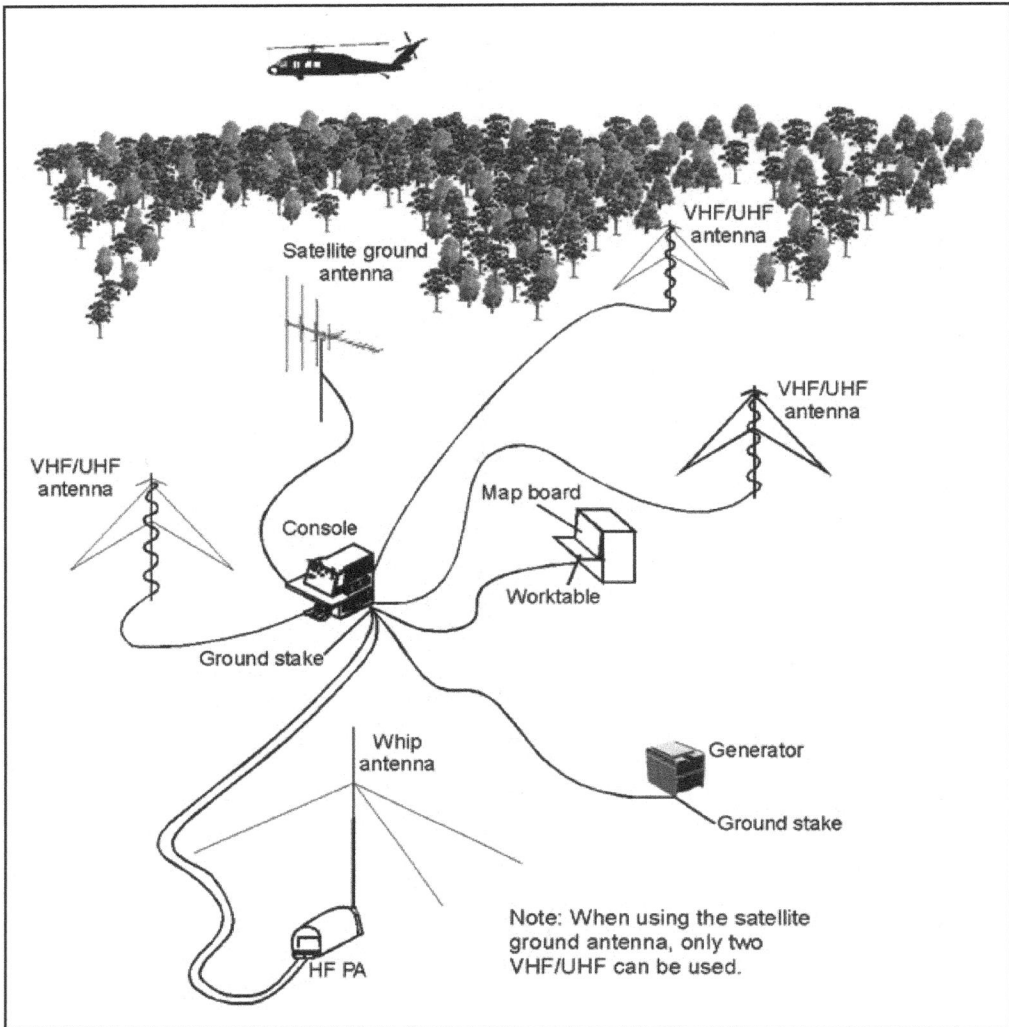

Figure 3-11. Ground based command and control console

Capabilities

3-192. The capabilities of the C2 console include the following:

- Provides the commander approximately 6 hours of on-station time (with ERFS mounted).
- Provides retransmission capability for VHF, UHF, and SINCGARS increasing the communications range for the supported unit.
- Can be configured for ground-based operations.
- VHF/AM and UHF radio can store up to 30 preset frequencies.
- Provides VHF and UHF scanning of up to four frequencies.
- Can store two SATCOM preset channels.

Limitations

3-193. The limitations of the C2 console include the following:

- **Requires an individual trained in operation of the console system for effective operation.** The crew chiefs of the aircraft are not C2 system operators; therefore the supported unit should have dedicated and trained console operators.
- **Removal from the aircraft is timely.** It takes at least one hour and four personnel to remove the C2 console from the aircraft for ground-based operations. Reinstallation in the aircraft requires special mounting hardware.
- **Limited FM communications.** With only one SINCGARS radio, the console can only load six FM frequency hop sets at a time. This limits the commander's ability to communicate, and retransmission capability is lost.

ARMY AIRBORNE COMMAND AND CONTROL SYSTEM CONFIGURATION

3-194. A2C2S consists of two components: an A-Kit and B-Kit. The A-Kit is permanently affixed to the airframe and consists of antennas, wiring, and aircraft interfaces (power, structural) enabling B-Kit installation onto the host platform. Once the A-Kit is installed, the airframe is designated EUH-60. The B-Kit (also referred to as the mission equipment package, airborne C2 system) consists of operator positions/workstations, computer systems, and the communications devices necessary to host and support the digital C2 process. Through its onboard ABCS, A2C2S provides continuous battlefield SA. It is also the source of digital information for nondigitized aircraft supporting the operation. The robust communications package on A2C2S provides maneuver commanders with on-the-move C2. The system supports three major operational functions—mission planning, mission execution, and mission support. Its primary function is monitoring execution of current operations while the main CP focuses primarily on planning future operations.

FEATURES AND PERFORMANCE

3-195. A2C2S provides—

- LOS communications through the latest version of the combat net radio (CNR) including SINCGARS-Advanced System Improvement Program, demand assigned multiple access for UHF SATCOM, HF radio with automatic link establishment, and Have Quick II/VHF/UHF.
- Beyond line of sight (BLOS) systems to include interface with the Blue Force Tracking-Aviation (BFT-A) system resident on the platform, which provides connectivity to the lower tactical internet for SA and C2 messaging and broadband (Ku-band or Ka-Band) communications systems. These systems support connectivity to the upper tactical internet and data transport for hosted ABCS and other hosted C2 systems while on the move.
- ABCS applications form maneuver, effects, intelligence, and SA (FBCB2 and BFT-A).
- Receive and view Army tactical UAS imagery for up to four user workstations for the commander and staff.
- Modular design (two or four workstation configuration) to allow the commander to configure the A2C2S to best support his C2 requirements.
- Ability to host current and emerging communication systems such as the Joint Tactical Radio System, Warfighter Information Network-Terrestrial, and military and commercial satellite systems.
- Common displays.
- Digital connectivity with all ABCSs.
- Airborne and ground operational modes.

INTERFACES

3-196. A2C2S utilizes a suite of secure communication systems providing voice and data communications. Voice capabilities include CNR (ground/air LOS and BLOS). Data capabilities include SA and C2 messaging, data synchronization, and collaboration. The radio requirements closely replicate the ground commander's TAC CP capability allowing the commander to operate the same nets and use the same TTP developed for ground CPs.

OPERATION AS A GROUND COMMAND POST

3-197. When operating as a ground CP, the preferred power source is commercial power. If commercial power is not available, a generator is the next preferred power source. If external power is not available, aircraft power is required. Extended ground times may require a ground power unit, which could be brought in via sling-load or tactical ground vehicle, such as a HMMWV with a generator kit.

INFORMATION FLOW

3-198. ATCCSs are primarily top-down planning tools. Once the execution phase begins, the primary flow of information is bottom-up via FBCB2. A2C2S draws real-time data from broadcast sources to determine changes to the enemy situation during the execution phase of a mission.

3-199. The operating environment increases stress on joint C2 as commanders are faced with unfamiliar scenarios in complex, uncertain, and rapidly changing situations. Simultaneously, joint C2 must support the increased demand for high quality information and conflict resolution that includes greater interagency, coalition, multinational, and NGO involvement.

3-200. A2C2S relies on the open sharing of SA and C2 information between joint and coalition warfighters as required by joint battle command. This enables A2C2S-information sharing with other service components and leverages relevant information from other command, control, communications, computers, ISR systems and sensors. The passing of information throughout the joint force and coalition community is key in achieving enhanced SA and information/situation dominance. A2C2S is dependent on multiple systems including, but not limited to, platform power, communications, computers and networking, position location devices, geospatial reference data, and subsystem/sensor integration.

SECTION V – AEROMEDICAL EVACUATION

3-201. Commanders of medical units in a theater of operations use modularity and economy of force to effectively allocate their resources to evacuate and treat sick, injured, and wounded Soldiers. A wounded Soldier's survival often depends on the time it takes to receive treatment. Rapid responsive care is essential to protecting the force and ensuring high survival rates on the battlefield.

Note. Refer to FM 4-02.2 for additional information on Medical Evacuation

---

3-202. Army aviation is responsible for command, control, and execution of the Army aeromedical evacuation mission. Each GSAB has an organic air ambulance company capable of supporting 24-hour operations. This company consists of a company HQ and four FSMTs with three aircraft each. The company can be individually or group deployed in support of tactical, operational, and strategic missions encompassing full spectrum operations worldwide.

MEDICAL EVACUATION

3-203. MEDEVAC is the timely, efficient movement and en route care by medical personnel of wounded, injured, or ill persons from the battlefield and/or other locations to MTFs. MEDEVAC applies to both air and ground evacuation and is a combat multiplier. Refer to FM 4-02.2 for additional information.

3-204. The U.S. Army is the only service that provides MEDEVAC consisting of dedicated ground and air platforms designed to provide en route care. These platforms are protected under the provisions of the Geneva Conventions from intentional attack by the enemy.

3-205. In contrast to a typical aviation mission cycle, continuous aeromedical evacuation coverage results in extended operational duty days that often exceed 24 hours in length. MEDEVAC units must plan and develop a detailed battle rhythm that addresses CRM and mission execution processes and TTP unique to 24-hour continuous evacuation operations.

3-206. A MEDEVAC crew cycle (figure 3-12) begins like any other mission planning; however, the location or time of execution is absent. Crews must manage rest cycles while ensuring procedures are in place to maintain battlefield SA for a rapid, safe execution when a 9-line is received. Units must establish unique crew rest cycles and briefing procedures for remote/split-based crews.

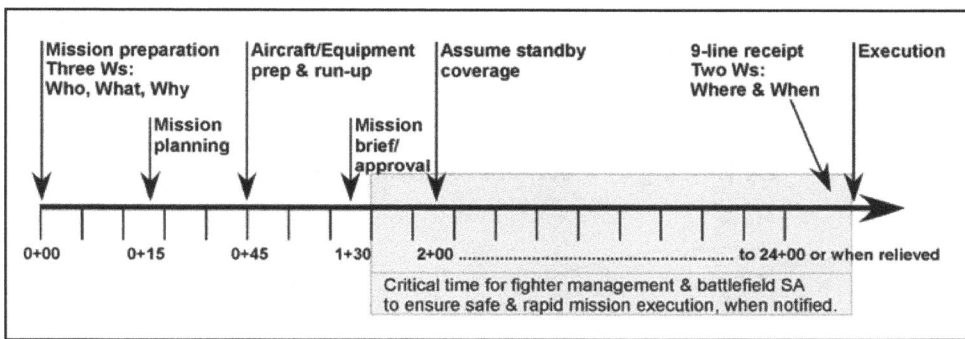

Figure 3-12. Example medical evacuation mission cycle

Dedicated Assets

3-207. Dedicated MEDEVAC assets include—
- Permanently allocated vehicles with no other assigned mission.
- Permanently allocated medical equipment for the purpose of en route care.
- Specifically trained medical personnel to provide en route care.

En Route Care

3-208. The provision of en route care on medically-equipped vehicles or aircraft enhances the patient's potential for recovery and may reduce long-term disability by maintaining and/or stabilizing the patient's medical condition. Recent world conflicts indicate extended distances from point of injury to treatment facilities make en route patient care more critical. Highly-proficient flight medics with standardized training are essential for patient stabilization, sustainment, and survival over extended distances.

FUNDAMENTALS

3-209. Army air ambulance companies are the only dedicated rotary-wing aeromedical assets within the Department of Defense (DOD). Air ambulance companies are assigned to the aviation brigade and provide intratheater evacuation to division, corps, and theater units. The speed, range, and flexibility of aeromedical evacuation moves patients directly to an MTF best equipped to treat the casualty. The HH-60 is used as the primary dedicated air ambulance.

3-210. The primary mission of the GSAB air ambulance company is patient evacuation; however, the company also provides—

- Patient movement between MTFs (patient transfers).
- Class VIII resupply.
- Joint blood program support.
- Medical C2.
- Movement of medical personnel and medical equipment.
- Air crash rescue support.

3-211. The air ambulance company executes a diverse set of missions. Their scope often crosses the mission boundaries of its aviation brigade. The air ambulance company may also call for support to a specific mission or unit external to the aviation brigade.

3-212. In accordance with Title 10 of U.S. Code, air ambulance assets are responsible for MEDEVAC in support of joint operations. In planning evacuation operations, the tactical, operational, and strategic scope of the mission, as part of the joint force, must be considered in CAB planning (figure 3-13).

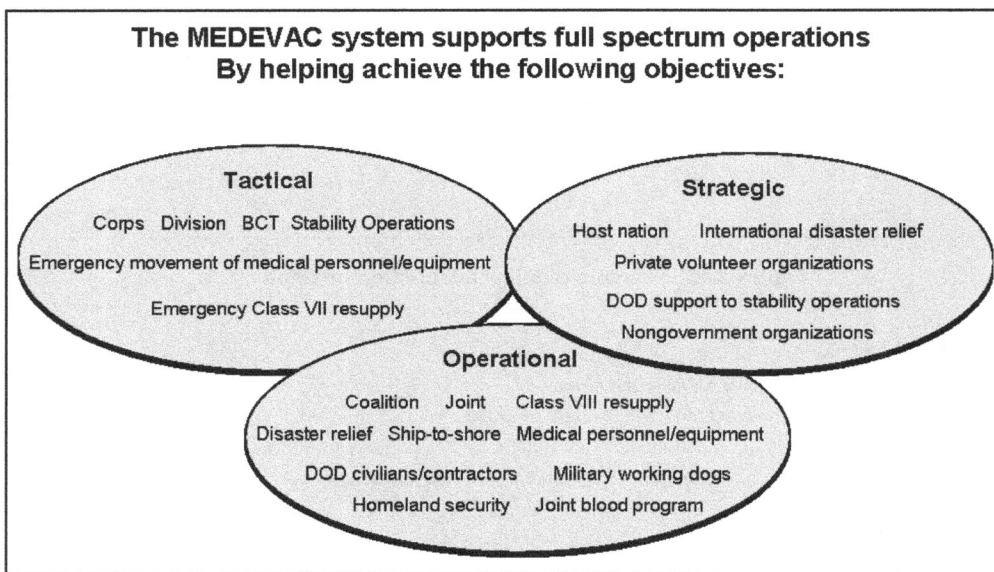

The MEDEVAC system supports full spectrum operations
By helping achieve the following objectives:

Tactical

Corps   Division   BCT   Stability Operations

Emergency movement of medical personnel/equipment

Emergency Class VII resupply

Strategic

Host nation   International disaster relief

Private volunteer organizations

DOD support to stability operations

Nongovernment organizations

Operational

Coalition   Joint   Class VIII resupply

Disaster relief   Ship-to-shore   Medical personnel/equipment

DOD civilians/contractors   Military working dogs

Homeland security   Joint blood program

Figure 3-13. Army medical evacuation mission spectrum

3-213. Air ambulance company joint missions during combat operations include—

- Evacuation of joint and coalition force casualties.
- Evacuation of enemy prisoner of war (EPW) casualties.
- Evacuation of civilian patients.
- Evacuation of contractors and government employees.
- Noncombatant evacuation.
- Shore-to-ship evacuation.
- Transfer of patients to Air Force aeromedical evacuation staging facilities.
- Evacuation of military working dogs.
- Support of PR operations.

3-214. Air ambulance joint missions during stability operations or civil support operations include—
- Support of natural disaster area evacuees.
- Support of disease and famine stricken areas.
- Support of areas struck by acts of terrorism.
- Evacuation of civilian patients in nations occupied by joint forces during stability operations.

PLANNING CONSIDERATIONS

3-215. Planning considerations for aeromedical evacuation operations often require unique and specific plans to support continuous and often decentralized operations. These include but are not limited to—
- Receipt and synchronization with the evacuation plan from higher.
- Support for CAB DS and GS missions.
- Logistics support for split-based operations.
- Battle rhythm/communication flow for receiving MEDEVAC missions.
- MOC coordination with all medical units for collecting medical information to develop and maintain SA of MTFs and patient regulation.
- Fighter management plan to support continuous operations.
- Identify and coordinate CASEVAC support when necessary.
- Rapid communications plan with risk approval authorities to ensure mission rebrief if required.

RECEIPT OF THE EVACUATION PLAN FROM HIGHER

3-216. The evacuation plan from higher integrates aeromedical evacuation with the Army medical system. To establish evacuation procedures, each level of command issues an evacuation plan through the orders process developed by evacuation planners at each level of command. On receipt of the higher HQ force health protection plan, the aeromedical evacuation support plan must be synchronized with Army aviation planners.

3-217. The evacuation order assigns—
- **GS mission responsibilities** such as patient transfers, blood, and medical resupply. For example, an air ambulance company collocated with a CAB supporting a division in reserve may be assigned a greater portion of the patient transfer mission due to lower expected casualties within its assigned DS division.
- **Joint and coalition force support responsibilities** such as an FSMT tasked to provide DS to a Marine Corps regiment
- **Any DS or GS taskings that takes air ambulance assets away from their CAB.** For example an FSMT could be tasked to specifically support a humanitarian mission occurring in a specific region of a combat zone.

SUPPORT PLAN FOR DIRECT SUPPORT AND GENERAL SUPPORT MISSIONS OF THE COMBAT AVIATION BRIGADE

3-218. The air ambulance company in concert with evacuation planners (MOC) of the CAB and GSAB must devise an allocation plan that can support all of the evacuation coverage areas and missions the evacuation order assigns to the CAB. Important considerations include—
- **MEDEVAC aircraft are a critical asset in today's operational environment.** Care must be taken on how to employ MEDEVAC assets as effectively and efficiently as possible.
- **FSMTs must retain flexibility in employment.** In both the DS and GS role, FSMT efforts should not be rigidly tied to any area or supported unit.
- **Air ambulance assets are a limited resource and located where they are most needed.** This can be with troops most often engaged in combat, high population density areas, areas of famine or disease with high civilian casualties, refugee areas, or geographically centralized locations.

- **FSMTs performing area support or GS accomplish the patient transfer mission that develops between MTFs, FSMTs and MTFs, and MTFs and intertheater movement locations.** These FSMTs are also responsible for the DS mission within their immediate vicinity.

PLAN FOR SPLIT-BASED OPERATIONS (IF APPLICABLE)

3-219. Air ambulance split-based operations can occur for a short time or the entire duration of a deployment/operation. CAB/GSAB commanders must consider the ramifications of this action and provide the necessary support with personnel, maintenance, communication and other equipment, vehicles, and a bench stock (BS) of several categories of supply.

3-220. FSMTs or an air ambulance company may be operating and collocated with a GSAB or be task-organized with a joint task force (JTF), marine expeditionary force (MEF), BCT, coalition, host nation, or other organizations such as the civilian disaster relief operations center.

3-221. When air ambulance companies or their FSMTs are task-organized apart from the GSAB, C2 may become difficult and a break in contact, short or long term, should be included in the plan. Solid SOPs, leadership skills, and command guidance are necessary to compensate for a temporary break in communications.

3-222. Air ambulance assets collocated with the CAB will be able to utilize the operations cell (battle captain) to grant launch authority if the CAB commander chooses. However, an FSMT or air ambulance company may be isolated from the CAB, and another measure will have to be used such as delegating launch authority and authorized briefers. For example, an air ambulance company supporting a Marine Corps division apart from the CAB will not have high and very high risk briefers who are PCs in the mission being performed; therefore, an alternate method must be assigned.

METHODOLOGY FOR RECEIVING MEDICAL EVACUATION MISSIONS AND LAUNCHING MEDICAL EVACUATION AIRCRAFT

3-223. Time is of crucial importance to MEDEVAC missions. MEDEVAC duty cycles are generally executed differently than other aviation missions but could be compared to a helicopter QRF mission cycle. Generally, aeromedical evacuation duty cycles are conducted as follows:

- Mission brief and risk assessment developed.
- Mission intelligence, ACO, SPINS, NOTAMs, and other information collected and incorporated in planning.
- Local area events and knowledge is shared among crews.
- Preflight and maintenance checks performed.
- Aircraft is run-up and set up in mission ready status with necessary mission equipment onboard.
- Crew stands by for MEDEVAC missions.

3-224. When missions are received—

- Crew analyzes the mission from the 9-line and determines risk level.
- Procedures must be in place to coordinate immediately for the next higher level of command to approve, if risk level is beyond what the crew is briefed,.
- Crew coordinates for other mission specific considerations (escort aircraft or extraction equipment).
- The goal is to launch as rapidly as possible (METT-TC dependent) to ensure safe, efficient execution of the mission.

3-225. MEDEVAC missions are received through a number of different communications venues (figure 3-14. page 3-43). An established communication net that provides adequate battlefield SA and the FSMT the ability to communicate during mission execution is essential. This is often a command net but could also be another reliable and dedicated communication system if available. The higher HQ maintaining SA over the operation could be the GSAB HQ for the air ambulance company or one of many options including: JTF, MEF, BCT, coalition, host nation, or a disaster relief operations center.

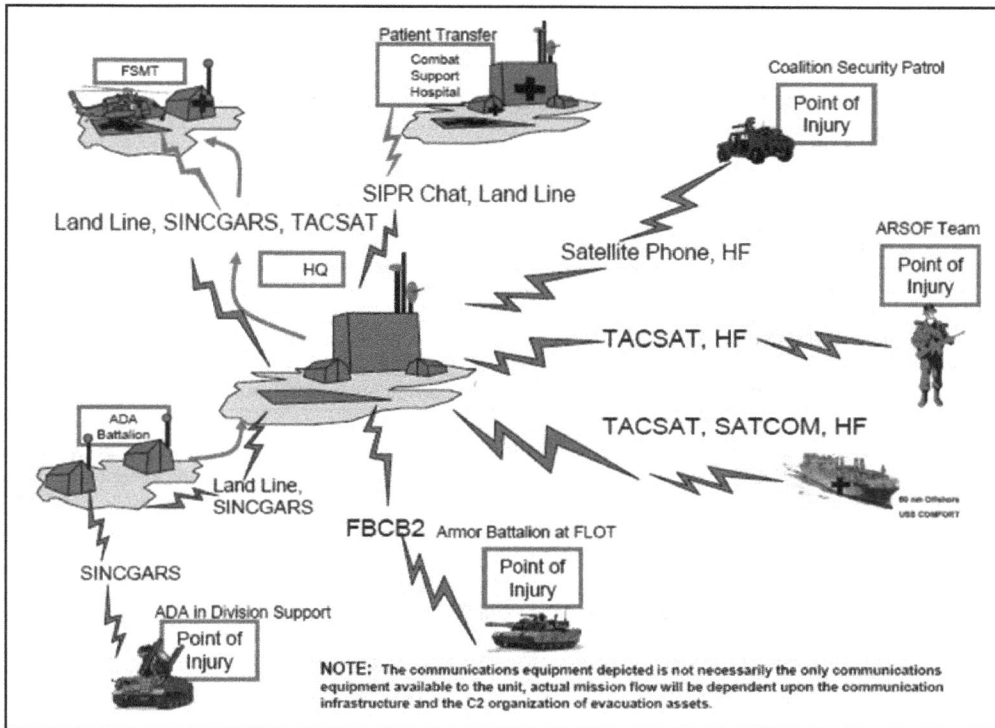

Figure 3-14. Medical evacuation mission communications

AIR AMBULANCE LAUNCH DECISION

3-226. The decision to launch air ambulance assets for a specific mission is determined by the theater evacuation order and launch authority policy.

Theater Evacuation Order

3-227. As part of the theater evacuation order, a standard procedure for the assignment of evacuation resources will be in effect. The order also specifies the tactical situations (enemy ground-to-air and air-to-air threat, enemy ground threat in the pick up area, and weather) that dictate the conditions for an air or ground ambulance launch. If a mission falls within the parameters of the theater evacuation order's protocol for aeromedical evacuation, then the mission is valid. No other mission or medical validations are necessary.

Launch Authority

3-228. The air ambulance crew(s) preparing for the MEDEVAC mission will obtain launch authority in accordance with the CAB commander's guidance. The launch authority decision is based on METT-TC (weather, enemy threat, crew endurance, and equipment available) for that particular mission.

Evacuation Requests

3-229. It is critical all commanders with C2 of MEDEVAC assets understand the categories of casualty precedence. Soldiers are evacuated by the most expeditious means possible dependent on their medical condition and assigned evacuation precedence. Anyone can request MEDEVAC; however, assignment precedence is paramount. Refer to table 3-7, page 3-44, for MEDEVAC categories of precedence.

Table 3-7. Medical evacuation categories of precedence

Priority I	URGENT	Evacuation as soon as possible within 2 hours to save life, limb, eyesight; prevent complications of serious illness; or avoid permanent disability.
Priority IA	URGENT SURGICAL	Requiring far-forward stabilizing surgical intervention prior to further disability.
Priority II	PRIORITY	Sick and wounded requiring prompt medical care within 4 hours otherwise patient will become an URGENT or suffer unnecessarily.
Priority III	ROUTINE	Sick and wounded requiring evacuation but whose condition is not expected to deteriorate within the next 24 hours.
Priority IV	CONVENIENCE	Patient movement is convenient but not necessary.

3-230. In most cases, the senior military person present requests MEDEVAC and assigns the appropriate medical precedence. The person sending the request may utilize the advice of the senior medical person at the scene, if one is present, regarding patient condition; however, no medical validation is required for MEDEVAC. The precedence assists the supporting medical unit and controlling HQ in determining priorities for committing evacuation assets. For this reason, correct assignment of precedence cannot be overemphasized; over classification remains a continuing problem. Patients are evacuated as soon as possible, consistent with available resources and pending missions.

MEDICAL OPERATIONS CELL COORDINATION WITH HIGHER ECHELONS OF MEDICAL AUTHORITY

3-231. The MOC, consisting of the GSAB and CAB staff medical planners, is the conduit for communication between higher echelons of medical C2 and the CAB. The MOC will—

- **Establish flight procedures specific to aeromedical evacuation missions within the CAB.** This could include special routes or corridors as well as procedures for escort aircraft link-up.
- **Ensure LOCs to supported units and higher echelons of medical command are available.** The MOC also ensures supported units understand MEDEVAC procedures and capabilities.
- **Facilitate MEDEVAC briefing and launch procedures.** Ensure there is 24-hour access to those able to launch high and very high risk missions.
- **Maintain awareness of the tactical and medical situation.** Coordinate with medical regulators at higher echelons to efficiently conduct GS and work in concert with adjacent units.
- **Assist the air ambulance company and GSAB/CAB to conduct aeromedical evacuation.**
- **Coordinate missions with supported command surgeons.** To ensure coordination of MEDEVAC efforts, the staff should keep command surgeons updated on aeromedical evacuation missions performed in their AO.
- **Consult and coordinate with supported command surgeons when air ambulances cannot be launched to execute a requested mission.** It is important the appropriate command surgeon is notified to ensure the mission can be accomplished by ground evacuation assets.

MEDICAL EVACUATION AIRCRAFT CAPABILITIES

UH-60A/L

3-232. The UH-60 continues to operate as the main helicopter platform for the majority of tactical Army aeromedical evacuations. The UH-60 can be equipped with a removable, high-performance internal hoist, and patient carousel capable of holding six litter patients. All medical equipment is carried on the aircraft and can be switched out.

HH-60A/L/M

3-233. The interior design of the HH-60 has maximum cabin space, placing sophisticated, life-saving instruments and equipment at the fingertips of the medical attendants. Normal cabin configurations of the HH-60 can accommodate up to four primary litter patients or six ambulatory (seated) patients. However, when necessary, two standardization agreement (STANAG) litters can be placed on the floor under the forward lifts for a total of six litter patients. The unique platform design also includes oxygen distribution and suction systems, an airway management capability, and provisions for stowing intravenous solutions. The interior also features the following capabilities:

- Oxygen-generating systems.
- NVG-compatible lighting throughout.
- An environmental control system.
- Medical equipment.
- Patient monitoring equipment.
- Neonatal isolettes.

SECTION VI – CASUALTY EVACUATION

3-234. Casualties will be evacuated by Army MEDEVAC resources if MEDEVAC assets are available. If available MEDEVAC resources are overwhelmed (such as in a mass casualty situation), some casualties may be transported on nonmedical vehicles. This is referred to as casualty evacuation (CASEVAC). CASEVAC should only be used when the number of casualties exceeds the capability of the MEDEVAC assets or when the urgency of evacuation exceeds the risk of waiting for MEDEVAC assets to arrive.

Refer to FM 4-02.2 for additional information on Casualty Evacuation and Medical Evacuation.

3-235. Sufficient advance CASEVAC planning is essential.. Proactive planning and rehearsals are a critical step to reducing risk when executing effective CASEVAC operations. All crewmemebers should be familiar with the location and capabilites of medical treatment facilites located within the area of operations.

> **WARNING**
>
> **Without aeromedically trained en route care, the casualty's medical condition may deteriorate during transport and an adverse impact on his prognosis and long-term disability may result.**

CASUALTY EVACUATION CLASSIFICATIONS

3-236. There are three general classifications of CASEVAC crews—vehicles, personnel, and associated equipment:

- **Dedicated.** Dedicated crews are identified and reserved for the CASEVAC mission exclusively. This tasking may be for a period of hours or months. Similar to a MEDEVAC crew, they will not be called on to perform another mission. This is the highest level of classification for CASEVAC.
- **Designated.** Designated crews are tasked to perform the CASEVAC mission on request. These crews may have a variety of priorities, CASEVAC not necessarily being the highest.
- **Lift of opportunity.** Crews performing a CASEVAC lift of opportunity have no specific prior designation as a CASEVAC platform. This does not indicate a lack of CASEVAC planning, but does not ensure CASEVAC resources will be available at any given time.

3-237. None of the above classifications are associated with any certain level of medical care. In any configuration, it is highly desirable to have aeromedically trained personnel onboard to administer treatment. Without this capability, further harm may come to the patient(s). Therefore, when executing CASEVAC, it is advisable that the least injured are evacuated using CASEVAC assets and most injured using MEDEVAC assets. Any available medical personnel at the pickup site can assist in determining priority for evacuation by available medical vehicles and aircraft.

3-238. During the planning process for CASEVAC, the same availability methodology used to assist CASEVAC crews must be used for en route medical care personnel. Onboard medical personnel can serve in a dedicated, designated, or lift of opportunity capacity. Due to the coordination necessary between the CASEVAC crews' parent unit and medical unit providing personnel for en route care, prior planning is especially critical.

3-239. Aeromedical care is a specialized task. Medical personnel not trained in this particular area of medicine may cause further harm to the patient. If possible, prior training/orientation should be coordinated when serving in the CASEVAC role.

CASUALTY EVACUATION AIRCRAFT CAPABILITIES

3-240. For any platform utilized for CASEVAC, significant preparations may be required to accommodate litters, medical attendants, and medical equipment. Well-planned CASEVAC operations take into account this additional time requirement. Units should also conduct CASEVAC aircraft reconfiguration rehearsals.

3-241. Aircrews conducting the CASEVAC mission should have medical SA. It is important to ensure crews understand the location and status of MTFs, their basic capabilities, and the severity of casualties onboard to help prevent further harm. This information is critical to ensure patients are evacuated to the correct facility that can provide proper treatment and care.

UH-60

3-242. UH-60s can provide CASEVAC support to the brigade and division. The number of casualties that can be transported by the UH-60 varies depending on aircraft configuration, such as seats in or seats out and other equipment onboard the aircraft. The UH-60 can carry three or four litters, depending on seating configuration. UH-60s can be used in a variety of CASEVAC missions including executing as far forward as possible to evacuate front line casualties on an armed platform due to the tactical situation.

CH-47

3-243. CH-47s can transport up to 24 litter patients or 31 ambulatory patients or some combination thereof in the following configurations:

- **Seats folded.** With seats folded up, the number of casualties transported is dependent on the type of casualty (ambulatory versus litter) and the severity of their injuries and wounds.
- **Seats down.** With seats folded down, the lifting capacity for litter patients will be reduced. Ambulatory capabilities in this configuration will be 30 seated ambulatory casualties and others loaded on the floor, as directed by the aircrew.
- **Litter configuration.** CH-47s can be equipped with a litter kit. This kit gives the CH-47 the capacity to transport 24 litter patients. When in the litter configuration, CH-47 seats are replaced with six tiers of litters, four litters high.

Note. The CH-47 litter support kit consists of poles and supports only. Litters and tie-down straps must be provided by the supported unit. Litters must be provided by medical assets belonging to the unit the CASEVAC aircraft are supporting.

SECTION VII – AIR TRAFFIC SERVICES

MISSION AND SUPPORT CAPABILITIES

3-244. ATS assets promote safe, flexible, and efficient use of airspace that is shared with a multitude of weapon systems. ATS companies maximize technology by coordinating airspace and providing recovery capabilities. For additional ATS information, see FM 3-04.120.

AIR TRAFFIC SERVICES COMPANY

3-245. An ATS company supports CABs by providing terminal area and en route airspace information and control services. ATS companies provide services to support CABs throughout full spectrum operations. ATS companies are composed of a control tower, GCA, AIC, and two tactical aviation control teams (TACTs). They also deploy as part of the CAB and are an integral part of brigade readiness.

3-246. ATS companies have the following capabilities:
- Deployable within 96 hours of notification and equipped and capable of operating in any environment.
- Control tower operations on 30 minutes of arrival in an AO and become fully operational within 1 hour of arrival.
- Provide self-sustaining operations for 72 hours upon arrival in an AO.
- Set up TACTs in austere/tactical environment operational within 15 minutes after arrival in an AO.
- Support aircraft recovery operations including PR, MEDEVAC, and assistance to aircraft in distress (battle damage, inclement weather, and disoriented aircraft).
- Provide airspace management operations in support of manned and unmanned air operations for its designated airspace sector by providing updates of airspace information.
- Provide navigational assistance to friendly aircraft.
- Coordinate ATC procedures with military C2 agencies and civilian agencies/organizations, including the Federal Aviation Administration and International Civil Aviation Organization
- Provide personnel for survey/reconnaissance party team ensuring air traffic procedures, ATS equipment emplacement criteria, and terminal instrument procedures (TERPs) are considered and addressed during site survey.
- Provide personnel as required for integrated aviation planning and management of air operations.
- Provide precision and nonprecision NAVAIDs.
- Provide essential SA information for use in activation and execution of the airfield base defense zone (BDZ).

- Provide ATS subject matter experts to assist with the CAB's mission area relating to the joint, interagency, interdepartmental, and multinational force.
- Provide ATS operations across the full spectrum of conflict to include civil support and homeland security operations facilitating restoration, revitalization, stability, and sustainment services.

OPERATIONAL CONSIDERATIONS

3-247. The type of operation determines equipment requirements, back-up capabilities, and the communications connectivity used. A CAB main operating base or division airfield is normally established by the terminal assets of the ATS company. Mission planning for ATS operations should incorporate close coordination and guidance from the CAB S-3. The following planning considerations should be utilized when preparing to conduct initial entry operations:

- **Type of mission.** This determines the section or sections of the company called on to complete the mission.
- **Length of operations.** Promote input by platoon sergeants and facility chiefs. Factors such as food, water, fuel, medical support, and life support issues (showers, laundry, and resupply of uniforms, boots, and other common table of allowances [CTA] 50-900 [TA 50]) must be well planned. Fighter management issues such as sleep and feeding plans must be considered.
- **Type of services required.** This involves instrument flight rules (IFR) recovery capability. A TERPs package must be developed and forwarded to the U.S. Army Aeronautical Services Agency for approval and certification. Emergency IFR recovery procedures are interim procedures developed for emergency use. The approval authority for this procedure is the CAB commander.
- **Support requirements.** Support requirements are determined by the type of services and communications required at the airfield and length of mission. Once established, these requirements must be met by the GSAB or CAB through division support and logistic channels. Some requirements may dictate the need for semipermanent facilities as well as commercial power if hardened facilities are used.
- **Future mission of the base.** If the base is used as a theater airfield later in the operation, ATS companies plan for and execute—
  - Site surveys and TERPs packages as required.
  - Terminal airspace coordination.
  - Development and publication of local airfield procedures.
  - NAVAID frequencies requests with timelines for their use.
- **Current combat airspace/additional airspace requirements.** Current combat airspace is a critical planning measure. During the planning process, a risk assessment is completed and control measures are implemented. Current and future combat airspace is disseminated to all airspace users, controllers, and aircrews during the mission brief.
- **Environment.** The operating environment impacts the planning process. Terrain determines equipment placement and may impact equipment capabilities based on LOS radio and NAVAID performance. Terrain can also dictate site layout for LZ or FARP operations and type of formation flight used during the mission. SOPs should address factors considered in the METT-TC mission planning risk assessment/management process.

SECTION VIII – PERSONNEL RECOVERY

3-248. The Army's PR philosophy is one of leadership and accountability. It comprises primarily the Soldier's Creed, directed responsibilities, and practical considerations. The Army conducts PR as a collection of architecture and activities designed to affect the recovery of personnel who are isolated, missing, detained, or captured (IMDC). PR is no longer just combat search and rescue (CSAR); it includes a special operation force or air asset centric operation designed primarily for the rescue of aviators. See FM 3-50.1 for more details.

3-249.   The Army PR function is defined as "the sum of military, diplomatic, and civil efforts to affect the recovery and return of U.S. military, DOD civilians, DOD contractor personnel, and/or other personnel, as determined by the Secretary of Defense, who are IMDC in an operational environment." PR is one of the highest priorities within the DOD.

3-250.   Army aviation's role in PR is in the execution of pre-established procedures and well-rehearsed operations to report, locate, support, recover, and repatriate IMDC personnel. Specifically, aviation is involved in the recovery of personnel within the unit's or supported units' AO when the IMDC personnel's location is known. Four principle methods of recovery are used when planning and executing recoveries:

- **Immediate recovery** is the sum of actions conducted to locate and recover IMDC personnel by forces directly observing the isolating event or, through the reporting process, determining IMDC personnel are close enough for them to conduct a rapid recovery. Immediate recovery assumes the tactical situation permits a recovery with the forces at hand without detailed planning or coordination.

- **Deliberate recovery** is the sum of actions conducted by Army forces when an incident is reported and immediate recovery is not feasible or was not successful. Weather, enemy actions, IMDC personnel location, and recovery force capabilities are examples of factors that may require the detailed planning and coordination of a deliberate recovery.

- **External supported recovery (ESR)** is the sum of actions conducted when immediate or deliberate recovery is not feasible or was not successful. ESR is either the support provided by the Army to other JTF components, interagency organizations, or multinational forces, or the support provided by these entities to the Army. CAS, ISR, and airborne C2 are examples of capabilities that may be required from different components to execute an ESR.

- **Unassisted recovery** comprises actions taken by IMDC personnel to achieve their own recovery without outside assistance. An unassisted recovery typically involves an evasion effort by IMDC personnel to get back to friendly forces or to a point where they can be recovered via another method. While the code of conduct requires IMDC personnel make every effort to evade or escape, commanders must strive to recover these personnel via one or a combination of methods.

ROLES AND RESPONSIBILITIES

3-251.   PR is a dynamic and unique mission including all levels of threat. The vast geographic area, variety of hostile defenses, and geographic separation of friendly forces demand thorough mission coordination. Each PR event has the possibility of becoming a joint mission depending on the situation of forces involved in a recovery. Some joint participants receive specialized training to execute their role in a recovery. A thorough understanding of the roles and responsibilities of all participants ensures recoveries that start as immediate or deliberate may be continued as externally supported with a minimum of confusion. This level of functionality and modularity requires an understanding of terms, recovery training, and action drill rehearsals at all levels.

Personnel Recovery Terms

3-252.   Any PR event has the possibility of becoming a joint mission. Additionally, the Army may be called on to participate in civil search and rescue (SAR) operations. Therefore, it is important to note key joint terms with regard to other services and civil SAR as well as the Army (table 3-8).

Table 3-8. Personnel recovery terms

Joint Terms	Army Terms	Civilian Terms
JPRC	JPRC	Rescue Coordination Center
PRCC	PRCC	Rescue Sub Center
PRO	PRO	SAR Mission Coordinator
OSC	OSC	OSC
Airborne Mission Commander	Operations Officer S-3/Battle Captain	Aircraft Coordinator
CSAR Unit	*	SAR Unit
Helicopter Recovery Force	Helicopter Recovery Force	SAR Unit
RESCORT	Attack Escort	**
RESCORT Commander	AMC (Attack)	**
JPRC – joint personnel recovery center PRCC – personnel recovery coordination cell PRO – personnel recovery officer OSC – on-scene commander RESCORT – rescue escort		* – No Army term ** – No civilian term

Battalion Role

3-253. The Army has detailed the PR planning process and equipment requirements in FM 3-50.1. In many cases, the battalion or TF HQ may act as C2 coordinator or facilitator for PR recoveries by providing assets, an OSC, coordination for recovery assets, or communication relay. Overall execute authority for deliberate recoveries should be outlined in the theater SOP and/or unit SOP.

3-254. Predeployment PR training/preparation for all personnel should include ISOPREP development, high risk to capture training and use of weapons, PR drills, and ground-to-air communication/signaling procedures. Aircrews should receive additional training on SPINS and ATO data, SOPs, and include PR battle drills. AHB and GSAB CP personnel should be trained on PR procedures and have rehearsed PR missions prior to deployment.

3-255. Commanders must ensure that only forces required to accomplish the recovery are put at risk. Additional forces may only complicate recovery planning and execution. Execution tasks for the battalion may vary based on the mission, level, and type of recovery. The Air Force utilizes an airborne mission commander in much the same way as the battalion operation staff functions. The difference being, the airborne mission commander is airborne. Some common execution tasks include—

- Appointing an OSC and coordinating OSC relief as the situation dictates. Communications capability, weapons load, fuel status, and aircraft limitations are considered when selecting the OSC. The initial OSC may be the wingman or a ground unit in the area.
- Locating low-threat areas where rescue assets can hold and egress.
- Determining the threat level in the isolated personnel's area.
- Obtaining evasive plan of action (EPA) data from flight operations and passing data to the recovery force, OSC, and PRCC.
- Coordinating and monitoring PR radio nets. Aircrews use an FM radio as the primary net if Army assets are only used during the operation. UHF/VHF becomes primary if the operation is inter-service or joint.
- Continuing to gather information from all sources and passing to higher in accordance with SPINS and PR plan.
- Managing flow of aircraft to and from the objective area.

3-256. Battalion operations will execute additional tasks based on the mission to include—

- Briefing the designated RESCORT or PR recovery force on missions with the potential for an isolating event. This may be a part of the briefing for the QRF or DART.
- Completing all necessary information in the rescue mission brief (RMB).
- Determining isolated personnel's available signaling devices.
- Conducting a thorough threat assessment and developing a threat map covering the following to permit protection of the recovery team:
    - Radar sites due to their ability to detect PR forces, intercept communications, and possibly direct hostile forces to the vicinity of isolated personnel.
    - Threats to primary rescue vehicles such as helicopters, antiaircraft artillery (AAA), man-portable AD systems, small-arms fire from ground forces, and armed enemy aircraft. Known or suspected enemy sites should be avoided at all times.
    - Location of ROZs for EW and airborne C2 platforms often required for PR missions.
    - Data concerning enemy weapons and troop deployments with terrain and weapon ranges noted. This provides mission planners with detailed information to plan ingress and egress routes for rescue vehicles with respect to enemy weapon systems and ground forces.
- Recommending air routes to and from the area. If threats are present, inform RESCORT of threat positions so threats can be circumvented or additional support assets requested.
- Making a go/no-go recommendation based on information gathered at the objective area.
- Preparing isolated personnel for pickup.

Company Role

3-257. The company's role in PR is at execution level. The commander must understand PR includes training of all aircrews and personnel in PR procedures for both execution of recovery and actions of company personnel if they become isolated. Procedures for immediate recoveries should be outlined in the unit TACSOP and rehearsed based on the type of airframe and circumstances for its use. This section will concentrate on procedures for a deliberate recovery or participation in an externally supported recovery. Personnel should be familiar with the following terms.

On-Scene Commander

3-258. The OSC is the person designated to coordinate recovery operations within a specified area. He does not have to be in an aircraft; he may be ground or vessel based, but he must be proficient in all PR procedures and have the ability to communicate with higher. While the Air Force qualifies a pilot to act as OSC, any Army aircrew may be called on to act in this capacity. Other responsibilities of the OSC include—

- Establishing and authenticating communication with isolated personnel.
- Locating isolated personnel and passing initial information to the AMC via the RMB.
- Conducting a threat assessment of the objective area (avoid highlighting the isolated personnel's location).
- Completing the OSC checklist.
- Determining the health/condition of isolated personnel and passing status to the AMC.
- Re-authenticating isolated personnel after OSC changeover only when the situation warrants.

Rescue Mission Commander

3-259. The rescue mission commander (RMC) is the designated AMC maintaining control of the entire recovery during the launch, en route, and terminal phase. Areas considered when selecting the RMC should include knowledge of the overall mission, capabilities of the helicopter recovery force, requirements for communication, night vision capabilities, and joint interoperability.

Recovery Force

3-260. The PR force consists of personnel that will affect the actual recovery of the isolated personnel. These personnel nclude—

- Security personnel for the area around the extraction point.
- Recovery personnel that authenticate and move the isolated personnel to the aircraft.
- Medical personnel that provide immediate assistance to the isolated personnel or injured security force personnel.

The size and composition of this force may vary with the mission supported or actual threat. During recovery operations, the RMC should be in the gun escort for SA at the objective; however, this is mission dependent.

Helicopter Recovery Force

3-261. The helicopter recovery force will consist of lift aircraft used to move the recovery force to and from the objective area and the recovered IMDC personnel back to friendly forces. The helicopter recovery force will designate an AMC. The helicopter recovery force AMC will coordinate all PR force efforts on the objective.

Gun Escort

3-262. Attack/reconnaissance assets utilized to provide security escort to the helicopter recovery force may also be called the RESCORT. The primary duty of the gun escort or RESCORT is to provide protection for the helicopter recovery force. The principles of air assault security are used in execution of this task. Priority is to avoid, suppress, and destroy targets posing a threat to the helicopter recovery force or recovery force on the ground.

TYPES OF ESCORT

3-263. Several types of escort methods may be used during the en route phase, but the tactics will depend on factors such as speed, altitude, distance, fuel, level of threat, weather conditions, and whether it is a day or night operation. Two common types of escort may be utilized (table 3-9):

- **Attached escort.** This method allows continuous visual or radar contact (AH-64D fire control radar [FCR]) of the helicopter recovery force.
- **Detached escort.** This method includes reconnaissance ahead of the helicopter recovery force, trail escort, or proximity escort. Detached escort requires knowledge of routes and planned timing or position calls.
  - **If the escort sweeps ahead of the helicopter recovery force**, it suppresses threats along the ingress route or redirects the helicopter recovery force to avoid enemy activity. Checkpoints or control points must be established to maintain SA and horizontal airspace deconfliction.
  - **Trail escort** employs the escort in a rear quadrant. This may be used for rapid linkup of the gun escort with the helicopter recovery force but delays response time to en route engagements and puts the trail elements at more risk.
  - **Proximity escort** is similar to trail escort but allows the gun escort to fly a parallel course to the helicopter recovery force. This provides an increased survivability from surface-to-air and air engagements and decreased probability of detection for both groups.

Table 3-9. Types of escort

	Attached	Detached
Advantages	Good SA of helicopter recovery force assets and status. Rapid response to threats. Mutual response from recovery force assets.	Does not highlight helicopter recovery assets. Allows flexibility in maneuver. Allows escort to maximize individual tactics.
Disadvantages	Escort may highlight the formation Increased potential for aircraft conflict due to formation. Decreased formation maneuverability.	May preclude continuous visual, radar, or radio contact. Helicopter recovery force may not be aware of or responsive to threats to assets. Potential for loss of mutual support.

SEQUENCE OF EVENTS

3-264. To effectively integrate into the PR architecture, the unit should ensure PR has been rehearsed exhaustively. The dynamic and unpredictable nature of this mission requires time and effort in preparation to reduce risk during execution. The gun escort mission includes but is not limited to—

- Rendezvous with the helicopter recovery force.
- Ingress.
- Conduct of security escort and/or suppression.
- Cover and/or suppression during the extraction.
- Egress security escort and/or suppression to a friendly or permissive threat environment.

Premission Planning

3-265. To effectively integrate a deliberate recovery into the PR architecture, the unit should ensure PR has been rehearsed exhaustively. The dynamic and unpredictable nature of this mission requires time and effort preparing to reduce risk during execution. A determination must be made immediately, based on predetermined factors, if the unit is capable of conducting the recovery or if the recovery should be conducted by externally supported assets.

3-266. Whether aircrews are being utilized as gun escort for a designated helicopter recovery force or are maintaining an on order status as part of QRF, friendly and enemy SA is of primary concern. Each aircrew should understand their role in the recovery operation. Knowledge of the helicopter recovery force procedures, PR force actions on the ground, and OSC procedures are critical.

3-267. Capabilities of the helicopter recovery force must be considered carefully. The threat and ability to provide forward firepower, locate the threat at night, and maneuver must be considered when determining formation, patterns, and actions on the objective.

3-268. Planning for a deliberate recovery is conducted from TF/battalion-level down to the aircrews performing the mission. Commanders must ensure missions are planned using only the forces required to gain the situational advantage required to execute the recovery. This may not be achieved by aviation assets only. Aircrews assigned PR missions must have adequate time for planning to ensure mission success. Information necessary to execute a PR mission includes—

- Call sign, type of aircraft, and number of personnel.
- Enemy situation.
- Last known location/position.
- FLOT penetration points/routes.
- ISOPREP and SPINS data for time of PR incident (SPINS will change immediately following PR incident).

3-269. Basic planning factors are the same regardless of the mission type or aircraft utilized. METT-TC and the following factors should be considered:

- Isolated personnel, location, and condition.
- Threat.
- Ingress/egress routes.
- Meteorology.
- Terrain.
- Navigation.
- Fuel (FARPs and aircraft ranges).
- Flight formation.
- ROE.
- SEAD plan.
- Elements of the personnel recovery (PR) TF.
- Deception plan.
- Security.
- Defining and coordinating action at the terminal objective area.
- LZ.
- Force requirements.
- EPA.
- Aircraft destruction criteria.
- Transload required after isolated personnel pickup. Y/N? If yes, where?
- Location (FOB/combat support hospital) where rescued personnel will be returned.

Notification

3-270. Notification procedures during an isolating event should be the same whether it is unit personnel or personnel outside the unit that have been isolated. Immediately following notification of a possible isolating incident, the operations section executes its immediate action steps that should include receiving or transmitting the IMDC's ISOPREP, EPA, and search and rescue incident report (SARIR) to/from the PRCC. This enables parallel planning at all levels and opens the LOCs to receive additional assets to aid in the recovery.

> *Note.* Updates or mission complete messages are sent to the PRCC in the SAR situation summary report format.

3-271. Aircrews that are part of the unit's designated PR helicopter recovery force should begin preparations for launch based on mission requirements. Local SOP should outline how this is accomplished to ensure each member of the aircrew has all information required to complete their part of the mission. Sensitive IMDC information, like the ISOPREP and EPA, should not be carried by the recovery force. The staff should brief the RMC on all aspects of the recovery and construct the RMB or order.

Launch and En Route

3-272. Following notification and passing of the RMB or order, the helicopter recovery force and gun escort are directed to launch. The execution authority for the recovery should be outlined in the SOP. Depending on the isolated personnel's location, the helicopter recovery force launches and is expected to hold at a point outside hostile fire range until permission to enter is given by the gun escort AMC. If the initial legs of the flight to the objective area are to be conducted in friendly territory, the helicopter recovery force proceeds without gun escort (provided they are not collocated) reducing the helicopter recovery force en route time once the execute order is given.

3-273. If not collocated, the gun escort or RESCORT conducts an aerial link-up with the helicopter recovery force and conducts the following tasks:

- Reconnoiters the planned ingress route.
- Provides security for the recovery force along the designated route to the HA.
- Passes all updates to the helicopter recovery force AMC.
- Escorts the helicopter recovery force to the objective area (isolated personnel's location).

3-274. Before the recovery force is established in the objective area, the gun escort or RESCORT sets the conditions at both the primary and alternate LZ for insertion of the recovery force. Conditions that must be met include—

- No armored vehicles in the objective area.
- No indirect fire affecting the LZ.
- No unit larger than squad size in the objective area.
- No weapon larger than 7.62-millimeter.

3-275. The gun escort AMC or RMC conducts an inventory of the isolated personnel's signaling devices, directs isolated personnel to prepare the appropriate device for identification, and briefs the pickup plan to all participants per the RMB or order. This briefing is completed prior to the terminal area phase.

Terminal Area Phase

3-276. During the terminal area phase, the gun escort attempts radio contact with the isolated personnel in an effort to determine their precise location. When radio contact is made and the gun escort clears the objective area, the helicopter recovery force moves from the HA to the objective area. The helicopter recovery force may require vectors from the HA to the objective area from the gun escort. Once visual contact is established, the helicopter recovery force assumes communication responsibility with the isolated personnel. The primary means of recovery is conducted by landing in the objective, but alternate means may be required.

3-277. The gun escort or RESCORT provides overwatch utilizing pre-established orbit patterns or from an ABF during the operation. The patterns or ABF should allow coverage of any avenues of approach into the objective area and permits the gun escort or RESCORT to observe the isolated personnel's position. This should be accomplished by establishing an inner area of security around the objective area then moving outward to form an outer band of security.

3-278. RMC, gun escort, or RESCORT continually reports to higher or relays through airborne C2 assets on the current situation and helicopter recovery force's location throughout the mission.

Reintegration Phase

3-279. Reintegration begins once the isolated personnel is in positive control. The level of reintegration required is determined during the MEDEVAC and, if appropriate, SERE debrief following an isolating event. It is important to note an isolating event is traumatic and each Soldier will react differently based on intensity and duration of the event. A miscalculation or lack of emphasis on complete reintegration of an isolated soldier has unpredictable results. A well-organized and efficient reintegration program includes but is not limited to—

- Medical evaluation and follow-up.
- SERE debrief.
- Psychological evaluation and follow-up treatment.
- Limited duty.
- Medical or psychological evacuation for continued care.

STABILITY AND CIVIL SUPPORT OPERATIONS

3-280. Stability and civil support operations are separate activities not necessarily involving armed conflict between organized forces. Stability operations are conducted outside the continental United States (OCONUS), whereas civil support is conducted inside the continental United States (CONUS). The battalion does not perform any unique missions during stability and civil support operations. It simply performs the same mission set described above within a different operational environment and with certain specific mission planning considerations.

3-281. During stability and civil support operations, the AHB and GSAB can expect to work with U.S. government, host nation, and international agencies. These agencies may not have the military-style chain of command to which U.S. Soldiers are accustomed. Prior coordination and flexibility are keys to mission success. The chain of command, support responsibility, reporting requirements, and authority to approve specific actions must be clearly understood by all parties prior to initiating the mission. Units must maintain liaisons with local police, ATC, and civil and military authorities.

PLANNING CONSIDERATIONS

3-282. AHB and GSAB commanders face challenges differing from those involved in conventional operations.

Mission Analysis

3-283. Perhaps the greatest obstacle for the commander to overcome in stability and civil support operations is defining the mission for the unit. When he receives the OPLAN, OPORD, or implementing instructions, mission analysis begins. The commander must pay particular attention to limitations placed on him by ROE or political considerations.

Task Organization

3-284. Task organization for stability and civil support operations is METT-TC driven. The commander must assess the battalion's capabilities versus the mission and determine if task organization is capable of accomplishing assigned missions. If the mission can not be completed, the commander should modify the organization.

Command Relationships

3-285. It is critical command relationships for stability and civil support operations be established early. Elements of the AHB or GSAB may deploy for stability and civil support operations without their parent HQ. It is also possible the aircraft may work for another service or U.S. nonmilitary agency, such as the Drug Enforcement Agency (DEA) or Federal Bureau of Investigation. A clear understanding of the command, control, and support relationship helps reduce confusion and allows the unit to integrate with their controlling HQ early and with proper resource support requirements.

Advance Party Operations

3-286. Advance party personnel need a comprehensive overview of their unit's mission, capabilities, requirements, and commander's intent prior to deployment. They must coordinate with the gaining or outgoing command, higher HQ, and local population. The commander must carefully select advance party personnel. For example, deploying to another country with an undeveloped logistics base may require the advance party be heavily logistics weighted and contain foreign language specialists, while other missions, such as counter-drug operations, can be weighted with operational personnel. Whichever the commander chooses, the advance party must receive guidance and focus prior to deployment. The advance party must also keep the commander informed as to their actions and current situation.

Split-Based Operations

3-287. The battalion, or some of its elements, will often deploy on stability and civil support operations into a theater having an immature logistics base. Logistics operations may be conducted in theater from the unit's home station. This is termed split-based operations. The commander who deploys on a split-based operation must consider the type of support required from home station. He must pay special attention to communications between the theater of operations and home station, and to the transportation means available to provide a timely flow of logistics.

SPECIAL CONSIDERATIONS

3-288. There are several key employment guidelines for the battalion commander to consider during the planning process. These guidelines are preparation, specialty augmentation, host nation requirements, ROE, and ROI.

Preparation

3-289. Battalion and companies should expect a wide range in the tempo of operations and plan accordingly. Staff must be able to adjust rapidly to many different operational considerations. They must plan ahead and have contingency plans for numerous situations not normally addressed in the unit's METL. These situations can be identified and trained at home station. Examples of situations include civilians on the battlefield, media relations, public affairs, and defense against terrorism.

Specialty Personnel Augmentation

3-290. Operational conditions of stability and civil support operations frequently require integration of specialty personnel with battalion staff including civil affairs, PSYOP, staff judge advocate (SJA), and special forces personnel. Besides specialty staff personnel, battalion may be required to operate with infantry, armor, artillery, engineer, sustainment, or a combination of these and other assets. Whatever the composition, staff must be fully integrated to coordinate and plan operations. LNOs from the battalion to other units and from supporting units to battalion are critical.

Host Nation Requirements

3-291. Airspace restrictions, flight clearances, refueling procedures, civil and military laws, environmental laws and regulations, radio frequency (RF) usage, ground convoy clearances, and product disposal procedures vary from country to country. The commander must adapt unit procedures to the host nation's operating environment and procedures. Serious complications can develop when host nation requirements are not met with repercussions ranging from mission restrictions to mission failure. In some situations, battalions conducting stability operations may be included on the air component commander's ATO to ensure SA and reduce the possibility of fratricide.

EMPLOYMENT

3-292. The majority of missions assigned to battalions during stability and civil support operations will either conform to or build on their standard mission roles (air assault, air movement, C2, ATC, MEDEVAC). Generally, the major differences in unit operations during stability and civil support operations will be in the C2 relationships between the battalion and its higher HQ, and the greater requirement for restraint in potentially hostile situations.

CATEGORIES OF OPERATIONS

3-293. During stability operations, the AHB and GSAB primarily perform their METL-related tasks and remain prepared for potential escalation to full armed conflict. During civil support operations, they use the capabilities of their combat systems to increase the effectiveness of the overall effort. Again, the AHB and GSAB must remain prepared for renewed hostilities or civil disorder. Many of these missions will be performed as an integrated piece of the overall U.S. military capability—often in conjunction with forces from other nations, other U.S. agencies, nongovernmental organizations, and United Nations forces. Therefore, leaders should familiarize themselves with joint operational procedures and terms.

Stability Operations

3-294. Combatant commanders employ Army forces in stability operations outside the U.S. and its territories to promote and protect U.S. national interests. Stability operations are designed to influence the threat and the political and information dimensions of the operational environment. These operations include developmental, cooperative activities during peacetime, and coercive actions in response to crisis. Stability operations are normally conducted in noncontiguous AOs. Army forces conduct the following five stability tasks—civil security, civil control, restore essential services, support to governance, and support to economic and infrastructure development (FM 3-0)

Civil Security

3-295. Civil security involves protecting the populace from external and internal threats. Ideally, Army forces defeat external threats posed by enemy forces that can attack population centers. Simultaneously, they assist host-nation police and security elements as the host nation maintains internal security against criminals and small, hostile groups. In some situations, there is no adequate host-nation capability for civil security and Army forces provide most of it. Civil security is required for the other stability tasks to be effective.

Civil Control

3-296. Civil control regulates selected behavior and activities of individuals and groups. This control reduces risk to individuals or groups and promotes security. Civil control channels the population's activities to allow provision of security and essential services while coexisting with a military force conducting operations. A curfew is an example of civil control.

Restore Essential Services

3-297. Army forces establish or restore the most basic services and protect them until a civil authority or the host nation can provide them. Normally, Army forces support other government, intergovernmental, and host-nation agencies. When the host nation or other agency cannot perform its role, Army forces may provide the basics directly. Essential services include the following:

- Emergency medical care and rescue.
- Preventing epidemic disease.
- Providing food and water.
- Providing emergency shelter.
- Providing basic sanitation (sewage and garbage disposal).

Support to Governance

3-298. Stability operations establish conditions that enable interagency and host-nation actions to succeed.

By establishing security and control, stability operations provide a foundation for transitioning authority to other government or intergovernmental agencies and eventually to the host nation. Once this transition is complete, commanders focus on transferring control to a legitimate civil authority according to the desired end state. Support to governance includes the following:

- Developing and supporting host-nation control of public activity, rule of law, and civil administration.
- Maintaining security, control, and essential services through the host nation. This includes training and equipping host-nation security forces and police.
- Normalizing the succession of power (elections and appointment of officials).

Support to Economic and Infrastructure Development

3-299. Support to economic and infrastructure development helps a host nation develop capability and capacity in these areas. It may involve direct and indirect military assistance to local, regional, and national entities.

CIVIL SUPPORT OPERATIONS

3-300. Civil support operations use battalions to assist civil authorities as they prepare for or respond to crises and relieve suffering. Assault and GS helicopter forces provide essential support, services, assets, or specialized resources to help civil authorities deal with situations beyond their capabilities. The purpose of civil support operations is to meet the immediate needs of designated groups for a limited time, until civil authorities can do so without Army assistance. In extreme or exceptional cases, U.S. forces may provide relief or assistance directly to those in need. More commonly, they help civil authorities or nongovernmental organizations provide support.

Homeland Defense

3-301. During CONUS declared disasters or emergencies, battalions may be called on to supplement efforts and resources of state and local governments. Such operations may include responding to natural or manmade disasters, controlling civil disturbances, conducting counter-drug activities, combating terrorism, or aiding law enforcement. The battalion may be employed to augment C2 requirements, provide security for air movement, search for casualties, and assess damage.

RULES OF ENGAGEMENT

3-302. ROE are designed to control the application of force. ROE are prepared and issued by higher HQ. Commanders must clearly understand ROE and ensure all Soldiers understand them. ROE situations should be rehearsed in detail prior to deploying or executing a mission. No situation should occur in which personnel are unsure whether to use force, and what types of force—to include deadly force—are warranted. For ROE assistance, the commander should consult with the SJA representative.

RULES OF INTERACTION

3-303. ROI embody the human dimension of stability operations; they lay the foundation for successful relationships with the numerous factions and individuals playing critical roles in these operations. ROI encompass an array of interpersonal communication skills, such as persuasion and negotiation.

3-304. ROI are tools the individual Soldier will need to deal with the nontraditional threats prevalent in stability operations including political friction, unfamiliar cultures, and conflicting ideologies. In turn, ROI enhance the Soldier's survivability in such situations. ROI, when applied with good interpersonal communication skills, improve military personnel's ability to accomplish the mission while reducing possible hostile confrontations.

3-305. ROI are based on applicable ROE for a particular operation; they must be tailored to specific regions, cultures, and/or populations affected by the operation. Like ROE, ROI can be effective only if thoroughly rehearsed and understood by every Soldier in the unit.

QUICK REACTION FORCE OPERATIONS

3-306. A QRF is any force poised to respond on very short notice. The QRF provides the TF commander an on call capability to react to contingencies within the AO. The QRF package is based on anticipated mission requirements and the crew and aircraft assets available. Due to the short-fused launch order, mission success requires extensive preplanning by QRF aircrews and the supporting operations cell.

PRE-POSITIONED QUICK REACTION FORCE

3-307.   The standard battalion pre-positioned QRF package includes two attack reconnaissance aircraft, two utility aircraft (UH-60), and ground forces. The parent CAB may also have two UH-60s, a MEDEVAC aircraft, and one heavy lift helicopter (CH-47) on call for support if required. The QRF maintains a readiness condition (REDCON) as established in the OPORD for the duration of the duty period. The standard QRF duty day is 14 hours allowing for 2 hours of mission planning and a 12-hour shift.

3-308.   Aircrews assigned as the QRF should not be tasked for additional missions. To reduce risk of aircrew fatigue while assigned to the QRF, the following steps are taken:

- Restrict QRF crewmembers from conducting rigorous physical training while on QRF.
- If the tactical situation allows, afford aircrews the opportunity to sleep during QRF duty period.
- Provide the QRF a separate environmentally-controlled staging area for all crews and personnel.
- Exempt QRF crews from conducting any other additional duties distracting from QRF readiness.
- The TF commander approves training flights during QRF duty period.

PRELAUNCH PLANNING CONSIDERATIONS

3-309.   The QRF AMC is the focal point of all coordination between the supporting staff and QRF. Prior to assuming the mission, the AMC—

- Obtains a tactical update brief and determines the status of the on-duty QRF elements and/or ongoing missions. This action determines the possibility of a relief-in-place or immediate launch.
- Obtains a weather brief for the duration of duty shift plus 2 hours.
- Files an EPA and flight plan for the entire QRF package. All mission planning except takeoff time, route of flight, duration of flight, and destination is completed.
- Completes a mission risk assessment and obtains approval from the TF/battalion commander. The mission risk assessment should approve no lower than medium risk operations. Approved operations include all tasks on the crew's CTL, all conditions (day, night, NVD), and all modes of flight that may be encountered during the duty period. Crews are briefed to operate in the worst weather forecasted during the duty period or go/no-go weather.
- Completes crew mission kneeboard packets for each aircraft providing all known information.
- Conducts an AMB with all known information and ensures each aircrew completes applicable crew and passenger briefings.
- Ensures all aircraft, crews, and support personnel assume designated REDCON level. All aircraft are preflighted and individual equipment checks complete prior to assuming mission. Depending on unit SOP and mission, aircraft are run-up with communications checks complete (includes spare aircraft).
- Ensures QRF package maintains REDCON level as briefed until alerted or relieved.
- Conducts static rehearsal of anticipated missions.
- Immediately informs controlling flight operations of any developments that will interfere with QRF launch.

ALERT PROCEDURES

3-310.   The battalion/TF commander establishes criteria for launching the QRF to avoid unnecessary alerts; however, the QRF is alerted as early as possible. Alert of the QRF criteria includes the following:

- QRF launch authority approves the mission.
- Mission is a "preapproved" immediate response mission.
- The battalion/TF commander determines alerting the QRF is justified in anticipation of launch approval.

3-311. When alerted, the QRF assumes the designated REDCON as quickly as possible and awaits either a launch order or stand-down order. Specific tasks necessary to assume the mission include the following:

- QRF AMC reports to the operations center for a mission brief. Crew packets are completed and printed for all aircrews. In some cases, the QRF is ordered to launch immediately and crews proceed with communications cards and products on hand received during initial QRF brief. The QRF AMC receives and briefs the mission via radio.
- PCs from each aircraft meet the AMC for a mission brief.
- Copilot and crewmembers from each aircraft run-up the auxiliary power unit, if required, and initialize all systems, mission equipment, and weapons. The communications check consists of all copilots checking in with the AMC's copilot when able.
- When the mission brief is complete, each PC reports to their aircraft to complete run-up, brief the crew, and conduct communications check with the AMC.
- Once the QRF package is at the appropriate REDCON level, the AMC reports to the operations center and awaits further instructions.

POST-LAUNCH PROCEDURES

3-312. Once ordered to launch, the AMC or flight lead requests priority handling from the control agency for takeoff and route of flight. This should be precoordinated and is usually based on call sign. As the mission progresses, the AMC updates the operations center and requests any additional follow-on forces. When the mission is complete, the QRF returns to the AA and assumes the designated REDCON level. The AMC reports to the operations center and debriefs the battalion/TF S-2 and/or S-3. Part of the debrief is a QRF status report with information as to how much mission time each crew has remaining and if any crews or aircraft need replacing.

AERIAL MINE DELIVERY OPERATIONS

3-313. Volcano-equipped UH-60 aircraft can dispense wider turn or block minefields or a single-pass narrower disrupt or fix minefield. Aircraft can dispense up to 960 mines in 18 seconds at 120 knots. Mines have a self-destruct feature that can be set for 4 hours, 48 hours, or 15 days. The owning aviation unit is responsible for transporting and mounting the air Volcano. Although aviation provides the equipment, engineers provide the mines. The unit must coordinate closely to ensure transport and delivery of mines to the upload site.

VOLCANO MINE DISPENSING SYSTEM

3-314. The Volcano system consists of the M139 mine dispenser, four launcher racks, M87 or M87A1 mine canisters, an electronic dispensing control unit (DCU), carrying cases, and special mounting hardware. The system for the UH-60 is identical to the ground Volcano version except for mounting hardware. Each system can dispense mines 35 to 70 meters from the aircraft flight path. The aircraft flies at a minimum altitude of 5 feet at speeds ranging from 20 to 120 knots.

M87 Mine Canister

3-315. The M87 mine canister comes with five antitank (AT) mines and one antipersonnel (AP) mine. Later M87A1 versions consist of six AT and no AP mines. They come in prepackaged, unalterable mine mixtures. A nylon web electronically connects mine groups in each canister and functions as a lateral dispersion device as mines exit the canister. Mine-mounted spring fingers prevent mines from coming to rest on the edge. On coming to rest, each mine has a delayed arming time. The AT mine takes 2 minutes and 15 seconds to arm, and the AP mine takes 4 minutes to arm.

M139 Mine Dispenser

3-316. The dispenser consists of four launching racks (two on each side) mounted in the UH-60 cargo-compartment door openings. Each rack holds up to 40 M87 mine canisters. Each canister contains 6 mines yielding a total capacity for the dispenser of 960 mines. The mounting hardware secures the racks to the UH-60 and provides for a jettison assembly that can propel racks away from the aircraft in an emergency.

Dispensing Control Unit

3-317. The DCU, the central control panel for air Volcano, is used by the operator to perform system fault isolation tests, select delivery speed, set self-destruct times, and initiate the system arming sequence. The start-stop firing switch, located on the DCU and cyclic, allows the DCU operator or pilot to initiate or stop mine dispensing. A DCU counter indicates the number of canisters remaining on each side of the aircraft.

PLANNING CONSIDERATIONS

3-318. The division or higher commander makes decisions to emplace Volcano minefields based on the tactical situation and recommendations from division staff. While the assistant division engineer (ADE) plans Volcano employment for most shaping and decisive operations, brigade commanders can request Volcano integration into their scheme of maneuver and may conduct the planning. Planners must develop good triggers with the Assistant Chief of Staff, Intelligence (G-2) or S-2.

3-319. On receipt of the WARNO, the Volcano-equipped unit begins planning and aircraft preparation. Aircrews, with battalion staff assistance, plan flight routes, J-SEAD, en route FS, attack reconnaissance aircraft security, CAS, and airspace deconfliction. Volcano planning is similar to that for a team insertion or small air assault using the reverse planning sequence. The resultant OPORD must contain defined triggers based on enemy actions. The S-2/S-3 establishes these triggers as DPs to increase aircraft REDCON levels for execution.

Aircrew Briefing

3-320. The division, brigade, or battalion staff briefs the aircrew on the Volcano mission. The aircrew brief includes times, locations, routes, J-SEAD, AH-64 or OH-58D security, minefield marking procedures, delivery technique, and minefield purpose. The purpose of the brief is to assist crews if improvision, based on the commander's intent, is necessary, such as if the threat proves too great at the preplanned minefield location or if navigation systems fail and require use of a clearer start or endpoint. The planning staff provides a minefield sketch for the aircrews.

Logistics Planning

3-321. The planning staff coordinates to have mines at the arming location at least 6 hours prior to the planned arming time. Three hours before departure time, aircraft reposition to the arming location where the aircrew and other personnel load the canisters into dispensers. Once loaded, aircraft must exercise care as to where they park so accidentally discharging mines do not threaten other aircraft, trucks, or personnel.

Reporting Requirements

3-322. As soon as possible after mission completion, aircrews give the ADE an exact dispensing time and start/end point coordinates for the minefield-dispensing strip. The aircrew uses the FM-secure or secure relay and scatterable minefield warning reporting format in accordance with FM 3-34.210. This allows the ADE to properly mark and determine safe distances away from the minefield. Aircrews verify ADE receipt of the entire message following mission completion.

CAPABILITIES AND LIMITATIONS

3-323. Capabilities of the air Volcano system are—

- Each aircraft carries 960 mines (800 AT, 160 AP mines, or all AT).
- Mines have three programmable self-destruct times (4 hours, 48 hours, or 15 days).

- The system lays minefields up to 1,115 meters long by 120 meters wide with 960 mines in as few as 18 seconds.
- The system provides commanders an offensive or defensive mine-dispensing capability.
- The system allows accurate emplacement of minefields at night.

3-324. Limitations of the air Volcano system are—

- The system weighs 6,413 pounds, placing the aircraft near or beyond maximum gross weight for many environmental conditions (crew may have to burn off fuel).
- Flight crews cannot operate the door gun with air Volcano installed.
- Aircraft cannot employ the ESSS or ERFS with air Volcano installed.
- It takes 3 to 4 hours to install the system on the UH-60.
- It takes a team of eight trained personnel 30 minutes to reload the canisters.
- Ground transport of the aviation unit's three air Volcano systems requires two 5-ton trucks that must come from internal assets with no TOE vehicle increase.

EMPLOYMENT PRINCIPLES

3-325. The system can emplace four minefield types—disrupt, fix, turn, block:

- **Disrupt.** With low lethality and density, the commander's intent is to confuse enemy formations with near randomness or denial of high-speed roads, bridge approaches, or masking terrain.
- **Fix.** These minefields are placed to permit synchronized ground force fires once encountered.
- **Turn.** Density and lethality are sufficient to influence the maneuver of enemy formations in another direction.
- **Block.** Density and lethality are sufficient to deny enemy use of terrain when emplaced with other natural and manmade obstacles.

     Both turn and block minefields have a probability of mine encounter exceeding 80 percent. The encounter probability for disrupt or fix minefields with less depth and width drops to 50 percent.

3-326. Typical turn or block minefields are dispensed in depth, perpendicular to the enemy direction of travel at a chokepoint. Disrupt or fix minefields are similarly perpendicular but may occur in a more offset manner in larger planned engagement zones along high-speed avenues of approach. Disrupt minefields fracture and break up enemy formations. This causes premature commitment of breaching assets, altering enemy C2 focus and timing. Fix minefields may slow or stop formations with multiple smaller minefields employed in depth in an engagement area (EA).

3-327. Mine-dispensing aircraft may increase minefield effectiveness by dispensing mines on reverse slopes masking aircraft and the minefield itself from approaching enemy forces. Similarly, mine-dispensing aircraft survivability improves with masked approaches to, and masked egress away from, the dispensing pass. Channeling terrain on both sides of a minefield masks the dispensing aircraft and also serves as a natural obstacle to hinder enemy bypass.

3-328. For narrow constricted enemy avenues of approach, an effective technique is to fly directly down the chokepoint pass in a snake-like path. This results in a minefield difficult to breach since it extends for hundreds of yards. This serpentine flight path is essential as no mines are dispensed within 35 meters of the aircraft, so a straight flight path will leave a natural breach. A second dispensing aircraft, mirroring the lead aircraft's movements 150 meters to its rear, will form an effective turn and block minefield.

3-329. Attack reconnaissance aircraft overwatch mine dispensing operations and fire smoke rockets to screen most likely enemy force positions from the flight path of mine-dispensing aircraft. Other high-explosive rockets and 30-millimeter gunfire directed at wood lines within range of the flight path can suppress hidden enemy forces. Refer to table 3-10 and table 3-11, page 3-65, for planning factors and emplacement times.

Table 3-10. Volcano planning factors

Minefield Type	Depth (Meters)	Front (Meters)	No. of Strips	Canisters Per Strip Per Side	Total Canisters	Minefields Per Load
Disrupt	140	278	1	40/20	40	4
Fix	140	278	1	40/20	40	4
Turn	340	557	2	80/40	160	1
Block	340	557	2	80/40	160	1

Table 3-11. Minefield emplacement times

Knots	Disrupt/Fix Minefield (Seconds)	Turn/Block Minefield (Seconds)	160 Canister Load (Seconds)
20	27	54	108
30	18	36	72
40	13	27	54
55	9[1]	18	39
80	6[1]	13[1]	27
120	4[1]	9[1]	18
Minefield Width (meters)	278.7 m (single strip)	557.5 m (each strip)	1,115 m (one long strip)
No. of Passes per Minefield	1	2 (for 2 strips)[2]	1
No. of Canisters per Pass	40	80 (each strip)	160

Notes:
1: Indicate problematic airspeed/time combinations for Volcano dispensing.
2: UH-60s operating in pairs can lay turn and block minefields in one pass, firing 80 canisters each.

Disrupt and Fix Minefields

3-330. Disrupt and fix minefields use one centerline 278 meters long and 140 meters wide and deep (figure 3-15). Aircrews move toward the start point, maintaining the ground speed selected in the DCU. The pilot initiates and concludes mine dispensing by pressing the cyclic launch switch. Such minefields employ just 40 canisters per location, allowing fully loaded aircraft to dispense up to four separate disrupt and fix minefields.

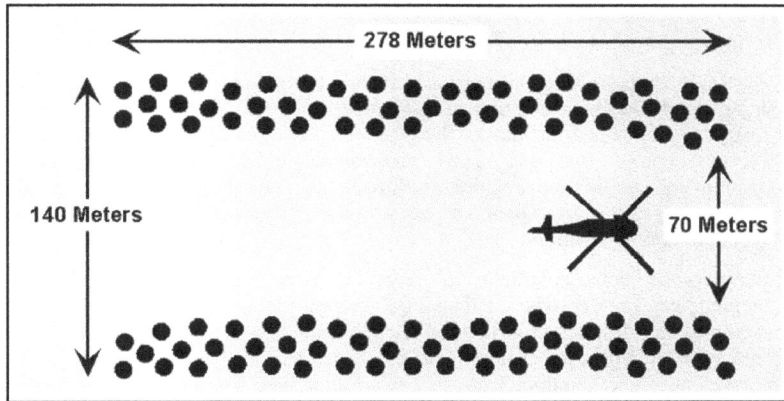

Figure 3-15. Disrupt and fix minefields

Turn and Block Minefields

3-331.   These minefields have greater density and use all 160 mine canisters at one location (figure 3-16, page 3-66). They are longer and wider than disrupt and fix minefields. To achieve the greater depth requires two parallel passes by one aircraft or one simultaneous parallel pass by two aircraft. The resulting minefield is 557 meters long and 340 meters wide and deep.

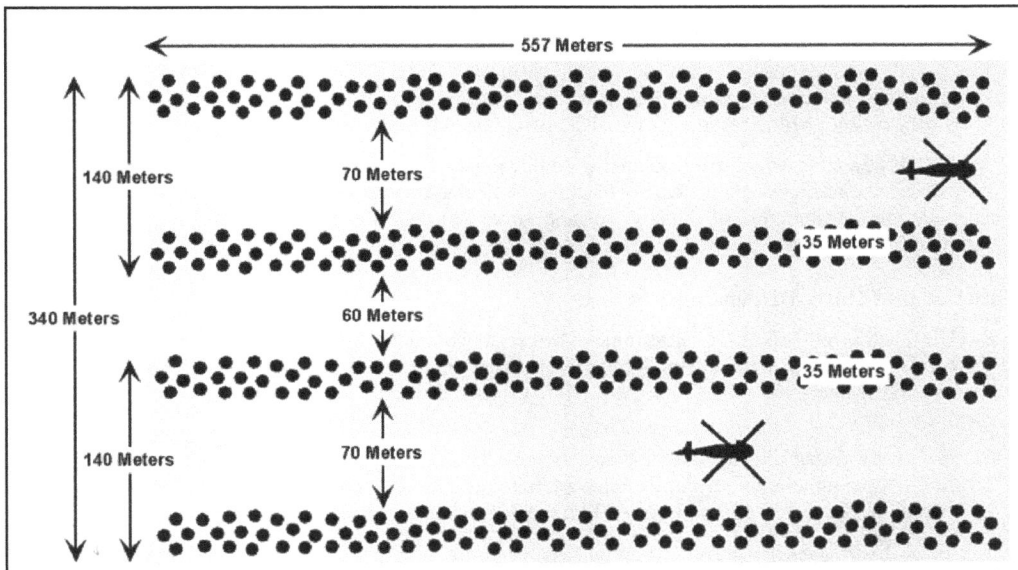

Figure 3-16. Turn and block minefield

AIR VOLCANO OPERATIONS

Air Volcano in Shaping and Decisive Operations

3-332. In shaping operations, deep air-emplaced minefield missions may require simultaneous insertion of LRS teams to mark the minefield and maintain observation of obstacles for subsequent MLRS and ATACMS fires and preplanned air attacks. Deep minefields may support operations in deep areas and assault helicopter maneuvers by fixing enemy forces or denying enemy reinforcements of an air assault objective. Shaping Volcano missions require attack reconnaissance aircraft security, J-SEAD, possible C2 aircraft support, and JSTARS/UAS support to assist in identifying enemy axis of advance and dispensing the corresponding minefield locations.

3-333. In decisive operations, minefields can block enemy withdrawal during exploitation and pursuit. Volcano minefields can protect exposed flanks by denying the enemy's use of an avenue of approach. Following minefield self-destruction, follow-on friendly forces can employ the same avenue of approach for parallel attacks or to bypass reconstituting units. Combat training centers continue to identify problems with late employment of Volcano minefields, lack of security, and inadequate planning, all of which lead to reduced Volcano aircraft survivability and minefield effectiveness.

Volcano in Offensive Operations

3-334. Volcano mines can block potential enemy avenues of approach to reduce surprises during friendly movement to contact. Minefields employed during attacks can secure an exposed flank or reduce vulnerability to counterattack. Routes away from objective areas can be mined to eliminate counterattack and withdrawal routes. Minefields employed during offensive operations will often have shorter four-hour self-destruction times to avoid disrupting friendly maneuver.

Volcano in Defensive Operations

3-335. Assault units can rapidly emplace minefields in the covering force area to delay and disrupt enemy formations. When employed to reinforce natural obstacles at chokepoints, minefields provide opportunities for friendly counterattacks. Minefields employed during defensive operations have long self-destruction times to delay the enemy during friendly strategic deployments. Minefields employed during periods of temporary defense before resuming offensive operations may employ the 48-hour self-destruct time.

3-336. A key consideration for defensive employment of Volcano is division planners preplan several minefield locations based on the enemy reaching particular DPs indicating its axis of advance. During IPB, DPs cue mission initiation of standby Volcano aircraft to dispense the preplanned minefield well before arrival of threat forces.

Deliberate and Hasty Dispensing

3-337. Factors of METT-TC determine whether to conduct deliberate or hasty mine dispensing. A deliberate run would involve a preliminary "dry run" rehearsal just before actual dispensing. It might involve having personnel dismount the aircraft to mark the minefield start and end point with flags or chemical lights.

3-338. Hasty dispensing involves either less time, less security, or a greater threat near the minefield location. Hasty minefields rely on detailed premission map and threat analysis and rehearsal at another location to ensure proper functioning of GPS/Doppler navigation systems.

3-339. LRS or scout personnel, which may precede the mine-dispensing mission, can emplace flags or chemical lights for mission aircraft. Crew chiefs or other aviation personnel can perform the same function concurrently, threat and time permitting.

3-340. When premarking is not an option, the most effective and preferred method is for planners to develop start and stop points for the minefield and pass these coordinates to the aircrews as an eight-digit grid. Aircrews fly precisely between the two points.

Air Volcano Delivery Techniques

3-341. It is imperative flight crews emplace Volcano minefields at the correct location. Failure to do so reduces or eliminates minefield effectiveness and increases fratricide risk. There are several techniques to help ensure proper minefield emplacement.

Visual Identification

3-342. During retrograde or covering force operations, engineer units can clearly mark minefield limits prior to the air-dispensing mission. As mentioned earlier, LRS teams, COLTs, or scouts can mark minefields in the same manner for deep and close missions.

Azimuth/Time Lapse

3-343. Speed may be essential to survivability during the mine-dispensing mission. Aircrews fly along a particular azimuth from a known start point for a predetermined time at a predetermined high speed to deliver the correct minefield dimensions. This is an effective method for night operations.

Azimuth/Canisters Fired

3-344. This technique focuses on ensuring mine-dispensing accuracy by tracking the number of mine canisters dispensed. At the start point along a predetermined azimuth and slower airspeed, the pilot initiates and continues dispensing until the DCU counter reaches the predetermined number of canisters.

Doppler/Global Positioning System

3-345. This technique is the most accurate. The aircraft navigation system can identify minefield eight-digit start and end points. The crew flies precisely between these points. This technique is particularly useful in desert and flat featureless terrain where map navigation/confirmation is ineffective. If time and threat permit, aircraft can actually land at start and end points to get accurate GPS readings, mark the minefield, and then fly the dispensing mission.

This page intentionally left blank.

Chapter 4

Sustainment Operations

This chapter describes maintenance and logistics doctrine. The role of these functions is maintaining and supplying the force during continuous operations. This chapter discusses how to coordinate for different levels of support, and how to request and receive support from the ASB. A thorough understanding of the mission and function is critical to successful aviation logistics and sustainment. Refer to FM 3.04.500 for more information on aviation maintenance and logistics operations.

SECTION I – FUNDAMENTALS

4-1. Aviation logistics organizations must be designed to place the right logistics resources at the right location and time. Aviation logistics organizations primarily consist of an ASB within CABs at division and theater levels, and an aviation maintenance company and FSC with each operational aviation battalion. These units collectively form the framework for aviation logistics in the Army's redesigned force structure.

Contents

4-2. It is essential for all leaders, not just logisticians, to understand the fundamentals for supporting military operations. By understanding how the logistician is trained, manned, and equipped for sustainment operations, the supported commander will know what to expect. The following paragraphs discuss logistics characteristics and methods of resupply.

LOGISTICS CHARACTERISTICS

4-3. Historically, success in battle is dependent on unity of effort between the tactical operation and its sustainment operations. The combat commander succeeds or fails by how well the logistics operators in the operational environment understand and adhere to logistics characteristics discussed in FM 4-0. These logistics (sustainment) characteristics are—

- Responsiveness.
- Simplicity.
- Flexibility.
- Attainability.
- Sustainability.
- Survivability.
- Economy.
- Integration.

4-4. In addition, how well the combat commander emphasizes accurate and timely reporting and incorporates logistics leaders into the planning and preparing process prior to execution impacts his success or failure.

METHODS OF DISTRIBUTION

4-5. A company uses voice or digital means to request resupply and report status. The method used is determined after an analysis of the factors of METT-TC. The three distribution methods of resupply are—

- **Supply point distribution.** Supply point distribution requires unit representatives move to a supply point to pick up their supplies using their organic transportation.
- **Unit distribution.** The ASB may use logistics convoys to conduct unit distribution operations. Unit distribution provides delivery of supplies directly to the unit. A unit representative meets the resupply package at the logistics release point (LRP) and guides the package to the battalion or company position.
- **Throughput distribution.** Shipments bypass one or more echelons in the supply chain and speed delivery forward. Throughput is more responsive to the user, provides more efficient use of transportation assets, and supplies are handled or transloaded less. Throughput is used frequently to resupply FARP operations. Throughput to forward areas leverages configured loads, containerization, information, force structure design, technological enablers, and C2 relationships to deliver sustainment from the operational level directly to the customer or its supporting unit.

SUPPLY OPERATIONS

4-6. The battalion is responsible for coordinating and requisitioning supplies for companies. Although companies do not have a TOE position for a supply sergeant or officer, it should be assigned as an additional duty. The assigned supply officer/sergeant assists the 1SG in obtaining and delivering supplies. Some items are handled internally, while coordination is made with the battalion S-4 for transportation assets (internal or external) to deliver bulky items. The commander ultimately establishes priorities for delivery; however, supplies and equipment in classes I, III, V, and IX are usually the most critical to successful operations.

4-7. To manage unit supply operations, the supply officer/sergeant uses commander's guidance, authorization documents (TOE/MTOE, hand receipts, TMs, and FMs), and external supply SOPs (ASB, aviation maintenance company, and/or FSC). The battalion SOP provides detailed procedures for requesting, receiving, storing, inventorying, issuing, and turning in supplies, equipment, and reparable parts.

4-8. Supply operations involve acquisition, management, receipt, storage, and issuance of all classes of supply except class XIII. FM 3-04.500, FM 4-0, JP 4-0, JP 4-03, and FM 10-1 contain additional information. Table 4-1 provides classes of supply.

Table 4-1. Classes of supply

Classes	Items
Class I	Subsistence, including free health and welfare items.
Class II	Clothing, individual equipment, tentage, tool sets and kits, hand tools, administrative, and housekeeping supplies and equipment (including maps). This also includes items of equipment, other than major items, prescribed in authorization/allowance tables and items of supply (not including repair parts).
Class III	POL, petroleum and solid fuels, including bulk and packaged fuels, lubricating oils and lubricants, petroleum specialty products, coal, and related products.
Class IV	Construction materiels, including installed equipment and all fortification/barrier materiels.
Class V	Ammunition of all types (including chemical, radiological, and special weapons), bombs, explosives, mines, detonators, pyrotechnics, missiles, rockets, propellants, and other associated items.

Table 4-1. Classes of supply

Classes	Items
Class VI	Personal demand items (nonmilitary sales items).
Class VII	Major items: A final combination of end products that is ready for its intended use (principal item) such as, aircraft, mobile machine shops, and vehicles.
Class VIII	Medical materiel, including medical peculiar repair parts.
Class IX/IX (A)	Repair parts and components, including kits, assemblies and subassemblies, reparable and nonreparable, required for maintenance support of all equipment.
Class X	Materiel to support nonmilitary programs, such as agricultural and economic development, not included in Classes I through IX.

CLASSES OF SUPPLY

Class I

4-9.   The battalion S-4 requests class I supplies automatically on the daily strength report. Class I ration requests are consolidated by the S-4 section and forwarded to the CAB S-4 or appropriate support area if operating independently. Extra rations are usually not available at distribution points; therefore, ration requests must accurately reflect personnel present for duty. The CAB S-4 section draws rations from the distribution point and issues them to the battalion. Company 1SGs have the added responsibility of ensuring all attached, OPCON, and DS elements within their respective AOs are included in the head count.

Class II

4-10. The supply officer/sergeant uses Unit Level Logistics System-Supply (ULLS-S4) to request class II supplies and equipment; expendable items, such as soap, toilet tissue, and insecticide, are distributed during LOGPAC operations. Section leaders and/or platoon sergeants submit requests to the supply officer/sergeant, who must obtain budget approval from the parent organization S-4 before submitting the ULLS-S4. The items are then distributed to the battalion using supply point distribution. In some cases, the items may be throughput from division or theater to subordinate battalions.

Class III

4-11. Units normally use fuel forecasts to determine bulk POL requirements. The company 1SG submits requests for POL to the parent organization S-4. Battalions consolidate company forecasts and estimate the amount of fuel required based on projected operations, usually for the period covering 72 hours beyond the next day. Battalion S-4s forward requests through the brigade S-4 to the appropriate distribution management center (DMC). Fuel trucks from the ASB return to battalion areas either as a part of the LOGPACs or to refueling points in FARPs.

4-12. Class III bulk for the CAB is delivered by sustainment brigade assets. The sustainment brigade can store a one-day supply of class III bulk. The fuel is stored and distributed from collapsible bladders or 5,000-gallon tanker trailers. Class III bulk normally is delivered to the ASB and routinely delivered by the sustainment brigade as far forward as the aviation BSA. However, it may be delivered as far forward as battalion FARPs in certain situations.

Class IV

4-13. Consisting of construction materiels, class IV items are used by battalions for fighting positions, perimeter defense, and access points. Commanders should ensure the SOP specifies vehicle loads for each item. The company supply officer/sergeant requests these items using ULLS-S4.

Class V

4-14. Normally, the S-4 requests ammunition from the appropriate DMC. Ammunition managers use combat loads rather than days of supply (DOS). Combat loads measure the amount of class V a unit can carry into combat on its weapons system. Once the request has been authenticated, the ammunition is distributed to the battalion FSC by the ASB's distribution company.

Required Supply Rate

4-15. Required supply rate (RSR) is the estimated amount of ammunition needed to sustain the operations of a combat force without restrictions for a specific period. RSR is expressed in rounds per weapon per day and is used to state ammunition requirements. The battalion S-3, in conjunction with the S-4, normally formulates the battalion RSR, although it is often adjusted by higher HQ.

Controlled Supply Rate

4-16. Controlled supply rate (CSR) is the rate of ammunition consumption (expressed in rounds per day per unit, weapon system, or individual) supported for a given period. It is based on ammunition availability, storage facilities, and transportation capabilities. A unit may not exceed its CSR for ammunition without authority from higher HQ. The battalion S-4 compares the CSR against the RSR, then remedies shortages by requesting more ammunition, sub-allocating ammunition, cross-leveling, or prioritizing support to subordinate units. The battalion commander establishes CSRs for subordinate units; the company commander ensures company requirements are anticipated, requested, and received.

Basic Load

4-17. The basic load is the quantity of ammunition authorized by the theater commander for wartime purposes and the amount required to be carried into combat by a unit. The basic load provides the unit with enough ammunition to sustain itself in combat until it can be resupplied. The unit basic load may not be the appropriate load to conduct operations based on contingencies. Any deviation from the unit basic load is requested early for approval and resourcing.

Combat Load

4-18. The combat load is the quantity of supplies, such as fuel or ammunition, carried by the combat system or Solider into combat. The commander knows the required combat load for each system and Soldier per individual mission requirement.

Class VI

4-19. Class VI supplies are made available through local procurement, transfer from theater stocks, or requisitioning from the Army and Air Force Exchange Service (AAFES). When a post exchange is not available, the S-1 is responsible for overseeing and submitting class VI requests.

Class VII

4-20. Class VII items are controlled through command channels and managed by the supporting DMC. Each echelon manages requisition, distribution, maintenance, and disposal of these items ensuring visibility and operational readiness. Units report losses of major items through both supply and command channels. Replacement requires coordination among materiel managers, class VII supply units, transporters, maintenance elements, and personnel managers. Class VII items are issued based on battle loss reports a company submits to its parent organization S-4. Each battalion should have a property book officer (PBO) to account for these items, any stay behind equipment, or other theater issued stock items received in the theater of operations.

Classes IX and IX (A)

4-21. Class IX supplies include repair parts and documents required for equipment maintenance operations. When a company orders repair parts, the platoon sergeant (ground components) and materiel manager/tech supply (air components) coordinate with the FSC supporting the specific requests. The company also obtains repair parts by exchanging reparable parts, including batteries for NVDs and manportable radios.

4-22. Class IX requisition begins with the unit filling requisitions from its combat spares. If the item is not stocked on the combat spares or is at zero balance, the requisition is passed to the supply support activity (SSA). This SSA fills the request from its authorized stockage list (ASL) or passes the requisition to the MMC. The ground maintenance sections of ASBs normally maintain the class IX ASL for ground equipment. The aviation support company (ASC) maintains the class IX (A) combat spares.

Class X

4-23. Division level or higher provides instructions for request and issue of class X supplies.

OTHER SUPPLY CONSIDERATIONS

Maps

4-24. Unit personnel submit requests for unclassified maps to the battalion S-4 and classified maps through the battalion S-2. If a digital topographic support system team is attached, personnel may also make customized AO maps upon request to the main CP.

Support by Host Nation

4-25. Logistics support and transportation may be provided by host nation organizations and facilities. Common classes of supply may be available and obtained from local civilian sources. Items may include barrier and construction materiels, fuel for vehicles, and some food and medical supplies. Requisition and distribution are coordinated through logistics and liaison channels.

SUSTAINMENT DURING COMBAT OPERATIONS

4-26. Sustainment operations are inseparable from decisive and shaping operations. Failure to sustain may result in mission failure. Sustainment operations occur throughout the AO, not just within the noncontiguous support areas. Sustaining operations determine how fast forces reconstitute and how far forces can exploit success. At the tactical level, sustaining operations establish the tempo of the overall operation.

4-27. Aviation logistics units should be trained, equipped, and manned to operate in a hostile environment while accomplishing their mission. The aviation unit commander must consider what level of force protection his unit can accomplish while still performing sustainment and support operations; for example destroy Level I, defeat Level II with assistance, and employment of a tactical combat force for Level III. This does not presume that 100 percent level of sustainment operations can occur 100 percent of the time. Sustainment may fluctuate depending on the threat level and enemy operations. If the enemy threat is stronger than the ability of the aviation logistics unit to destroy or defeat it, then the prudent commander knows other forces are required to sustain logistics operations at the level desired or risk their destruction.

4-28. Aviation logistics leaders must understand the concepts of battle command as discussed in chapter 2 of this manual. This requires logistics Soldiers gain and sustain competency in executing individual and collective level combat tasks required for their unit and its associated operational environment.

4-29. Maneuver commanders must be willing to allocate combat power as an essential part of the sustainment mission. This allows maneuver forces to defend high risk aviation logistics units and open and maintain as necessary ground and aerial LOCs. It may take the form of combat unit(s) escorting logistic convoys, attaching a combat unit to reinforce the perimeter defense, or occupying an area with sufficient force for a stated period of time to eliminate an air or ground threat.

4-30. The implied task for the aviation unit commander is to possess the requisite skills necessary to integrate the maneuver commander's forces into his security plan. All logistics leaders must also be capable of defending an assigned AO by employing organic assets. As appropriate, the aviation logistics commander should coordinate with the CAB or battalion S-3 for assistance in development of the area defense plan.

SECTION II – MAINTENANCE

PRINCIPLES

4-31. Maintenance is a combat multiplier. When enemy forces have relative parity in numbers and quality of equipment, the force combining skillful use of equipment with an effective maintenance system has a decisive advantage. This force has an initial advantage in that it enters battle with equipment likely to remain operational longer. A subsequent advantage is it can repair damaged equipment, make it operational, and return the equipment to the battle faster.

4-32. Well-trained and equipped forward maintenance elements are critical to success of the maintenance concept. They must have the proper personnel, equipment, and tools as well as immediate access to high usage replacement parts. Field maintenance units concentrate on rapid turnaround of equipment to the battle, while sustainment-level maintenance units repair and return equipment to the supply system.

4-33. The maintenance system is organized around forward support. All damaged or malfunctioning equipment should be repaired onsite or as close to the site as possible.

SUPPORT SYSTEM STRUCTURE

4-34. The maintenance support system is a two-level structure—field maintenance and sustainment maintenance.

Field Maintenance

4-35. Field maintenance is performed by aviation brigade personnel assigned to flight companies, aviation maintenance companies, and ASCs. The aviation maneuver battalion's assigned flight companies perform authorized maintenance procedures within their capability. Aviation maintenance companies assigned to aviation maneuver battalions provide maintenance support to all flight companies. As compared to the ASC, operational flight battalions are more agile, flexible, and mobile as they have reduced sets, kits, outfits, tools, and special tools (SKOT).

4-36. Both the aviation maintenance company and ASC perform field-level maintenance; however, the aviation maintenance company is limited to unit maintenance while the ASC is equipped with additional SKOT and is authorized to perform intermediate maintenance. On a case-by-case basis, the aviation brigade may obtain specialized repair authorization from Aviation and Missile Command (AMCOM) to perform limited depot repairs on specific equipment classified as depot level according to the maintenance allocation chart (MAC).

Sustainment Maintenance

4-37. According to FM 4-0, sustainment maintenance is the Army's strategic support. The strategic support base is the backbone of the National Maintenance Program (NMP) and the sustainment maintenance system. At this level, maintenance supports the supply system by economically repairing or overhauling components. Maintenance management concentrates on identifying the needs of the Army supply system and developing programs to meet the supply system demands.

4-38. Sustainment maintenance support is divided and primarily performed by three separate entities: the original equipment manufacturers and their contract field service representatives; Army depots, located at fixed bases in the CONUS; and NMP sources of repair.

4-39. Figure 4-1 shows a graphic depiction of two-level maintenance, which illustrates the supported and supporting relationships of field to sustainment maintenance.

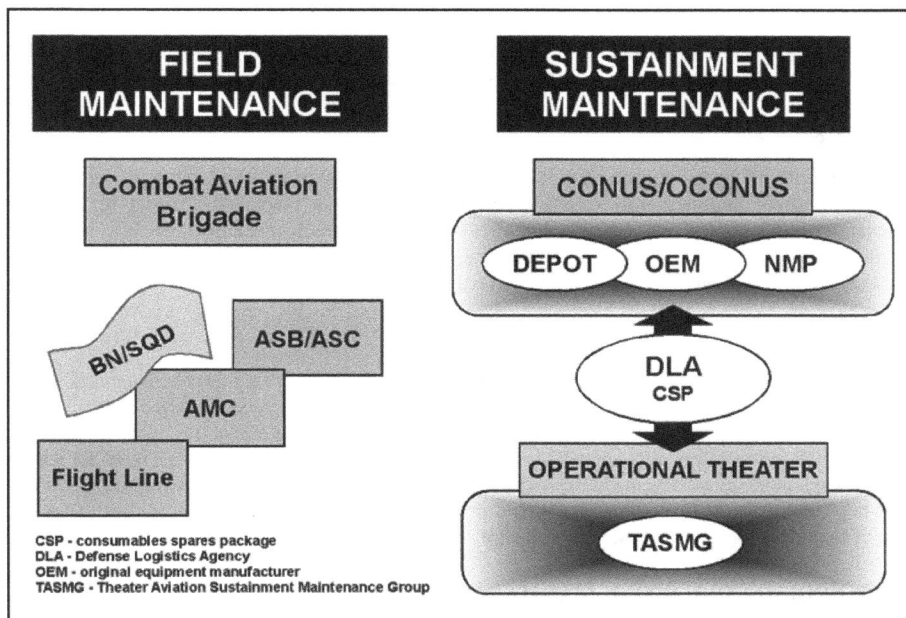

Figure 4-1. Two-level aviation maintenance and sustainment

AVIATION MAINTENANCE OPERATIONS

4-40. As Army aviation transforms, the aviation maintenance company within each battalion will continue to provide unit maintenance above the capability of the flight companies. The ASC assigned to the ASB will continue to provide primarily intermediate maintenance and secondary backup unit maintenance to the battalion.

4-41. Aviation maintenance is performed on a 24-hour basis. The governing concept is to replace forward and repair rearward so units can rapidly return aircraft for operational needs. Emphasis is on component replacement rather than repair. Such replacement requires increased stockage of line replaceable units (LRUs) and quick change assemblies. Damaged or inoperable aircraft requiring time-consuming repair actions are handled in more secure areas toward the rear. FM 3-04.500 provides more detail.

MANAGEMENT BALANCE

4-42. The flying hour program and operational readiness rates must be balanced ensuring bank hours (hours remaining per aircraft until phase) are available to meet the operational needs required during a deployment and/or training. Commanders and maintenance officers evaluate available resources and adjust them accordingly. The problem, plan, people, parts, time, and tools (P4T2) concept may assist in this evaluation. Another tool available for managing aircraft maintenance is the flowchart.

Flowchart

4-43. The flowchart is a simple but effective method maintenance officers use. Unit Level Logistics System-Aviation (ULLS-A) provides a flowchart outlining bank time to assist maintenance managers in scheduling maintenance. The flowchart—

- Prevents an unnecessary backlog of scheduled maintenance inspections under normal conditions.
- Prevents a corresponding sudden surge in requirements for aircraft parts.
- Allows the unit maintenance officer a degree of control over individual aircraft hours flown.
- Provides a graphic depiction of future scheduled maintenance requirements.

Operational Readiness Rate

4-44. The ability of an aviation unit to perform its wartime mission is numerically represented by its aircraft operational readiness rate. Higher operational readiness rates are a direct result of effective maintenance and logistics management by all aviation maintenance leaders, officers, and technicians. Reducing aircraft downtime proportionally increases aircraft availability providing the battalion commander with needed aircraft to continue and win the fight (refer to FM 3-04.500).

SCHEDULED MAINTENANCE

4-45. Scheduled maintenance takes place anytime an aircraft phase, progressive phase maintenance, and preventive maintenance services, to include scheduled component replacement, are to be conducted. To ensure minimum disruption to the supported unit's mission (training/tactical), a scheduling system that promotes efficient workflow is needed. This ensures customers receive their aircraft with the least possible delay. Many factors must be considered when production control develops a scheduling system. These factors may include the current workloads and priorities of supported units, availability of tools, and the supply of major components, parts, and hardware.

PHASE AND PROGRESSIVE PHASE MAINTENANCE

4-46. The modular force is changing the levels of responsibility and management of phase/periodic maintenance scheduling and flow. A methodical and purposeful flow of aircraft scheduled maintenance events increases overall readiness.

4-47. Ongoing operations, training exercises, and deployments can have a major impact on readiness (for example, flying too many aircraft into scheduled maintenance at a critical time). OPTEMPO, deployments, training, and availability of resources (tools, maintenance personnel, repair parts, special equipment) must be considered when planning phase maintenance.

UNSCHEDULED MAINTENANCE

4-48. Aircraft scheduled for daily mission (training/tactical) requirements may on occasions experience unexpected malfunction, premature component breakdown, or battlefield damage causing the aircraft to undergo unscheduled (reactive) maintenance. Unplanned aircraft system, subsystem, or components malfunctions or breakdowns will prompt production control to coordinate for unscheduled (reactive) maintenance to bring affected aircraft to a fully mission capable status. It is the production control officer's responsibility to prioritize, manage, and track unscheduled repairs having a negative effect on the total mission capability of the attack reconnaissance battalion (ARB). Maintenance platoon leadership is ultimately responsible for conducting maintenance repairs to affected aircraft systems, subsystems, and components in accordance with established maintenance publications and references.

DEFERRED MAINTENANCE

4-49. The production control officer prioritizes maintenance actions by weighing them in terms of which maintenance procedures must be performed immediately and which procedures can be postponed for a later time. When maintenance procedures are postponed, this action is commonly referred to as deferred maintenance. Deferred maintenance actions must be performed when an aircraft goes down for unscheduled maintenance or an airframe is scheduled for a preventive maintenance service or phase. Regardless, deferred maintenance actions cannot be delayed indefinitely; it must be coordinated and scheduled to be performed at the earliest opportunity. The commander is the approval authority for all deferred maintenance actions and should be notified immediately when the status of aircraft flightworthiness changes.

AIRCRAFT RECOVERY, EVACUATION, AND BATTLE DAMAGE ASSESSMENT AND REPAIR

Battlefield Management of Damaged Aircraft

4-50. BDAR/recovery operations are normally planned and coordinated in conjunction with PR operations. Recovery operations move an aircraft system or component from the battlefield to a maintenance facility. Recovery may require on-site repair for a one-time flight or movement by another aircraft or surface vehicle. In extreme circumstances, only portions of inoperative aircraft may be recovered. An aircraft is cannibalized at a field site only when the combat situation and aircraft condition are such that the aircraft would otherwise be lost to enemy forces. See FM 3-04.500 and FM 3-04.513 for more detailed information on aircraft recovery.

Responsibility

4-51. The battalion is responsible for coordinating aircraft recovery, while it is the aviation maintenance company who is responsible for conducting the recovery. A successful recovery operation is a highly coordinated effort between the owning organization, its ASB support, other supporting units, and ground element where the operation is to take place. If recovery is beyond the aviation maintenance company team's capability, ASB support is requested. Overall, control of recovery rests with the CAB CP.

Recovery Teams

4-52. Aviation battalions prepare for aircraft recovery contingencies by designating a DART. The DART, at a minimum, includes an MP, maintenance/shop platoon personnel, aircraft assessor, and technical inspector. The technical inspector may also be the assessor. All members must be trained to prepare aircraft for recovery as this is a unit responsibility. The team chief ensures rigging equipment and quick-fix BDAR kits (tools, hardware, POL products, repair parts, and TMs) are kept ready for short-notice recovery missions. Aircraft recovery can turn into PR if the tactical situation changes; recovery teams are integrated into the QRF. FM 3-04.513 contains a sample aircraft recovery and evacuation SOP.

Planning Considerations

4-53. Assessment of the following factors facilitates selection of the best COA:
- Location of downed aircraft.
- Types of special equipment packages installed on aircraft.
- Amount of damage to aircraft.
- Weapon munitions onboard the aircraft and requirement for explosive ordnance disposal (EOD).
- Tactical situation and proximity to enemy.
- Time available (planning time for aviation maintenance company preparation and rigging is 30 to 60 minutes, which may vary based on METT-TC).
- Weather.
- P4T2.

Courses of Action

4-54. The unit SOP provides guidance required to determine which of the following actions is appropriate for the situation:

- Make combat repairs, defer further maintenance, or return aircraft to service.
- Make repairs for one-time flight and fly aircraft to an appropriate maintenance area.
- Rig aircraft for recovery (by ground or air) and arrange for transport.
- Selectively conduct controlled exchange, destroy, or abandon aircraft in accordance with TM 750-244-1-5 and unit SOP.

Aerial/Ground Recovery

4-55. General procedures are typically covered in unit SOPs. FM 3-04.513 provides detailed procedures for preparing and performing recovery operations for specific aircraft. FM 3.04-120 provides doctrinal guidance on requirements, procedures, and C2 tasks involved in planning, coordinating, and executing airspace control functions. Parallel planning using P4T2 for a ground recovery should occur while any aerial recovery operation is ongoing.

Planning

4-56. Recovery operations and, to a lesser degree, maintenance evacuations can easily be detected and attacked by enemy forces. Units must plan command, control, and coordination for recovery operations in advance. Recovery and evacuation procedures must be included in unit SOPs, contingency plans, OPORDs, and AMBs.

Aircrew

4-57. Depending on the enemy situation, crew status, and aircraft communications, the following items or additional pertinent information will be obtained from the pilot or aircraft operator:

- Aircraft mission design series and tail number.
- Crew status and condition (are they able to conduct evacuation of aircraft).
- Describe extent of damage (is aircraft airworthy).
- Enemy activity.
- Aircraft altitude when it went down.
- Approximate fuel remaining in aircraft.
- Pilot-reported weather.
- Time and place of last-known position.
- Heading since last-known position.
- Airspeed when aircraft went down.
- Navigation equipment capability.
- NAVAID signals received.
- Visible landmarks.
- Number of people onboard.
- Point of departure and destination.
- Emergency equipment on hand.
- Weapons available, if any.

Destruction of Aircraft and Associated Equipment

4-58. Destruction of aircraft and associated equipment that cannot be recovered and are in danger of enemy capture may be destroyed according to TM 750-244-1-5. The authority for destruction will be delineated and included in SOPs and OPORDs. If possible, aircraft are cannibalized before destruction.

The higher HQ command assigned to a theater of operations, on a mission basis, mandates recovery and evacuation of enemy, allied, and other U.S. services' aircraft using higher-echelon assets.

VEHICLE AND GROUND EQUIPMENT MAINTENANCE AND RECOVERY OPERATIONS

MAINTENANCE SUPPORT STRUCTURE

4-59. Ground maintenance support for each battalion is provided by their organic FSC. Sustainment level units provide maintenance assistance as required.

PREVENTIVE MAINTENANCE CHECKS AND SERVICES

4-60. The operator or crew and organizational maintenance personnel perform unit maintenance including scheduled and unscheduled unit-level maintenance, repair, and PMCS. PMCS maintains operational readiness of equipment through preventive maintenance and early diagnosis of problems.

FIELD MAINTENANCE

4-61. Field maintenance units are tailored to the weapons systems of the supported unit and provide organizational and DS levels of maintenance with a multi-capable mechanic. They provide extensive maintenance expertise, component replacement, and limited component repair.

SUSTAINMENT MAINTENANCE

4-62. Sustainment maintenance is characterized by extensive component repair capability. It repairs damaged systems for issue through the supply system such as classes II, VII, or IX items. This level of maintenance is normally found at theater or depot level.

VEHICLE AND EQUIPMENT RECOVERY PROCEDURES

4-63. The recovery manager coordinates recovery operations with overall repair effort to best support the commander's priorities and tactical situation.

Recovery Principles

4-64. When the unit recovers its equipment but lacks the physical means to recover an item, it requests assistance from the supporting maintenance element. Management of recovery operations is centralized at battalion whenever possible.

4-65. Maintenance personnel repair equipment as far forward as possible within limits of the tactical situation, amount of damage, and available resources. Recovery vehicles return equipment to the rear no further than necessary, usually to the maintenance collection point of the supporting maintenance unit.

4-66. Recovery missions interfering with combat operations or compromising security are coordinated with the tactical commander.

SECTION III – BATTALION SUSTAINMENT UNITS

FLIGHT COMPANY

4-67. Flight line or company maintenance activities primarily maintain Army aircraft by conducting scheduled maintenance. Unscheduled maintenance is conducted within the unit's capability. Strict and disciplined company operations allow assigned aircraft to be maintained according to prescribed policies and procedures. An atmosphere of "pride of ownership" enhances the quality and standard of assigned company aircraft and improves overall unit readiness.

4-68. Crew chiefs perform aircraft launch and recovery operations, and maintain aircraft logbooks in accordance with Army guidance and unit SOPs. They perform both scheduled and unscheduled unit maintenance to include replacement of major subsystem components, maintenance operational checks, and main and tail rotor vibration analysis. Battalion flight companies receive backup support from the aviation maintenance company to perform both scheduled and unscheduled maintenance.

4-69. Leaders must strictly adhere to established standards and maintenance procedures. The assigned flight crews must conduct detailed preflight and postflight inspections according to applicable TMs. The crew must ensure all identified deficiencies and malfunctions are promptly and accurately entered into the aircraft logbook.

AVIATION MAINTENANCE COMPANY

4-70. The aviation maintenance company is organic to AHBs and GSABs assigned to CABs. The aviation maintenance company consists of three modular aviation maintenance platoons: the HQ platoon, aircraft maintenance platoon, and aircraft CRP.

4-71. The purpose of the aviation maintenance company is to provide field level maintenance to enable CAB aircraft to sustain aviation combat power. The aviation maintenance company is organized to provide quick, responsive, internal maintenance support and repair within its capability and in accordance with the MAC. The aviation maintenance company troubleshoots airframe and component malfunctions and performs maintenance and repair actions. It conducts BDAR and recovery operations within its capability and is assisted by the ASC.

4-72. The aviation maintenance company provides mobile, responsive BDAR and DART operations support through forward maintenance teams (FMTs). FMTs repair aircraft onsite or prepare them for evacuation. The aviation maintenance company commander and production control officer coordinate and schedule maintenance at forward locations of the battalion. Members of the FMT must be able to diagnose aircraft damage or serviceability rapidly and accurately. FMT operations follow these principles:

- Teams may be used for aircraft, component, avionics, or armament repair.
- When the time and situation allow, teams repair onsite rather than evacuate aircraft; this includes BDAR.
- Teams must be 100 percent mobile and transported by the fastest means available (usually by helicopter).
- Teams sent forward may be oriented and equipped for special tasks to include recovery operations; type of aircraft recovery will depend on the assets available.

4-73. In some situations, normal maintenance procedures must be expedited to meet operational objectives. In such cases, the unit commander may authorize the use of aircraft combat maintenance and BDAR procedures. Aircraft combat maintenance and BDAR are an aviation maintenance company responsibility with backup from supporting ASC units.

4-74. The BDAR concept uses specialized assessment criteria, repair kits, and trained personnel to return damaged aircraft to the battle as soon as possible. Often, these repairs are only temporary. Permanent repairs may be required when the tactical situation permits. This method is used to meet operational needs. It is not used when the situation allows application of standard methods.

HEADQUARTERS PLATOON

4-75. The HQ platoon contains a HQ section, production control section, QA section and technical supply section. This platoon provides for internal management and quality of repairs, and logistics support within the battalion. The technical supply section operates the logistics Standard Army Management Information System (STAMIS), requisitions class IX (A) spares, and manages the battalion prescribed load list (PLL). Oversight is provided by the battalion AMO assigned to the S-4.

MAINTENANCE PLATOON

4-76. The maintenance platoon provides quick, responsive internal maintenance support and repair turnaround within its capability. When assigned to support aircraft managed under the phase maintenance concept, the maintenance platoon is primary provider of this scheduled maintenance within the battalion. The maintenance platoon operates and maintains aviation ground support equipment (AGSE), and operates and performs unit level maintenance on aviation ground power units, generators, and ground support equipment.

COMPONENT REPAIR PLATOON

4-77. The CRP contains assigned aviation repair specialty military operational specialties (MOSs) to include avionics, armament, powerplant/powertrain, hydraulics, pneumatics, and sheet metal repair assets. The CRP diagnoses airframe and component malfunctions and performs maintenance, repair actions, and removes and installs LRUs within its capabilities.

FORWARD SUPPORT COMPANY

4-78. An FSC is assigned to each operational aviation battalion and consists of a HQ platoon, distribution platoon, and ground maintenance platoon (see chapter 1 for organizational structure). The FSC commander provides all logistics (less medical) to the aviation battalion and is the senior multifunctional logistician at aviation battalion level. The FSC is designed to provide ground, air, missile, and AGSE systems support; refueling and rearming support; and necessary logistics support. The FSC also coordinates with the ASB for additional logistics as required. Each of the FARPs can be task organized to support continuous operations by providing support for maintenance, armament, and rearming and refueling. The FSC also maintains 2 DOS of class I, provides field feeding and distribution support, maintains class IX (ground) repair parts, and conducts ground maintenance, while maintaining one combat load each of class III (B) and V for its supported battalion.

HEADQUARTERS PLATOON

4-79. The HQ platoon of the FSC consists of a HQ section and field feeding section.

Headquarters Section

4-80. The HQ section of the FSC provides C2 to assigned and attached personnel. It ensures subordinate elements follow the policies and procedures prescribed by the FSC and battalion commanders. It directs the operations of its subordinate sections as well as the overall logistics operations (less medical) in support of the battalion.

Field Feeding Section

4-81. The field feeding section is found in the FSC of each aviation battalion. The field feeding section provides class I food service and preparation (from the BSA) for the battalion. This section prepares hot meals and distributes prepackaged or prepared food, or both, from the BSA. It can provide one "heat-and-serve" meal and one "cook-prepared" (A or B ration) meal per day.

DISTRIBUTION PLATOON

4-82. The key activity of the distribution platoon is the conduct of LOGPAC operations to the battalion and getting replenishment sustainment stocks from sustainment brigade units. The distribution platoon also provides supply and transportation support to the battalion. The distribution platoon provides classes II, III (P, B), IV, V, VI, and VII to the battalion. The distribution platoon has the ability to conduct simultaneous classes III and V retail support to the companies, HHC, and FSC itself and delivers hot meals to the company area. The distribution platoon operates FBCB2 and STAMIS to support supplies ordering and receipt.

Forward Arming and Refueling Point Operations

4-83. The FSC commander is responsible for accomplishing the FARP mission. He assists the S-3 in formulating the FARP plan and coordinates fuel and ammunition requirements with the S-4. The FSC commander requests additional FARP support from the ASB. The increased tempo of operations and/or density of traffic may require ATS assets. The FSC commander may request a TACT from the GSAB ATS company to perform this mission. In addition, a SO certifies the FARP prior to use. If an SO is not available, a pilot of the first aircraft in the FARP certifies the FARP according to the FARP checklist in the unit SOP. See FM 3-04.104 for more information on FARP operations.

Forward Arming and Refueling Point Location

4-84. The FARP location is METT-TC dependent and a function of the battalion S-3. The FARP should be located as close to the AO as the tactical situation permits. The intent is to reduce aircraft travel distance or time, thereby increasing aircraft time on station while simultaneously striking a balance that exposes the FARP to the least possible risk.

4-85. Commanders can employ and configure their assets as the mission dictates to complete mission requirements. The commander can choose to have one large FARP or several small FARPs. If a FARP must be located behind enemy lines, the following factors should be considered:

- Composition of the FARP should be austere.
- Security will be limited because the FARP will be emplaced for a very short time.
- A thorough map reconnaissance and intelligence update must be accomplished for the area.

4-86. The FARP is usually located as far forward as 18 to 25 kilometers (METT-TC dependent) behind the FLOT. This distance increases aircraft time on station by reducing the travel times associated with refueling. If possible, the FARP is kept outside the threat of medium-range artillery. Movement and resupply of the FARP are conducted by ground or aerial means. The FARP should remain in one location for only three to 6 hours; however, these times may be reduced by the factors of METT-TC. The size of the FARP will depend on the number of aircraft that will use the FARP and the type of refueling equipment (FARE/AAFARS or heavy expanded mobility tactical truck [HEMTT]) available. Four to eight refueling points are normally sufficient for continuous mission sustainment.

4-87. Ammunition palletized load system trucks with mission-configured loads push supplies down to where FARP elements meet them at LRPs. When possible, the FSC commander coordinates for direct delivery to the silent FARP to avoid transloading. Units travel to supply points for fuel or receive throughput from higher echelon 5,000-gallon tankers for transloading.

GROUND MAINTENANCE PLATOON

4-88. The ground maintenance platoon is organic to the FSC of each aviation battalion. Field maintenance units are tailored to weapons systems of the supported unit to provide maintenance expertise for component replacement and limited component repair.

4-89. The FSC's maintenance platoon provides field maintenance to itself and its battalion. The platoon consists of a HQ section, maintenance control section, recovery section, maintenance and service section, and FMTs. The maintenance platoon provides C2 and reinforcing maintenance to the FMTs. The FMTs provide field maintenance and BDAR to the companies. The platoon maintains a limited quantity of combat spares (PLL, shop, and BS) in the maintenance control section. The maintenance platoon's supply section is capable of providing class IX support (combat spares) to each company and the HHC. It also provides exchange of reparable items.

HEADQUARTERS AND HEADQUARTERS COMPANY

ORGANIZATION

4-90. The HHC supports a higher HQ commander and his staff. It provides personnel and equipment for C2 functions of battalion, and security and defense of the CP. The HHC also provides unit-level personnel service, UMT, logistics, and CBRN support.

4-91. Organization and capabilities of the battalion HHC are two of the most important factors in determining how the HHC supports its respective organizations. Force transformation restructured composition of the HHC by eliminating most sustainment assets except for the medical treatment team. With the new HHC organization, remaining sustainment assets are now part of the ASB and FSC.

4-92. The typical aviation battalion HHC consists of a command group, staff, company HQ section, supply section, communications/automation section, UMT, and medical treatment team. The company command group consists of the commander, 1SG, CBRN NCO, and decontamination specialist (as shown in chapter 1).

Supply Section

4-93. The supply section consists of a battalion supply sergeant, battalion armorer, and supply specialist. The supply section manages distribution of supplies in support of the battalion. It utilizes Unit Level Logistics System-Ground and Standard Army Retail Supply System-Level 1 (SARSS-1) interfaces providing supply receipt and issue management for all classes of supplies except class VIII (medical).

Communications Section

4-94. The communications section consists of a communications section chief, team chief, LAN manager, transmission system operator-maintenance specialists, signal support system maintenance specialists, and radio retransmission operators. The communications section plans, coordinates, and oversees implementation of communications systems. It performs unit-level maintenance on ground radio and field wire communications equipment and installs, operates, and maintains the radio retransmission site. The communications section monitors the maintenance status of signal equipment, coordinates preparation and distribution of the SOI, and manages COMSEC activities. The communications section's responsibilities include supervision of electronic mail on both unclassified and classified nets and the LAN.

Unit Ministry Team

4-95. The UMT is comprised of a chaplain and chaplain's assistant. The team provides religious support to all personnel assigned or attached to the battalion and company. The chaplain advises all unit commanders on religious, moral, and Soldier welfare issues, and establishes liaison with UMTs of higher and adjacent units.

Medical Treatment Team

4-96. The HHC's medical treatment team provides health service support (HSS) to battalion. At battalion level, the medical section consists of a flight surgeon, physician's assistant, and health care specialists.

4-97. The medical treatment section consists of two treatment teams (teams A and B). They operate the BAS and provide Level I medical care and treatment. This includes sick call; emergency medical treatment (EMT); preventive medicine; and advanced trauma management for wounds, injuries, or illness. The flight surgeon, physician assistant, health care sergeant and specialists provide EMT and assist with advanced trauma management procedures related to their occupational specialties. The treatment teams can operate for limited times in split-based operations in DS of battalion units.

4-98. The medical treatment team usually operates under direction of the battalion CP. Health care specialists provide medical treatment under supervision of the flight surgeon or physician's assistant. Battalion health care specialists monitor health and hygiene of the battalion, train the battalion's combat life saver personnel, and treat casualties requiring additional care during TACOPS. Medical personnel also provide training in basic first aid and buddy aid, train and direct unit personnel to assist in handling mass casualties, and assist the commander to ensure assigned and attached personnel meet all deployment readiness criteria.

4-99. They also coordinate with the supporting medical platoon in the ASB to assist in MEDEVAC from the point of injury to the Level I MTF/BAS and beyond. The medical sergeant keeps the S-1 and 1SGs informed of casualties' status, and coordinates with the S-4 for nonstandard evacuations as needed.

AVIATION SUPPORT BATTALION

4-100. The ASB is the primary aviation logistics organization above the aviation battalion. The ASB is organic to the CAB and provides all logistics functions necessary to sustain the AHB and GSAB during operations.

4-101. The battalion receives logistics from various elements depending on the logistics organizational structure at brigade's and division's supporting sustainment brigade. Battalion XOs are responsible to their respective commanders for overwatching sustainment operations and inserting themselves where appropriate to ensure successful sustainment operations for the battalion. The battalion S-4 identifies logistics requirements for the maneuver plan and provides them to the FSC, ASC, or ASB commander as appropriate for the level of command.

AVIATION SUPPORT BATTALION ORGANIZATION

4-102. The ASB (figure 4-2) consists of four companies: headquarters and support company (HSC), distribution company, network support company (NSC), and ASC. The ASB provides aviation and ground field maintenance, network communications, resupply, and medical support. The HSC provides medical support and conducts field-ground maintenance and recovery. The distribution company functions as an SSA and distributes supplies to subordinate units of the CAB. The NSC provides network and signal support to the CAB HQ. The ASC provides intermediate maintenance and support for on-aircraft and critical off-aircraft field level maintenance and maintenance of UAS. The ASC also conducts BDAR and provides backup support to the aviation maintenance company.

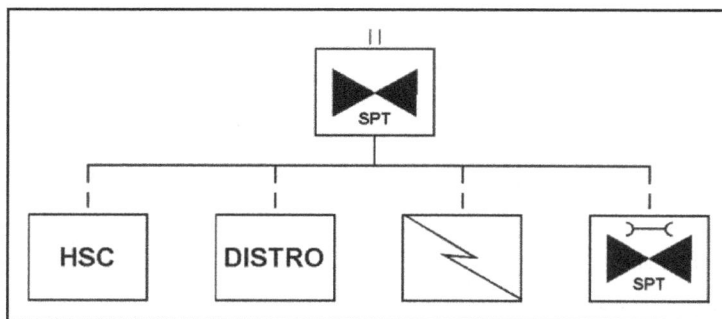

Figure 4-2. Aviation support battalion

Headquarters and Support Company

4-103. The battalion HSC contains a typical battalion staff structure with a command section, S-1 section, consolidated S-2/S-3 section, S-4 section, UMT, S-6 section, and a support operations section. The battalion HQ provides command, control, and intelligence and administration support for all organic and attached ASB units. The battalion HQ also plans, directs, and supervises logistics support for the battalions of the aviation brigade. The ASB has an organic Combat Service Support Automation Management Office that provides support to the entire brigade's automation, including the ULLS-A system.

4-104. The support operations section is organized to coordinate logistics support and provide distribution management to the aviation brigade. The support operations section is also manned to accomplish contracting, medical logistics, petroleum, ammunition, movement control, transportation, and mortuary affairs functions.

Support Company Section

4-105. The support company portion of the HSC provides ground maintenance, medical, supply, and food service support for units organic and attached to the ASB.

Maintenance Platoon

4-106. The maintenance platoon is responsible for field level maintenance of all ASB organic ground equipment.

Medical Platoon

4-107. The medical platoon provides Level I enhanced medical care. The platoon is organized into a HQ, treatment, and evacuation sections. The medical platoon provides the following capabilities:

- EMT and acute trauma management for wounded and diseased and nonbattle injury patients.
- Sick call services.
- Ground ambulance evacuation from supported units.
- Mass casualty triage and management.
- Limited patient decontamination.

Distribution Company

4-108. The distribution company provides a single source for all supply (less class VIII) and transportation operations. The distribution company includes a fuel and water platoon, supply platoon, and transportation platoon.

Fuel and Water Platoon

4-109. The fuel and water platoon has the capability to store and distribute 105,000 gallons (1 DOS) of fuel for the brigade using three load-handling system modular fuel farms. Additionally, the platoon has the capability to set up and run multiple refuel points for brigade aircraft. The fuel and water platoon also has the capability to purify 30,000 gallons of water daily and can store 18,000 gallons of water. The platoon has an organic quartermaster petroleum QA team assigned to provide QA testing for bulk aviation fuel. The team performs quality evaluation and provides technical assistance for handling, storing, sampling, and identifying petroleum products and their containers.

Supply Platoon

4-110. The supply platoon has an SSA and ammunition transfer holding point (ATHP) section. This platoon provides classes II, III (P), IV, V, VI, VII, IX and IX (A) DS to the brigade. The supply platoon receives, stores (limited), and issues classes II, III (P), IV, and IX. It receives and distributes classes I and VI under distribution-based doctrine of pushing supplies to the FSCs and aviation maintenance companies, and receives and issues class VII as required. The platoon also maintains classes II, III (P), IV and IX ASLs for the brigade. The ATHP section supports class V operations and operates the brigade ATHP.

Transportation Platoon

4-111.   The transportation platoon's purpose is to add organic transportation and distribution capability to the brigade and increase mobility of the ASB. The transportation platoon also has the ability to transport classes V and IX to supported FSCs and ASCs.

Network Support Company

4-112.   The NSC provides 24-hour operations supporting the aviation brigade network. It provides signal elements designed to engineer, install, operate, maintain, and defend the network. It extends defense information systems network services to the brigade and its subordinate elements and provides basic network management capabilities. During military operations, the company executes its technical mission under functional control of the brigade S-6 based on brigade OPORDs or other directives. The S-6 directs actions and movement of signal elements in support of brigade operations. The network signal company commander maintains command authority over the company's assigned operational platoons or attached elements.

Aviation Support Company

4-113.   Aircraft maintenance above aviation battalion level is provided by the ASB's ASC. The ASC is comprised of three platoons: HQ, aircraft repair platoon (ARP), and CRP. Modularity within the ASC is based on a contact support team concept and utilizes five shop equipment contact maintenance (SECM) vehicles per platoon. The ASC is capable of supporting split-based operations. It primarily performs intermediate maintenance in accordance with the MAC; however, it also provides backup unit maintenance in support of aviation battalions. The ASC provides aviation logistics support operations for battalions. It supplies aviation and ground equipment maintenance in a sustained combat environment to include UAS and ATC equipment. The ASC also performs production control and QA, conducts maintenance management, and provides MP functions. Additionally, ASCs have six man electro-optics test facility augmentation teams assigned.

Headquarters Platoon

4-114.   The HQ platoon contains a production control section, QA section, and technical supply section. This platoon provides internal management of repairs, quality of repairs, and logistics support within the ASB. The technical supply section operates logistics STAMIS, requisitions class IX (A) spares, and manages the ASB PLL. Oversight is provided by the battalion AMO assigned to the S-4.

Aircraft Repair Platoon

4-115.   ARPs assigned to an ASC provide field-level maintenance support in accordance with the MAC. Furthermore, ASC's ARP has the capability to perform limited sustainment-level maintenance in support of the aviation maintenance company's maintenance program. The ASC's ARP also provides technical assistance and maintenance support, when requested by supported aviation maintenance companies and coordinated through the ASC's production control office. This support entails performing field level repairs to include intermediate and, when authorized, sustainment-level (limited depot) repairs according to applicable TMs, including electronic technical manuals (ETMs)/interactive ETMs. AMCOM logistics assistant representatives (LARs) will issue a letter of authorization that authorizes ASC ARP maintainers to perform a one-time sustainment level maintenance repair. The ARP has modular maintenance contact teams to support battalion-level deployments. ARP personnel, with maintenance officers/technicians, perform in-depth troubleshooting and diagnostics of aircraft systems, subsystems, and components. The ARP also provides repair personnel for technical assistance, contact teams, and aircraft recovery teams. CRP personnel may be attached to ARPs (contact and aircraft recovery teams) to expedite repair of critical components to assist ARP personnel in providing rapid turnaround of unserviceable aircraft. The ARP section provides modular support to the aviation maintenance company using contact maintenance teams. The modular support is based on a contact support team concept using five SECM vehicles per platoon.

Component Repair Platoon

4-116. CRPs assigned to an ASC provide field-level maintenance component repair support functions to the aviation maintenance company's assigned aircraft and corresponding aircraft systems. Furthermore, ASC's CRP can provide unit-level component repair support, when requested by the aviation maintenance companies and coordinated through the ASC's production control office. The CRP performs airframe, LRU, and component repairs to aircraft systems at the ASC. These maintenance procedures entail performing field-level maintenance repairs according to applicable TMs and the MAC. Furthermore, CRPs are capable of performing limited sustainment. AMCOM LARs will issue a letter of authorization, which authorizes ASC CRP maintainers to perform a one-time sustainment level maintenance repair. Continuous component repair support of aviation maintenance companies and the reparable exchange (RX) program will increase availability of serviceable aircraft repair parts, thus reducing the customers' aircraft downtime. Sustaining a balanced approach to the battalion's component repair support program and RX program will provide aviation maintenance companies with required aircraft repair parts when needed.

AVIATION SUPPORT BATTALION MISSION

4-117. The ASB distributes supply classes I, II, III, IV, V, VIII, IX and IX (A). It performs field maintenance and recovery, both air and ground, and possesses HSS assets to conduct force health protection Level I enhanced for battalion. It carries logistics stocks exceeding the organic carrying capability of the AHB and GSAB that is generally 1 DOS for most classes of supply, except for classes III (B) and V where it is one combat load for brigade. The FSCs have the same type of carrying capacity relative to support of their battalion. The ASB plans and coordinates for the CAB's logistics requirements in coordination with the brigade S-4 during the brigade's MDMP. The ASB executes replenishment operations for the FSCs and aviation maintenance companies in concert with the operational plan developed by brigade. The ASB is the parent battalion HQ for the network signal company in support of brigade HQ.

SECTION IV – STANDARD ARMY MANAGEMENT INFORMATION SYSTEMS

STANDARD ARMY MAINTENANCE SYSTEM

4-118. This system includes Standard Army Maintenance System-Level 1 (SAMS-1) and Standard Army Maintenance System-Level 2 (SAMS-2). Refer to FM 3-04.500 for more information.

4-119. STAMIS consists of computer hardware and software systems that automate diverse functions based on validated customer requirements. STAMIS facilitate vertical and horizontal flow of logistics and maintenance status information to units Army wide. Figure 4-3, page 4-20, illustrates the systems that make up the STAMIS architecture. See FM 3-04.500 for more information.

STANDARD ARMY MAINTENANCE SYSTEM-1

4-120. SAMS-1 enables automated processing of DS/GS maintenance shop production functions, maintenance control work orders, and key supply functions. Requisitions are prepared automatically and automatic status is received from SARSS-1. SAMS-1 interfaces with other systems, such as Unit Level Logistics System (ULLS) and Standard Army Retail Supply System-Objective (SARSS-O). It also provides completed work order data to logistics support activity for equipment performance and other analyses.

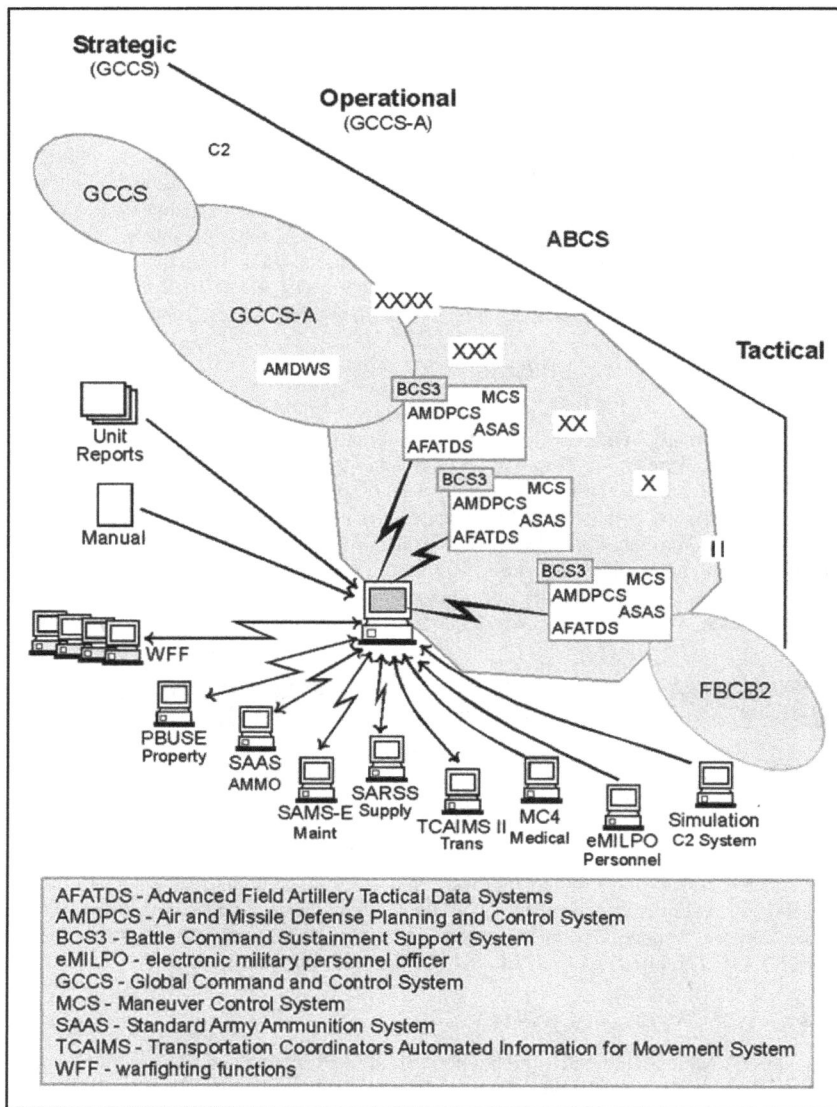

Figure 4-3. Standard Army Management Information System architecture

STANDARD ARMY MAINTENANCE SYSTEM-2

4-121. SAMS-2 is an automated maintenance management system used at FSC and ASB level. It enables monitoring of equipment nonmission capable status, and controlling and coordinating maintenance actions and repair parts usage to maximize equipment availability. SAMS-2 receives and processes maintenance data to meet information requirements of the manager, and fulfill reporting requirements to customers, higher SAMS-2 sites, and the wholesale maintenance level. Data can be accessed instantly to enable management control, coordination, reports, analysis, and review. SAMS-2 provides maintenance and management information to each level of command from the user to the wholesale and DA levels.

STANDARD ARMY MAINTENANCE SYSTEM-ENHANCED

4-122.   Standard Army Maintenance System-Enhanced (SAMS-E) automates maintenance functions, readiness reporting, unit status reporting functions, and unit-level supply. It provides day-to-day weapon system and subcomponent readiness status, and maintenance and related repair parts information. It facilitates management functions from the tactical DS/GS-level maintenance activities and the support field and sustainment maintenance concept (two levels of maintenance). SAMS-E is assigned to ASC and FSC. SAMS-E consists of SAMS-1 and SAMS-2 applications and supports sustainment, TOE, and organizational-level maintenance elements. SAMS-E eliminates duplicate processes but includes critical unit-level functions of equipment operator and qualification, equipment dispatch, equipment PMCS, scheduling and recording, equipment fault records, organizational work order number generation, Army Oil Analysis Program, and Army Materiel Status System reporting. SAMS-E allows multiple unit identifier code/Department of Defense Activity Address Code (DODAAC) and stock storage in multiple locations. In addition, SAMS-E—

- Automates unit-level class IX (repair parts) functions.
- Enables same-day processing of requisitions to source of supply, thus minimizing order-ship time.
- Integrates supply and maintenance applications to eliminate redundant functions.
- Automates demand history and stockage-level computations to avoid out-of-stock or excess conditions.
- Uses both Federal Logistics (FEDLOG) and the Standard Army Retail Supply System (SARSS) catalog update.
- Identifies units as either direct or indirect (supported customer).
- Generates a work order automatically when an operator-level fault is initiated and the part received.
- Changes management of unit data from DODAAC-based to unit identifier code-based selection and entry.
- Retains the man-hour accounting on/off switch as an option in case of deployment.
- Provides password protection to the operational processes and data elements.

PROPERTY BOOK AND UNIT SUPPLY ENHANCED

4-123.   Property book and unit supply enhanced (PBUSE) is the Army's Web-based, state-of-the art, sustainment property accountability system. PBUSE features provide standard property book system-redesign functionality and data access by permission control system for both garrison and tactical environments. When tactical requirements dictate and direct connection to the Web is not possible, the system operates in a disconnected standalone mode. On completion of a standalone tactical requirement, the system is reconnected to the Web for resynchronization of the user's data to the central database. PBUSE reduces the footprint and infrastructure requirements by consolidating two baselines into one. The system functionality provides much efficiency for the logistics community. With PBUSE, the commander has a real-time view of assets and accurate visibility of the unit's property book account operating on the AKO portal, which allows him to access the system for queries without having to depend on the PBO to gather, prepare, and present the information. PBUSE also provides—

- Real-time total asset visibility throughout all levels of Army management.
- Automatic Logistics Army Authorization Document System (LOGTAADS) updates; LOGTAADS is a by-product of an MTOE. LOGTAADS, an electronic version of the MTOE, updates PBUSE and other property book accounting systems.
- Elimination of unique item tracking reporting through automatic serial number tracking.

- Automated catalog changes.
- Unit transfer/TF/split operations.

STANDARD ARMY RETAIL SUPPLY SYSTEM

4-124. SARSS is a multiechelon supply management and stock control system that operates in tactical and garrison environments. SARSS comprises SARSS-1 (at the SSA), SARSS-2 aircraft, or corps/theater automated data processing service center (CTASC), and SARSS-Gateway. SARSS provides supply-related data to the Integrated Logistics Analysis Program (ILAP) system at various functional levels. SARSS supports ULLS, Standard Army Maintenance System (SAMS), PBUSE, nonautomated customers, and the dual-based operations concept. SARSS is fully integrated from the user through theater Army level. It can support worldwide deployment of combat forces to contemporary operating environments to include stability and civil support operations missions.

SARSS-1

4-125. SARSS-1 is the standard supply system used for receipt, issue, replenishment, and storage operations. It operates at the ASB's SSA and combat sustainment support battalions. SARSS-1 in each supply echelon is capable of sustaining prime support responsibilities for each customer's unit. Each customer unit can interact directly with any SARSS-1. SARSS-1 is the system of record. It maintains accountable balances and is supported by a SARSS-2A activity. It depends on SARSS-2B for catalog support and computation of stockage levels.

SARSS-2AC/CTASC

4-126. SARSS-2A performs time-sensitive supply functions. These include management of controlled items, lateral search of stocks to fulfill unsatisfied customer's requirements from subordinate SARSS-1 activities, and redistribution of excess. SARSS-2AC operates on CTASC hardware. SARSS-2AC/CTASC performs time-sensitive supply management functions for referral, excess disposition, and management for classes II, III (P), IV, VII and IX (Air). It manages redistribution of supplies. SARSS-2AC/CTASC also maintains a custodial availability balance file that provides visibility of SARSS-1 assets to include both divisional and nondivisional functions.

SARSS-2B

4-127. SARSS-2B performs management functions that are not time sensitive. These include document history, demand analysis, and catalog updates at installation and with the U.S. Property and Fiscal Officer. It supports subordinate SARSS-1 and SARSS-2A by performing stockage-level computations, tailoring catalog files, and maintaining active and inactive document history data.

SARSS-GATEWAY

4-128. SARSS-Gateway is an interactive/batch-oriented transaction processor that routes transactions to and from each interfacing STAMIS. It provides a communications network, and the capability to send transactions to the defense automatic addressing system (DAAS). It provides the appearance of a seamless, near real-time supply system to unit-level supply and maintenance activities. SARSS-Gateway provides customer access to all assets available within a specified geographical area. Requests are electronically transmitted from customers to a gateway computer, where lateral search/issue decisions are made based on the ABF residing there. If assets are not available, the gateway forwards the request to the wholesale SOS and provides status to customers on the actions taken.

ULLS-AVIATION

4-129. The ULLS-A program will enhance the Army's ability to more accurately track and control aviation maintenance, logistics, and aircraft forms and records. The ULLS–A program is designed to be user friendly while reducing man hours through complete automation. The ULLS-A is an innovative tool that assists aviation maintenance personnel with various tools to enhance aircraft reporting, status, and flying hours according to Army regulation (AR) 700-138. Furthermore, ULLS-A can process aircraft transfers, maintain operational and historical records, process class IX (A) repair parts, and enhance maintenance operations overall. In addition, ULLS-A automates BS listings by shop codes (stocked and maintained manually with an automated reordering process), PLL, reportable component management, and maintenance management processes performed by production control. ULLS-A is currently the system of record for all PLL/BS and The Army Maintenance Management System-Aviation operations at the unit level. ULLS-A enhances and supports those tasks associated with controlled exchange of reportable components.

4-130. ULLS-A at the aviation maintenance company is configured into a network operation. A notebook computer assigned to line companies facilitates those tasks previously performed on the manual logbook. Army aviation units are normally supported by three workstation computers (production control, quality control, and technical supply) and a file server (database) positioned in the production control office. These automated systems comprise the LAN. Tasks and activities performed by quality control and production control are transferred to the aircraft notebook. These procedures will ensure the ULLS-A is current and reflects the latest maintenance and logistics status assigned to the airframe.

4-131. ASCs are provided with an ULLS-A that supports those activities necessary to perform field maintenance support for customers and operational readiness float/return to fleet aircraft. If an aircraft is work ordered to an ASC, the logbook and laptop computer assigned to the aircraft will accompany the aircraft to track and record all performed maintenance actions. The ULLS-A provides production control with the ability to generate and manage ASC-level work orders and post statuses to the maintenance request register. ULLS-A provides the vehicle to produce and manage internal work orders (intrashop), which are printed and supplied to the ASC component and ARPs.

INTEGRATED LOGISTICS ANALYSIS PROGRAM

4-132. ILAP is the standard management tool used by the Army that collects, integrates, and displays logistics and financial data. ILAP operates at all echelons of the Army to provide management capability to unit, corps, installation, component, and theater levels. Financial data are pulled from Defense Finance and Accounting Service data sites. Logistics data are obtained from appropriate supply and maintenance sites. The cross-functional data are integrated and aggregated to upper echelons to provide summary decision support views and detailed information drill-down capabilities to the document detail level. This process of assembly and aggregation affords Army departmental users the opportunity to do Army-level analysis and data query. ILAP augments the STAMIS. Managers at all levels execute their duties more efficiently and effectively by using ILAP data. ILAP is most useful for managers who require data from disparate and isolated sources as ILAP virtually eliminates the time required for retrieval, integration, and display to support management analysis.

DEFENSE AUTOMATIC ADDRESSING SYSTEM

4-133. The logistics information processing system, maintained by the DAAS, is DOD's central repository for information on the status of requisitions. It also augments the global transportation network in monitoring the status of nonunit cargo shipments.

AVIATION LIFE SUPPORT SYSTEM

4-134. Commanders ensure mission-required ALSE is on hand in sufficient quantities, and equipment is in serviceable condition. To meet the Army's demanding transformation requirements, newer and more complex integrated systems are being fielded. These systems demand better maintenance planning, higher maintenance skills, and dedicated facilities.

4-135. Commanders are required to establish an ALSS maintenance management and training program budget to meet resource requirements. Funding for equipment, supplies, and repair parts is imperative. When preparing the budget, review AR 95-1, CTA 8-100, CTA 50-900, CTA 50-970, and applicable MTOEs and tables of distribution and allowances.

Appendix A

Aircraft Survivability

Aircraft survivability is a primary concern throughout mission planning and execution. Army aircrews operate in an extremely hazardous environment of highly lethal AD threats. The array of enemy AD systems includes radar, IR, optical/electro-optical (EO), laser, and directed-energy weapons (DEWs). Proper use of ASE, combined with careful route planning and movement techniques, greatly reduces the enemy's ability to effectively engage Army helicopters.

SECTION I – THREAT WEAPON SENSORS

A-1. The four major types of threat weapon sensors—radar, IR, DEW, and EO—must be man portable or transportable by land, sea, or aerial platforms. The actual sensor-type and guidance package for each threat should be determined and its inherent capabilities and limitations understood. These threat weapon sensors are discussed below.

RADAR

A-2. Direct-threat radar weapons require LOS to hit the target. These radar weapons are either fire-controlled AAA or, for missile systems, controlled by command, semiactive radar homing, active-radar homing, track via missile, or ground-aided seeker. Radar weapons must detect, acquire, track, launch and guide (or fire a ballistic solution), and assess damage. Radar systems have trouble with ground clutter. To pick out targets from ground clutter, radar systems can detect movement using a moving target indicator, Doppler (continuous-wave radar), or pulse Doppler. Some modern radar systems can and do track not only the movement of the aircraft but also the rotor blades. A few older radar systems had blind speeds—called a Doppler notch—where they could not detect an aircraft flying a specific speed toward or away from the radar. However, modern radar systems cancel blind speeds. Even with older radar systems, aircraft had difficulty maintaining constant speed and angle to or from one radar; it is impossible to be in Doppler notch of more than one radar. Radar systems can be detected, avoided, decoyed, jammed, and destroyed by direct and indirect fires—self, artillery, and antiradiation missiles.

INFRARED

A-3. All IR direct-threat weapons require LOS be established before launch; the in-flight missile must maintain LOS with the target until impact or detonation or the proximity fuse. IR missiles require the operator visually detect the target and energize the seeker before the sensor acquires the target. The operator must track the target with the seeker caged to the LOS until it is determined the seeker is tracking the target and not background objects such as natural or manmade objects. The IR sensor is also susceptible to atmospheric conditions (haze or humidity), the signature of the aircraft and its background, flares, decoys, and jamming. Generally, IR systems are difficult to—

- Detect before launch (passive sensor).
- Predict location (portability).
- Respond to (short time of flight after launch).
- Hard kill (requires shooting at an in-flight missile).

LASER AND DIRECTED-ENERGY WEAPONS

A-4. Laser weapons/DEWs have two distinct categories—laser-guided or laser-aided weapons and pure laser weapons/DEWs. Laser-guided or laser-aided weapons use laser for ranging, tracking, or guiding functions of conventional explosive missiles or projectiles. Pure laser weapons/DEWs use laser and other forms of DEW to inflict damage to aircraft or its sensors (the aircrew's eyes may be damaged). Pure laser weapons/DEWs are not required to burn a hole in the target to destroy it—although these weapons are reaching such capability. Simply igniting fuel vapor near vents or burning through fuel lines is effective as well as glazing cockpit glass so aircrew cannot see out. Inherently, laser weapons/DEWs are of short duration, hard to detect, extremely hard to decoy or jam, and hard to kill. Fortunately, they rely on LOS and atmospheric conditions and have a somewhat short range.

OPTICAL/ELECTRO-OPTICAL

A-5. Optical/EO sensors are used as primary or secondary sensors for all weapon systems. Although they rely on LOS, they are, with very few exceptions, completely passive. They are limited by human eyes, atmospheric conditions, distance, jitter, and in many cases, darkness. The optical/EO sensors are the most difficult to detect, seldom decoyed, and can be jammed in the sense of obscurants but, when located, hard to kill.

SECTION II – OPERATIONAL EMPLOYMENT CONSIDERATIONS

A-6. Aircraft survivability functions must be included throughout mission planning, rehearsal, execution, and recovery operations. Intelligence drives operations. Mission planning begins with receipt of situation and mission and continues through completion of mission execution and AAR. From receipt of enemy situation and mission, it is important to plan and integrate aircraft survivability functions.

A-7. For ASE to provide effective protection, configuration settings must be optimized for known and suspected threats. TACOPS ensure optimum ASE configuration settings are prepared and briefed for each flight. TACOPS give consideration for each system and settings for specific theater of operation.

MISSION PLANNING

A-8. ASE and EW must be considered in all phases of mission planning and execution. Figure A-1, page A-3, illustrates roles and responsibilities of ASE planning.

A-9. Once initial analysis of information is completed, the battalion S-2 notifies the battalion TACOPS and begins the planning cycle. The level of planning involved is always predicated on time, information, and personnel available. OPORDs for military operations are extensive in scope and contain information acting as a baseline for most unit operations.

A-10. The generation of the OPORD begins upon receipt of enemy and friendly situation, mission, and commander's intent. The EW annex is created to support the OPORD using this information. Enemy and friendly situations are further defined with emphasis on EW capabilities; each one finds, fixes, jams, deceives, disrupts, or destroys the other. Once the situation is clearly defined, the mission is analyzed to evaluate risk to friendly forces while accomplishing the mission within prescribed guidelines. After risk assessment is complete, risk reduction techniques are specified in the execution instructions. These techniques require commander's approval if mission constraints need to be altered significantly from the original intent. The next step is to determine service support for EW and the command and signal guidance necessary to accomplish the EW phase of the mission.

A-11. ASE settings depend on accurately analyzing enemy AD threat. Knowing the threat is critical to effective passive and active countermeasures. Unit TACOPS provide ASE settings/codes for training and deployment.

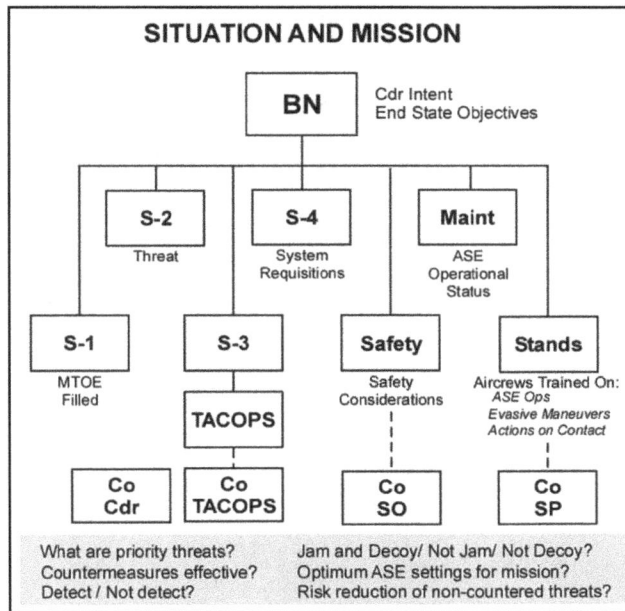

Figure A-1. Roles and functions

AIRCRAFT SURVIVABILITY EQUIPMENT RISK ANALYSIS

IDENTIFYING RISK

A-12. To perform a thorough risk assessment, detailed information regarding threat system operating procedures, tactics, system capabilities, and locations must be analyzed to determine enemy advantages or disadvantages in use of EW. Capabilities and limitations of friendly EW systems are compared to threats to assess the risk level associated with the mission. S-2s and TACOPS officers identify the following:

- Operating frequencies of radar threats.
- RF threats that can or cannot be detected.
- RF threats radar jamming equipment will affect (includes the extent of success jamming has).
- RF threats that can be decoyed (includes the extent of success decoying has).
- IR threats that may be encountered.
- IR threats that can be jammed or decoyed (effectiveness of jamming and decoying).
- Laser threats that can or cannot be detected.
- Optical/EO threats.

ELECTRONIC INTELLIGENCE PRIORITY INTELLIGENCE REPORTS

A-13. The company sends electronic intelligence (ELINT) PIR to battalion requesting specific threat emitter data on any templated EW/AD threats. Tabular data associated with any radar hits should also be requested.

ASSESSING RISK

A-14. Companies prioritize threat systems and optimize ASE settings for highest priority threats. Level of risk is determined based on threat and ASE capabilities, limitations, and mission as shown in DA Form 7573 (Aircraft Survivability Equipment [ASE] Risk Management Worksheet Survivability Risk Analysis) (figure A-2). The highest risk is used to determine overall risk to the mission. If risk due to IR threats is high, then overall mission risk would continue to be high risk. The risk assessment worksheet is used to determine what is causing the highest risks so controls can be developed to reduce those risks.

AIRCRAFT SURVIVABILITY EQUIPMENT (ASE) RISK ASSESSMENT WORKSHEET
SURVIVABILITY RISK ANALYSIS

For use of this form, see ARTEP 1-113 MTP and ARTEP 1-126 MTP; the proponent agency is TRADOC.

1. AIRCRAFT TYPE	2. MISSION	3. DATE *(YYYYMMDD)*

4. MISSION PROFILE

	a. < 100' AGI	b. > 100' AGI	
NIGHT	☐ LOW	☐ MEDIUM	
DAY	☐ MEDIUM	☐ HIGH	VALUE ________

5. IR THREATS

	a. SUPPRESSED	b. UNSUPPRESSED	
IRCM	☐ LOW	☐ MEDIUM	
Non-IRCM	☐ MEDIUM	☐ HIGH	VALUE ________

6. RF THREAT

	a. WARNING	b. NO WARNING	
RFCM	☐ LOW	☐ MEDIUM	
Non-RFCM	☐ MEDIUM	☐ HIGH	VALUE ________

7. EO THREAT

	a. Low Visibility and Contrast	b. High Visibility and Contrast	
MASKING	☐ LOW	☐ MEDIUM	
NO MASKING	☐ MEDIUM	☐ HIGH	VALUE ________

8. LASER/DEW THREAT

	a. WARNING	b. NO WARNING	
NO MASKING	☐ LOW	☐ MEDIUM	VALUE ________
	☐ MEDIUM	☐ HIGH	

9. OVERALL RISK. If overall risk is medium or high, reevaluate mission profile, ASE or flight routes.

☐ LOW ☐ MEDIUM ☐ HIGH HIGHEST VALUE ________

10. PRIORITY THREATS

IR	RF	EO	LASER/DEW
☐ A	☐ A	☐ A	☐ A
☐ B	☐ B	☐ B	☐ B
☐ C	☐ C	☐ C	☐ C
☐ D	☐ D	☐ D	☐ D

11. ASE CONFIGURATION SETTINGS

ALQ-144A Suppressed: ________ Unsuppressed: ________

ALQ-162 Jam Program: ________

APR-39A(V)1 OFP: ________ EID: ________

APR-39(V)2 Low/High: ________ Theater Position: ________

M-130 Chaff Program ________ UH-60: ________ EH-60: ________ ALQ-156: ________

IFF: Mode 1: ________ Mode ________ Mode ________ Mode 4: ________

IR = Infrared | IRCM = IR Countermeasures | Suppressed = IR Paint and Exhaust | RF = Radio Frequency | RCFM = RF Countermeasures | EO = Electro-Optical

Sample

DA FORM 7573, JUNE 2005 APD V1.01

Figure A-2. Sample aircraft survivability equipment risk assessment worksheet

DEVELOP CONTROLS

A-15. Optimum ASE configuration settings for each aircraft type and threats in the mission area are determined based on doctrinal assets and requested ELINT PIR. Threats that are highly lethal and not countered by ASE are identified and PIR are developed and submitted by the S-2 to higher HQ. Additional requirements include—

- Briefing the S-3 and higher commander on any medium or high risks associated with executing the planned mission.
- Using AMPS to display high threat areas.
- Making recommendations to higher commander to reduce risk to include—
  - Adjusting routes, LZs, PZs, and/or HAs.
  - Adjusting time of mission.
  - Employing artillery and smoke to reduce threat to aircraft.
  - Requesting joint EW assets.

A-16. Apply risk management techniques to minimize risk and enhance probability of survival. These measures include—

- Planning mission time earlier or later to take advantage of night operations.
- Requesting escort aircraft to suppress threats.
- Planning J-SEAD at critical points to reduce vulnerability.
- Preparing LZ/PZs with indirect fires.
- Altering flight routes to avoid known AD areas.
- Employing deception plan to include false insertions.
- Altering formation size to reduce signature.

IMPLEMENT CONTROLS

A-17. Commanders and aircrews must take an active role in reducing risks by implementing controls and supervising their implementation to include—

- Commanders ensure ASE/EW considerations and configuration settings are briefed to all aircrews and maintenance personnel.
- Aircrews ensure ASE settings are correct during preflight ASE checks.
- Aircrews ensure IFF codes are activated and deactivated at proper times and locations during mission execution.
- Commanders collect debriefings from aircrews during AAR.
- Aircrews report all ASE/EW abnormalities experienced during flight (ambiguities, false alarms, equipment failures).

A-18. Commanders ensure all ASE/EW data are entered into AMPS for the next mission (threat data, countermeasure responses, locations of false alarms, and friendly systems reported as threats).

MISSION BRIEF

A-19. The ASE/EW mission briefing disseminates information and instructions to aircrews prior to the mission. At least 4 hours prior to mission execution, the AMC requests an ELINT update. The briefing alerts aircrews to risks associated with threats, optimum ASE settings, and a review of tactics specific to the mission. These tactics include evasive maneuvers, actions on contact, multi-ship breakup and reformation procedures, and ROE for countermeasure weapons employment. Figure A-3, page A-6, illustrates an example of ASE/EW mission brief format.

```
┌─────────────────────────────────────────────────────────────────────┐
│                       ASE/EW BRIEFING FORMAT                          │
├─────────────────────────────────────────────────────────────────────┤
│  OVERALL RISK:      Low        Medium         High                    │
├─────────────────────────────────────────────────────────────────────┤
│  CAUSED BY:          Mission profile                                  │
│                      ASE suite                                        │
│                      Threat                                           │
├─────────────────────────────────────────────────────────────────────┤
│  ASE and IFF configuration settings:                                  │
├─────────────────────────────────────────────────────────────────────┤
│  ASE can detect:                                                      │
├─────────────────────────────────────────────────────────────────────┤
│  ASE cannot detect:                                                   │
├─────────────────────────────────────────────────────────────────────┤
│  ASE can jam:                                                         │
├─────────────────────────────────────────────────────────────────────┤
│  ASE cannot jam:                                                     │
├─────────────────────────────────────────────────────────────────────┤
│  Primary threats:    IR                                              │
│                      RF                                               │
│                      EO                                               │
│                      Laser/DEW                                        │
├─────────────────────────────────────────────────────────────────────┤
│  Risk-reduction measures:                                             │
├─────────────────────────────────────────────────────────────────────┤
│  Changes to standard TTP:                                            │
├─────────────────────────────────────────────────────────────────────┤
│  QUESTIONS:                                                           │
│                                                                       │
│                                                                       │
└─────────────────────────────────────────────────────────────────────┘
```

Figure A-3. Sample aircraft survivability equipment/electronic warfare mission brief format

MISSION EXECUTION

A-20. During conduct of the mission, it is important for aircrews to be familiar with ASE SA displays and expected threat indications. Some actions must be performed without delay. When visual indications of a gun or missile are fired at an aircraft, or ASE indicates a radar track or launch, the aircrew has only seconds to perform an action that will prevent the aircraft from being hit. Three distinct parts of reacting to threat engagements are—

- Indicating (determines immediate action and deploys to cover).
- Performing evasive maneuver and expend countermeasures (if applicable), if masking terrain is not readily available.

● Performing actions on contact (decision to continue or abort mission).

CREW COORDINATION

A-21. Crew coordination must be rehearsed to perform evasive maneuvers. Standardized terminology, such as "missile three o'clock, break right" and "break left" should be used to avoid confusion. At other times, indications do not require evasive maneuvering, such as radar search or acquisition.

MULTI-SHIP CONSIDERATIONS

A-22. Formations and spacing intervals should be selected to provide all aircraft maneuver space necessary to evade hostile fire. Standardized terminology, such as "Team 2 break right, missile" or "Team 1, tracers, three o'clock, break left", should be used to alert the flight to your actions. Briefings should include procedures for evasive formation breakup and how to reestablish formation after breaking engagement. It is important for one aircraft in the formation to communicate its ASE indications to the other aircraft since it may be the only one receiving indications due to terrain, narrow radar beam, altitude, or maintenance problems. Refer to FM 3-04.203 for more information.

SECTION III – AIRCRAFT SURVIVABILITY EQUIPMENT/ELECTRONIC WARFARE TRAINING

A-23. The company commander is responsible for training management and documentation of the company's ASE/EW program. This section discusses the ASE/EW management process and training responsibilities within the company.

A-24. The company ASE/EW program will undergo periodic inspections (command inspection program, U.S. Army Forces Command [FORSCOM] aviation resource management survey [ARMS], Directorate of Evaluation and Standardization, division "fly-away" inspections, and external evaluations). When inspections of this nature are conducted, ARMS evaluation guidelines are used as evaluation criteria.

TRAINING ASSETS

A-25. ASE/EW training must be conducted on an on-going basis to ensure aircrews are ready to operate on today's and tomorrow's battlefield. Training should be conducted at individual, crew, and collective levels. Company commanders are required to designate CBAT requirements in accordance with TC 1-210. Commanders, TACOPS, ASE officers, and unit standardization personnel plan and implement training. Table A-1 gives the assets that are available for ASE/EW training at levels indicated.

Table A-1. Training assets

	Individual	Crew	Collective
Academic training and study	X	X	
ATM flights	X		
CBAT	X	X	
Man portable RF/IR/ultraviolet simulators		X	X
Combat training centers (CTCs)		X	X
EW ranges		X	X
EW threats	X		
Synthetic flight training system	X		

TRAINING RESPONSIBILITIES

COMPANY COMMANDER

A-26. The commander is responsible for planning, executing, and documenting the company ASE/EW program. Other responsibilities include—

- Integrating CBAT into unit ATP.
- Providing necessary equipment to conduct CBAT training.
- Ensuring compliance with procedures for safekeeping and storage of classified materiel.
- Ensuring compliance with security regulations.
- Incorporating IFF training and verification plan into all unit collective training events.

COMPANY TACTICAL OPERATIONS OFFICER

A-27. The company TACOPS officer is authorized per MTOE. The TACOPS officer is school trained with an "I" ASI. The TACOPS officer's responsibilities include—

- Ensuring optimum ASE reprogramming is completed for the area of responsibility (settings may be changed during routine maintenance exchanges).
- Advising the commander regarding ASE/threat analysis.
- Performing tactical route mission planning.
- Tracking all ASE equipment assigned to company.
- Ensuring procedures for storage and safekeeping of classified materiels are followed.
- Conducting monthly inventories of all ASE/EW hardware and software and forwarding results of inventory to battalion TACOPS officers and S-2.
- Maintaining the security clearance access roster and monitoring usage of CBAT.
- Ensuring a designated, secure area is available for CBAT AT training. These areas must meet all security requirements.
- Reporting completion of CBAT requirements to company SP.
- Assisting with threat and countermeasures briefs, and in establishment of unit level ASE training.
- Developing and maintaining unit ASE/EW SOP.
- Ensuring unit complies with FORSCOM ARMS ASE checklist.

COMPANY STANDARDIZATION INSTRUCTOR PILOT

A-28. The company SP assists the commander in implementation of the unit ASE/EW training plan. Other responsibilities include—

- Assisting commander by developing training programs and/or STX scenarios using flight simulators and aircraft to train and evaluate crew ASE/EW qualification and proficiency.
- Ensuring individual IATFs accurately reflect individual training.

Appendix B

Army Aviation Air-Ground Integration

Operations must be integrated so air and ground forces can simultaneously work in the operational environment to achieve a common objective. Integration maximizes combat power through the synergy of both forces. The synchronization of aviation operations into the ground commander's scheme of maneuver may also require integration of other services or coalition partners. It may require integration of attack reconnaissance, assault, and cargo helicopters as well. This appendix addresses considerations for AHB/GSAB units operating independently, or simultaneously, with attack reconnaissance units in support of ground forces during various types of operations including shaping, decisive, and sustaining operations.

SECTION I – COMBAT IDENTIFICATION

B-1. Combat identification is the process of attaining an accurate characterization of detected objects in the operational environment sufficient to support an engagement decision. The combat identification process has three key purposes: to identify and classify targets in the AO; to allow for the timely application of the appropriate weapon system(s) on targets classified as enemy; and the mitigation of fratricide and collateral damage to noncombatants.

B-2. The combat identification process is a series of progressive and interdependent steps (or actions)—target search, detection, location, and identification—that lead to the decision process to engage or not engage. The detect, identify, decide, engage, and assess (DIDEA) process provides an iterative, standardized, and systematic approach supporting the application of specific combat identification and ROE performance steps to target engagement activities. Individual actions of the DIDEA process are summarized in table B-1.

Table B-1. Key terms and meaning

Detect – The acquisition and location of an object in the operational environment can entail the use of visual, sensor, radar, electronic signals measurement, or other means for detecting.
Identify – A systematic process supporting the characterization of detected objects as friend, enemy, neutral, or unknown. This is the primary step where specified combat identification tasks are accomplished. It commences after an object is detected and located, and provides a systematic process whereby the attributes of a detected object are systematically processed to support a friend, enemy, neutral, or unknown determination. In some cases, the characterization process may need to be further refined to include specific class, type, and nationality determinations.
Decide – Determination of appropriate application of military options and weapons resources on identified objects. This is the most generic step within the process and is the primary step where specified ROE application takes place. Specific sub-steps within the decide phase will vary depending on the weapon system/platform and mission application. In some cases the decision may be made to employ military options other than weapons systems (such as the repositioning of ISR assets for further monitoring of identified objects).

Table B-1. Key terms and meaning

In those cases where a weapons resource application is being considered, this phase would primarily address the following questions: • Can I engage? (ROE application) • If multiple targets, what to engage first? (severity of threat, commander's intent/high pay-off targets.) • What is the best weapons system to engage with? (lethal/nonlethal, munitions effect, collateral damage assessment.)
Engage – Specific application of military options/weapons resources. In this step the mechanical process of carrying out the decision made in the previous step takes place.
Assess – Did the applied weapons resources bring about the desired effect? In this step we assess the effects of the engagement phase against desired outcomes. If the desired outcome was not achieved, a decision to re-engage the target could be made.

GROUND UNIT AND AVIATION TASK FORCE COORDINATION

B-3. Ground maneuver commanders must understand that aviation forces can provide a significant advantage during operations. In addition, ground maneuver planners must understand that the unique capabilities of Army aviation require unique planning and coordination. Army aviation forces must be fully integrated in MDMP to ensure effective combined arms employment. Effective combined arms employment also requires aviation and ground maneuver forces synchronize their operations by working from a common perspective. Refer to FM 3-06.11 for additional information.

SUPPORT FOR GROUND MANEUVER UNITS

B-4. Utility and cargo helicopters, such as the UH-60 and CH-47, have weapon systems (7.62-millimeter or .50-caliber) that can aid in suppression of enemy forces when operating in urban terrain. However, their primary role is transporting personnel, equipment, and supplies to these critical urban areas. Utility and cargo helicopters can provide a distinct advantage by placing personnel and weapon systems at critical locations at critical times to surprise and overwhelm the enemy. Utility and cargo helicopters can also transport needed supplies to urban areas inaccessible to ground transportation. Ground units may also receive support from a variety of attack reconnaissance helicopters including the AH-64 and OH-58D. Attack reconnaissance helicopters can provide area fire to suppress targets, and precision fire to destroy specific targets or breach structures. Attack reconnaissance helicopters can also assist with ISR and communications using their advanced suite of sensors and radios.

GROUND MANEUVER UNIT PLANNING REQUIREMENTS

B-5. The ground maneuver brigade, through their ALO and BAE, provides the aviation HQ necessary information to meet planning requirements. Initial planning and the information to be passed to the aviation HQ include the location of the HA, air axis, and route or corridor for entry and exit through the brigade and battalion sector. Other planning requirements may include—

• Establishing a command relationship between supported unit and supporting aircraft.
• Giving initial task and purpose to aircrews.
• Giving ABTF current situation estimate (intelligence and operations).
• Reviewing any updates to the joint AC2 structure.
• Passing call sign and frequencies for ground elements.
• Establishing any control measures (recommended HAs, ROZs, no-fire areas, LZs, PZs, or EAs).

WEAPONS INTEGRATION

ACTIONS EN ROUTE TO THE OBJECTIVE

B-6. The ground maneuver HQ informs its units in contact when aircraft are inbound. En route to the HA, the AMC contacts the ground maneuver element on the FM command network for a SITREP on enemy and friendly forces.

B-7. A battalion close fight SITREP may consist of—

- Enemy situation (composition and disposition to include threat to aviation, recent enemy contacts, and threats to ground maneuver element).
- Friendly situation (including any AC2 deconfliction with UAS or indirect fires in vicinity of the operation).
- Recommended routing to the contact.
- Restrictions or constraints.

AVIATION FLIGHT CHECK-IN

B-8. It is essential to positively identify locations of friendly units and supporting aircraft. Aircrews confirm, with each other or wingmen, their positive location. Ground elements must be extremely careful when verifying any position information.

B-9. The aviation flight usually checks in using the command net of the unit having the element in contact or as directed in the mission briefing. Upon initial radio contact, the aviation flight lead executes a check-in. The flight's location may be expressed by grid coordinates or position with respect to a known point or common graphics. At check-in, the flight lead provides—

- Initial contact (aircraft present location).
- Flight composition, location, and ETE for arrival at supported unit's AO.
- Munitions available (include type and amount of ordinance).
- Station time/special capabilities (such as NVGs, TIS, and AIM-1).
- A request for ground SITREP, which includes UAS activity.

B-10. Table B-2 illustrates ground element responsibilities.

Table B-2. Ground element responsibilities for flight check-in

Situation	Enemy	Friendly
Mission	Task	Purpose
Coordinating instructions	Friendly location	Friendly marking
	Enemy location	Enemy marking (how friendly units will mark the enemy)
	C2 net for confirmation/ commands	Clearance of fires approval authority on the ground (call sign, location, and frequency)

B-11. The aviation flight, if required, selects and occupies a holding or orbit area within FM communications range until required coordination is complete. High-density altitudes may preclude hovering by a fully-loaded aircraft. The AMC informs the ground unit leader of the orbiting pattern or series of positions his team will occupy.

B-12. The AMC provides the ground maneuver unit leader with his concept for the operation. This briefing may be as simple as relaying direction of aircraft approach or attack route (if supported by attack reconnaissance helicopters) and time required to move to the recommended LZ. On completion of coordination with the lowest unit in contact, the flight departs the holding or orbit area.

Synchronization of Weapons

B-13. The main reason for using several weapons systems at once is to overwhelm the enemy with more than it can counter. When possible, units sequence employment of CAS, indirect fires, direct fires, and CCA so closely they seem simultaneous in fire effects. This action may be conducted as a joint air attack team (JAAT) if supported by attack reconnaissance aircraft. Mission fires are lifted or shifted at the most advantageous time for ground elements to overwhelm the objective before the enemy can offer effective opposition.

B-14. Army aviators may be key in controlling employment of multiple weapons systems due to their vantage point in the operational environment and ability to quickly relocate. Aviation units must routinely train with ground units so they can effectively employ other Army and joint weapons systems.

INTEGRATED OPERATIONS

B-15. True integration occurs when the commander effectively uses every available asset to the fullest extent. The following are some available assets and capabilities:

- CAS elements destroy enemy formations and installations.
- Attack reconnaissance and ground units search in front of the ground force, confirm enemy strengths and weaknesses, protect flanks, and allow the commander to orient on threats or exploit opportunities.
- Tank, mechanized infantry, light infantry, and air assault units—accompanied by AD and engineer elements, as appropriate—forcibly take and occupy key terrain or deny terrain to the enemy.
- Attack reconnaissance helicopters maneuver to attack enemy forces and deny terrain for limited periods.
- UH-60 helicopters move troops, light vehicles, light artillery, and supplies; they can also emplace minefields and augment C2.
- CH-47 helicopters move troops, medium vehicles, medium artillery, and supplies.
- Artillery provides indirect fires to disrupt and destroy enemy formations; aviation and ground forces also employ artillery for immediate suppression of enemy elements until they can maneuver and eliminate the threat (J-SEAD, SEAD, and on-call FS).

POSITIVE LOCATION/TARGET IDENTIFICATION

COMMAND AND CONTROL TECHNIQUES

B-16. Effective C2 techniques with Army aircraft during air-ground operations include the following:

- **Reference point technique** uses a known TRP or an easily recognizable terrain feature.
- **Grid technique** uses grid coordinates to define the point.
- **Sector/terrain technique** uses terrain and graphics available to both air and ground units.
- **Phase line technique** uses graphics available to both air and ground units.

MARKING

B-17. There are various ways to mark a location or target (table B-3, page B-5). The effectiveness of vision systems on helicopters compares to those found on ground vehicles. During the day, vision systems of aircraft allow accurate identification of targets. During periods of reduced visibility, resolution is greatly degraded, requiring additional methods of verification. This situation requires extra efforts from the ground unit and aviation element.

Table B-3. Methods of marking friendly and enemy positions

Method	Day	Night	NVGs	NVS	Friendly Marks	Target Marks	Remarks
Smoke	Go	No Go	Marginal	No Go	Good	Good	Easy ID. May compromise friendly position, obscure target, or warn of FS employment. Placement may be difficult because of terrain, trees, or structures.
Smoke (IR)	Go	Go	Go	No Go	Good	Good	Easy ID. May compromise friendly position, obscure target, or warn of FS employment. Placement may be difficult because of terrain, trees, or structures. Night marking is greatly enhanced by the use of IR reflective smoke.
Illumination, Ground Burst	Go	Go	Go	No Go	NA	Good	Easy ID. May wash out NVDs.
Signal Mirror	Go	No Go	No Go	No Go	Good	NA	Avoids compromise of friendly location. Depends on weather and available light. May be lost in reflections from other surfaces (windshields, windows, or water).
Spot Light	No Go	Go	Go	No Go	Good	Marginal	Highly visible to all. Compromises friendly position and warns of FS employment. Effectiveness depends on degree of ambient lighting.
IR Spot Light	No Go	No Go	Go	No Go	Good	Marginal	Visible to all NVGs. Effectiveness depends on degree of ambient lighting.
IR Laser Pointer (below .4 watts)	No Go	No Go	Go	No Go	Good	Marginal	Effectiveness depends on degree of ambient lighting.
IR Laser Pointer (above .4 watts)	No Go	No Go	Go	No Go	Good	Good	Less affected by ambient light and weather conditions. Highly effective under all but the most highly lit or worst weather conditions. IR zoom laser illuminator designator-2 is the current example.
Visual Laser	No Go	Go	Go	No Go	Good	Marginal	Highly visible to all. High risk of compromise. Effective, depending on degree of ambient light.
Laser Designator	Go	Go	No Go	Go	NA	Good	Highly effective with precision guided munitions (PGMs). Restrictive laser-acquisition cone and requires LOS to target. May require precoordination of laser codes. Requires PGM or laser spot tracker equipped.

B-18. Some U.S. weapons can kill targets beyond ranges that thermal, optical, and radar acquisition devices can provide positive identification. Both aviation and ground forces may become overloaded with tasks in the heat of battle. Simple positive identification procedures must be established and known to all.

Marking Friendly Positions

B-19. A method of target identification is direction and distance from friendly forces. Friendly forces mark their own positions with IR strobes or tape, NVG lights, smoke, signal panels, body position, MRE heaters, chemical lights, and mirrors. Marking friendly positions is the least desirable method of target location information and should be used with extreme caution. Marking friendly positions can be a more time-consuming process than directly marking a target and can reveal friendly positions to the enemy.

Marking Enemy Positions

B-20. Target marking aids aircrews in locating targets the unit in contact desires them to attack. Ground commanders should provide the target mark whenever possible. To be effective, the mark must be timely, accurate, and easily identifiable. Target marks may be confused with other fires on the battlefield, suppression rounds, detonations, and marks on other targets. Although a mark is not mandatory, it assists in aircrew accuracy, enhances SA, and reduces risk of fratricide.

Marking by Direct Fire

B-21. Direct-fire weapons can deliver a mark. Although this method may be more accurate and timely than an indirect fire mark, its use may be limited by range and the visibility of the weapon's burst effect. Aircraft may be used to deliver a mark. A burst of machine gun fire to the left or right of the target as a marking round may be an option. This method may alert the enemy but is a good way to verify the target with reduced risk of friendly casualties. Ground units may also mark targets with direct fire using tracers, M203 smoke rounds, or other means as coordinated by the unit.

Marking by Indirect Fire

B-22. Artillery or mortar fires are effective means of assisting aircrews in visually acquiring targets. Before choosing to mark by artillery or mortars, observers should consider the danger of exposing these supporting arms to enemy indirect-fire acquisition systems and additional coordination required. Marking rounds should be delivered as close to target as possible with smoke being the last round. Marking rounds are most effective when delivered within 100 meters of target, but those within 300 meters are generally effective enough to direct armed aircraft. If the situation requires a precise mark, observers or spotters can adjust marking rounds early ensuring an accurate mark is delivered. This action may, however, alert the enemy to an imminent attack.

Backup Marks

B-23. Whenever a mark is provided, a plan for a backup mark should be considered. For example, direct fire may be tasked to deliver the primary mark, while a mortar may be assigned responsibility for the backup mark.

INFRARED MARKING

B-24. IR pointers, as well as other IR devices, can be used to mark targets at night for aircrews using NVGs. Unlike laser designators, these IR devices cannot be used to guide or improve accuracy of aircraft ordnance. IR pointers may expose friendly units to an enemy with night-vision capability and should be used with caution. Ground units should initiate IR marks when the aircrew request "SPARKLE" and continue until the aircrew transmits "STOP" or the weapon hits the target.

TARGET MARKING BREVITY LIST

B-25. Table B-4 lists standard brevity terms.

Table B-4. Brevity list

Term	Meaning
Blind	Observer has no visual contact with friendly aircraft or ground position. Opposite of VISUAL.
Contact	Observer: (1) Has sensor contact at the stated position. (2) Acknowledges sighting of a specified reference point.
No Joy	Aircrew does not have visual contact with the target/bandit/landmark. Opposite of TALLY.
Rope	Observer is circling an IR pointer around an aircraft to help the aircraft identify the friendly ground position.
Snake	Aircrew calls to oscillate an IR pointer about a target.
Sparkle	Observer acknowledges: (1) Air-to-surface target marking by IR pointer. (2) Air-to-surface target marking by gunship/forward air controller (airborne) (FAC[A]) using incendiary rounds.
Steady	Aircrew calls to stop oscillation of IR pointer.
Stop	Aircrew calls to stop IR illumination of a target.
Tally	Observer acknowledges sighting of a target, aircraft, landmark, or enemy position. Opposite of NO JOY.
Visual	Observer is sighting a friendly aircraft or ground position. Opposite of BLIND.

OTHER OPERATIONS

SPECIAL OPERATIONS

B-26. Training at home station with SOF may not be practical or available. SOF may already be in theater, but their activities may not be published. Commanders must be aware of SOF location and plan for establishment of a communications link with these units to coordinate operations.

B-27. SOF are usually well trained in the use of all assets. This expertise should make coordination with them flow easily, but in some instances, the aviation force leader may have to use emergency coordination measures.

OPERATIONS WITH NONTRADITIONAL FORCES

B-28. Commanders must train their leaders and Soldiers to be flexible and prepared to conduct liaison with and support elements not traditionally included in home station training. These organizations may include the Central Intelligence Agency, Department of State, DEA, domestic and foreign police agencies, and indigenous forces. General checklists may be developed to address concerns. Often, these other agencies may not be aware of aviation capabilities. LNOs must be ready to advise and assist the supported element.

CLOSE COMBAT OPERATIONS

B-29. During close combat, attack reconnaissance aircraft and/or utility or cargo aircraft may engage targets near friendly forces, thereby requiring detailed integration of fire and maneuver of ground and aviation forces. To achieve desired effects and reduce risk of fratricide, air-ground integration must take place at company, platoon, and team levels. Close-combat engagements also require a higher training standard for aerial weapons delivery accuracy.

Close Combat Attack

B-30. Effective planning, coordination, and training between ground units and armed aircraft maximize capabilities of the combined arms team while minimizing risk of fratricide. The key to success for enhancing air-ground coordination and subsequent execution of the tasks involved begins with standardizing techniques and procedures. To prepare for close combat, basic tasks—such as how to find a ground unit's position at night—must be solved during home station training. Operations in unfamiliar terrain must not be hampered by the question of how to find the unit. It is found by one of various methods already practiced in training. CCA is a mission and should not be confused with a maneuver.

Close Combat Attack Briefing

B-31. CCA kneeboard card briefings (table B-5) follow joint standard five-line format, with minor modifications for Army helicopters. This briefing provides clear and concise information in a logical sequence enabling aircrews to employ their weapons systems. It also provides appropriate control to reduce risk of fratricide.

Table B-5. Sample close combat attack kneeboard briefing card

CLOSE COMBAT ATTACK BRIEFING (Ground to Air)
1. Observer-Warning Order: "_____. THIS IS _____. FIRE MISSION. OVER." 　　　　　(Aircraft)　　　　　　　　　　　　　　(Observer call sign)
2. Friendly Location/Mark: "MY POSITION _____. MARKED BY_____." 　　　　　　　　　(TRP, Grid)　　　　　　　　　(Strobe, Beacon, IR Strobe.)
3. Target Location: "_____." 　　　　　(Bearing [magnetic] and Range [meters], TRP, Grid.)
4. Target Description/Mark: "_____. MARKED BY _____. OVER." (Target Description)　　　　　　(IR pointer, Tracer)
5. Remarks: "_____." 　　　　(Threats, Danger Close Clearance, Restrictions, At My Command.)
AS REQUIRED: 1. Clearance: Transmission of the fire mission is clearance to fire (unless Danger close). Danger close ranges are in accordance with FM 3-09.32. For closer fire, the observer/commander must accept responsibility for increased risk. State "CLEARED DANGER CLOSE" on line 5. This clearance may be preplanned. 2. At my command: For positive control of the gunship, state "AT MY COMMAND" on line 5. The gunship will call "READY FOR FIRE" when ready.

Emergency Coordination Measures

B-32. Aviators may be required to assist ground personnel who are not fully familiar with aviation assets. Key personnel who habitually handle coordination for aviation support may become casualties or simply not be available. These situations require close attention, careful communications, and initiative on the part of the aviator to place fire on targets or deliver other support as necessary. An assault pilot may be required to coordinate an attack mission or call indirect FS.

B-33. Pilots must ask appropriate questions of the requestor with emphasis on positive identification of location. Possibilities include the following:

- Where is ground unit's position? What are the GPS coordinates? Are those coordinates verified with another GPS?

- Can ground unit mark its position with smoke, tracers, or other methods? If smoke is used, aircrew verifies color after deployment.
- What assistance does ground unit need (FS, extraction, or resupply)?
- Where is the target? What are the grid coordinates or relationship of the target to a readily identifiable natural or manmade feature?
- How far is the target from ground unit and in what direction? If the observer is not familiar with meters, aircrews ask the observer to try football or soccer field lengths estimating distances.
- What is the target? Is it personnel, vehicles, equipment, or buildings? What is the size of the enemy force, and what is it doing?

B-34. Aviators may have to fly helicopters near friendly troops to deliver ordnance onto the target. Factors reducing the potential for fratricide include—

- PGMs.
- FS coordinating measures.
- Planned or hasty coordination and control measures.
- Knowledge of GTP.
- Knowledge of exact location of friendly troops.
- Composition of friendly forces (number and type of vehicles, types of uniforms if nonstandard or coalition/host nation forces, Army or police).
- Knowledge of exact location of aircraft.
- Positive identification of targets.
- Familiarity between supported and aviation units.

MISSION TRAINING

B-35. Integration starts at home station with—

- Development of common SOPs among aviation and ground maneuver units.
- Habitual combined training, including battle drills, to help all team elements maintain awareness of locations and needs of other elements.
- Integration of AHB and/or GSAB into the ground maneuver unit's STX/field training exercise (FTX).

B-36. Training, procedural standardization, and familiarity of team members greatly accelerates planning and coordination, especially in unfamiliar environments. A team built in this manner establishes battle efficiency sooner and maintains a higher tempo of combat operations. Familiarity and compliance with joint procedures are essential in allowing seamless integration with other services' ground and air units.

B-37. Commanders must insist on a high degree of combined arms training with habitually supporting units. Air and ground units regularly train and execute battle drills together making coordination and reaction in combat instinctive. Although aviation may not be available for every exercise, ground maneuver units need to understand how to effectively integrate all aviation systems in their operations. Commanders can further ensure effective integration into ground maneuver through officer professional developments, NCO professional developments, and capabilities and limitations briefings with ground maneuver units.

B-38. When units are unable to create a desired habitual relationship, planning and coordination processes are longer and more detailed. Rehearsals are essential for success. In-country training exercises should also be accomplished whenever possible. The probability of mistakes is increased unless coordination, planning, rehearsals, and training are conducted. Commanders must apply risk-management procedures throughout planning and execution.

MISSION PLANNING

B-39. Mission planning encompasses mission training, rehearsal, and execution. During planning, a company commander analyzes the OPORD using TLP (identifying specified, essential, and implied tasks), visualizes the operational environment at various stages, develops a plan, and prepares the unit to conduct the operation. During split-based operations, platoon and section leaders must utilize these same TLP prior to conducting operations supporting the maneuver commander's intent.

B-40. Training exercises validate planning, training, and rehearsal, while the outcome of these exercises assists the commander in pinpointing where to place emphasis for future training and where to focus sustainment training (figure B-1).

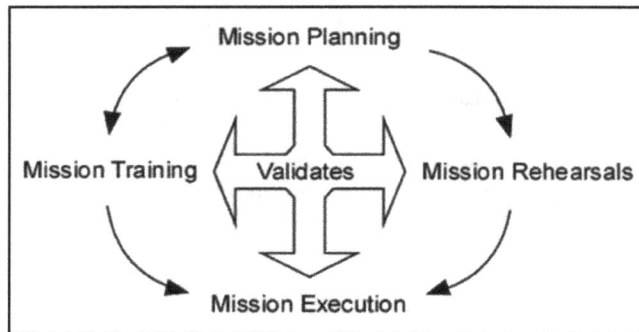

Figure B-1. Mission planning through execution cycle

B-41. Mission recovery ensures readiness for subsequent missions. Recovery includes munitions reconfiguration, refueling, maintenance, CP movement, and crew changes.

Minimum Planning Requirements

B-42. Minimum information required by an Army aviation team to ensure accurate and timely support includes—

- Situation including friendly forces' location, enemy situation (highlighting known ADA threat in the AO), mission request, and tentative LZ coordinates.
- Updating brigade- and battalion-level graphics via maneuver control system, AMPS, or radio communications. Updating critical items such as limit of advance, fire control measures, and maneuver graphics ensures better integration into the friendly scheme of maneuver.
- FS coordination information including location of DS artillery and organic mortars, and call signs and frequencies.
- Ingress/egress routes into the AO, including PPs into sector or zone, and air routes to the HA or LZ.
- Call signs and frequencies of the battalion in contact, down to the company in contact; air-ground coordination must be done on command frequencies to provide SA for all elements involved.
- GPS and SINCGARS time coordination. Care must be taken to ensure all units are operating on the same time schedule. All units should use GPS time that is the most accurate. A common error is for some ground units and aviation operations centers to set SINCGARS time by ANCD/CYZ 10 instead of GPS time. This results in ground and air communication failure due to time/synchronization error.

Digital transmission of information, such as coordinates, is faster and more accurate, if available. Voice communications are necessary to verify information and clarify needs and intentions.

LIAISON WITH THE GROUND MANEUVER FORCE

B-43. The BAE is a planning and coordination cell whose major function is incorporating aviation into the ground commander's scheme of maneuver. The BAE focuses on providing employment advice and initial planning for aviation missions, UAS, airspace planning and coordination, and synchronization with the ALO and FSCOORD. The BAE also coordinates directly with the CAB or supporting aviation TF for detailed mission planning. The liaison demands on aviation units are reduced by implementation and use of the BAE.

B-44. Although the BAE will conduct many of the functions traditionally performed by LNOs, aviation LNO teams remain a critical part of the process and must be staffed appropriately. While the members of the BAE work directly for the BCT commander as permanent members of his staff, aviation LNO teams represent the supporting aviation TF at a designated maneuver HQ only for the duration of a specific operation. Effective employment of LNOs is imperative for coordination and synchronization. Often aviation LNO teams will coordinate with the BAE and then proceed to a supported ground maneuver battalion. An example would be an aviation LNO team in support of an infantry battalion performing an assault to seize a key piece of terrain as part of a mechanized BCT scheme of maneuver.

B-45. Aviation LNOs must embody competence and credibility, and act as skillful representatives for their respective aviation TFs. A commander must exercise extreme care in choosing his LNOs since his unit is judged by their performance. The LNO must be capable of changing focus and approach depending on location and who he is supporting at the time. Above all, the LNO must be knowledgeable and mission focused toward the supported unit.

B-46. LNO teams maintain and provide current—

- Aviation unit locations.
- Aircraft/equipment status.
- Crew availability and fighter management cycle status.
- Class III/V status.
- METL training status.
- Continuous updates to the aviation commander and staff on the BCT's plan.

Refer to TC 1-400 for more information on BAE/liaison operations.

DECONFLICTION

B-47. Deconfliction is a continual process for ground, aviation, and other supporting units. During planning and execution, aviation units must deconflict their operations with friendly units by coordinating—

- Indirect fires, including mortars and possibly NSFS.
- CAS.
- UASs.
- ADs.
- Smoke operations.
- Other internal aviation operations.
- Nonorganic aviation operations.
- Other services' delivery systems such as supply drops.

SECTION II – FRATRICIDE PREVENTION

B-48. Air and ground assets require effective integration in conducting operations successfully and minimizing potential for fratricide and civilian casualties. Integration starts at home station with implementation of effective tactical SOPs, habitual relationships, and training. It continues through planning, preparation, and execution of the operation.

FRATRICIDE

B-49. Fratricide is the employment of friendly weapons and munitions, used with the intent to kill enemy forces or destroy its equipment or facilities, which results in unforeseen and unintentional death or injury to friendly, neutral, or noncombatant personnel. Fratricide is a type of accident and is a real and grim consequence of war. Its effects can spread deep within a unit and are devastating.

CAUSES OF FRATRICIDE

B-50. Contributing factors to fratricide include but are not limited to—
- Incorrect target identification.
- Incomplete planning and coordination.
- Equipment failure or improper procedures.
- Poor land navigation.
- Loss of communications.
- Position-reporting errors.

B-51. Weapons systems can detect, engage, and destroy targets at maximum range. However, weapons-sighting equipment cannot provide high resolution of targets at extended ranges, especially during limited-visibility conditions. The increasing use of common equipment by allied and hostile nations increases the probability of fratricide.

FRATRICIDE RISK CONSIDERATIONS

B-52. There are two types of risk: (1) losing men and equipment to accomplish the mission and (2) choosing a COA that may not be successful or may succeed but fails to achieve the desired effect. A commander must take such risks with prudence. Prudent risk taking emphasizes operational functions with the proper balance of administrative functions; for example—
- Understanding capabilities and limitations of units and components.
- Understanding the enemy, and identifying and creating opportunities to exploit enemy weaknesses.
- Pursuing actions that gain or retain the initiative.
- Planning for a mission or unit training.
- Training with supporting branches (joint and combined arms).
- Participating, supervising, and observing unit training.

B-53. The format for fratricide risk factors in figures B-2, page B-13, and figure B-3, page B-15, parallels the five-paragraph OPORD. The considerations/factors, key to fratricide reduction, are structured where they would likely appear in the OPORD. This is neither a change nor an addition to the OPORD format.

Fratricide Risk Factors

Paragraph 1: Situation

   a. Threat forces:

      Equipment and uniform similarities.

      Language.

      Deception capabilities and past record.

      What similarities could lead to fratricide?

      Location.

   b. Friendly forces:

      Similarities or differences (allied forces language, uniform, and equipment [combined operations]).

      Differences in U.S. Service's equipment and uniform (joint operation).

      What similarities could lead to fratricide?

      What differences could prevent fratricide?

      Deception plan.

      Location of unit and adjacent units (left, right, leading, follow-on).

      Location of neutrals and/or noncombatants.

   c. Attachments/Detachments:

      Do attached elements know above information?

      Do gaining units supply above information to detached elements?

     Own forces:

      Status of training (individual, crew, unit) proficiency.

      Fatigue (at time of the operation, sleep plan).

      Acclimatization to AO.

      Equipment (new, old, and mix: status of NET).

      MOPP requirements.

     Weather:

      Visibility (light data and precipitation).

      Hot, cold (effect on weapons, equipment, and Soldiers).

     Terrain:

      Topography and vegetation (such as urban, mountainous, hilly, swamp, prairie, jungle, forest, woods).

      Obstacles, avenues of approach, key terrain, observation, cover and concealment.

Paragraph 2: Mission

      Is this mission, with associated tasks and purpose, clearly understood?

Paragraph 3: Execution

   a. Task organization:

      Has unit worked under this organization before (familiarity)?

      Are SOPs compatible with the task organization (especially with attached units)?

     Uniform and equipment:

      Are special markings/signals needed for positive ID (such as cat's eyes, chem. lights, panels)?

      What special weapons and/or equipment are to be used?

      Do they look/appear like enemy weapons and/or equipment?

   b. Concept of operations:

     1. Maneuver:

      Are main and supporting efforts identified to ensure awareness of greatest fratricide danger?

Figure B-2. Fratricide risk factors

2. Fires (direct and indirect):

Are priorities of fires identified?

Target list(s).

Fire execution matrix/overlay.

Location of denial areas (minefields/family of scatterable mines [FASCAM]) and contaminated areas (such as improved conventional munition [ICM], CBRN).

Are aviation and CAS targets clearly identified?

Direct fire plan.

Final protective fire.

Sector limits (check/verify).

3. Engineer:

Barrier breaching:

Are friendly minefields, including FASCAM- and ICM-contaminated areas, known?

Are obstacles, along with approximate time for reduction/breaching, identified?

4. Tasks to each subordinate unit:

Are friendly forces identified, as appropriate, for each subordinate maneuver element?

5. Tasks to CS and sustainment units:

Are friendly forces identified to support and sustainment units?

6. Coordinating instructions:

Rehearsals:

Will one be conducted; is it necessary?

Are direct and indirect fired included?

Is a backbrief necessary?

Constraints and Limitations:

Are appropriate control measure clear and in the OPORD/overlay?

Control measures might include all or some of the following: AA, attack position, line of departure (LD), axis of advance/avenue of approach/direction of attack, phase lines, objective(s), movement times, restrictive fire line, fire support coordination line (FSCL), zone of engagement, limits of advance, main supply route, coordination points, listening post/observation post (LP/OP), challenge and password.

Are these control measures known by everyone who has a need to know?

What is the plan for using control measures to synchronize the battle and prevent fratricide?

Target/vehicle ID drills.

What is the immediate action drill/signal for "cease fire"/"I'm friendly" if coming under unknown/unfriendly fire?

Is there a backup action?

Is guidance included in handling dud munitions (such as ICM and cluster bomb units)?

Paragraph 4: Service Support

Ensure trains location(s) and ID marking(s) are known by everyone.

Ensure medical/maintenance personnel know routes between trains and units.

Paragraph 5: Command and Signal

a. Command:

Where is the location of the command and key staff?

What is succession of command?

Figure B-2. Fratricide risk factors

b. **Signal:**

Do instructions include signals for special and emergency events?

Do instructions include how to identify ourselves to aircraft?

Do instructions include backup for code words/visual signals for all special and emergency events?

Are SOI/communications-electronics operating instructions (CEOI) distributed to units (higher, owner, left, right, leading, following)?

Figure B-2. Fratricide risk factors

FACTORS		ASSESSED RISK LEVEL		
		LOW X 1	MEDIUM X 2	HIGH X 3
MISSION	**UNDERSTAND PLAN**			
	Commander's Intent	CLEAR	⟷	FOGGY
	Complexity	SIMPLE	⟷	COMPLEX
	Friendly Situation	CLEAR	⟷	UNCLEAR
	ROE	CLEAR	⟷	UNCLEAR
	BACKBRIEFS	THOROUGH	⟷	HASTY
	CONTROL MEASURES			
	Command Relationships	ORGANIC	⟷	JOINT/HASTY
	Audio	LOUD/CLEAR	⟷	JAMMED
	Visual	WELL-SEEN	⟷	OBSCURED
	Graphs	STANDARD	⟷	NOT UNDERSTOOD
	SOPs	STANDARD	⟷	NOT USED
	LOs	PROFICIENT	⟷	UNTRAINED
	Location-Navigation	SURE	⟷	UNSURE
ENEMY	**ENEMY SITUATION**	KNOWN	⟷	UNKNOWN
	COMBAT VEHICLE RECOGNITION			
	State of Training	TRAINING	⟷	UNTRAINED
	Vehicle Appearance to U.S. Vehicles			
	Friendly Units	SIMILAR	⟷	DIFFERENT
	Enemy Units	DIFFERENT	⟷	SIMILAR
	EXPLOIT ENEMY WEAKNESSES			
	Neutralize Strengths	EFFECTIVE	⟷	INADEQUATE
	CHALLENGE/PASSWORD			
	DISCIPLINE	HIGH USE	⟷	LOW USE
TROOPS	**TRAINING**	MOS QUALIFICATION	⟷	UNTRAINED
	FITNESS	RESTED/FIT	⟷	TIRED/BATTLE WEARY
	MORALE	HIGH	⟷	LOW
	UNIT PROFICIENCY	TRAINED	⟷	UNTRAINED
	HABITUAL RELATIONSHIPS	YES	⟷	NO
	INSPECTIONS	CONDUCTED	⟷	NOT CONDUCTED
	BUDDY SYSTEM	USED	⟷	NOT USED
	SAFETY DISCIPLINE	HIGH	⟷	LOW
TERRAIN	**SEASONAL HAZARDS**	GOOD WEATHER	⟷	EXTREME WEATHER
	DETAILED NAVIGATION PLAN	REDUNDANT NAVAIDS	⟷	NO NAVAIDS
	INTERVISIBILITY	GOOD	⟷	POOR
	OBSCURATION	NONE	⟷	EXTREME
	BATTLE TEMPO	SLOW	⟷	FAST
	POSITIVE TARGET ID	100 PERCENT	⟷	0 PERCENT
TIME	**PLANNING TIME**	ADEQUATE	⟷	INADEQUATE
	FULL TLP	FULL	⟷	ABBREVIATED
	REHEARSALS	FULL	⟷	NONE
	RECONNAISSANCE	THOROUGH	⟷	NONE
	SLEEP PLANS	GOOD	⟷	POOR
	***OVERALL FRATRICIDE ASSESSMENT**	** 37-61	57-91	87-111

* Commander may use numbers as the squadron decreases.
** In this example, each risk factor counts as one. These numbers are multiplied by the value assigned to each column (LOW-1, MEDIUM-2, HIGH-3). By weighing each factor, an overall score can assist in determining the risk.

Figure B-3. Risk reduction and/or fratricide prevention assessment

SECTION III – BRIGADE COMBAT TEAMS

ORGANIZATION

B-54. Maneuver BCTs are the Army's basic instrument of tactical execution. Figure B-4 provides an overview of the three types of maneuver BCT organization. See FM 3-90.6 for additional information.

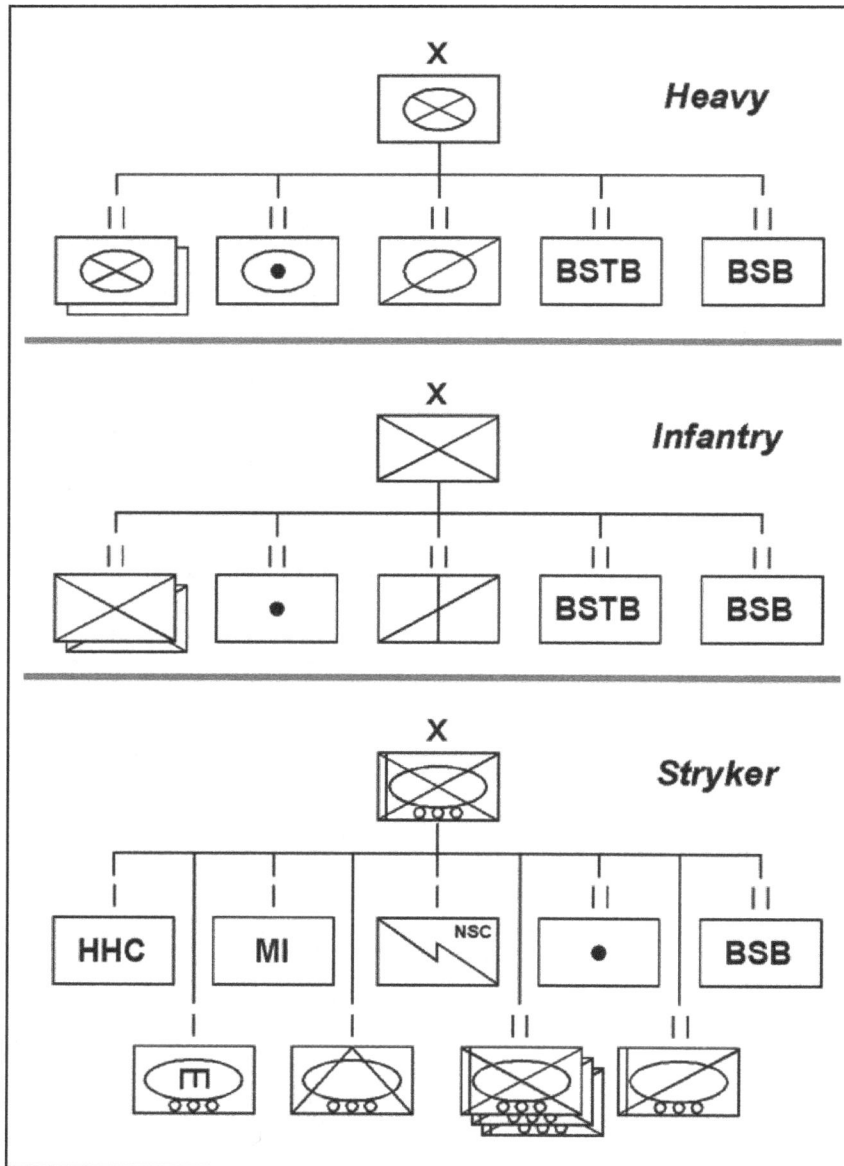

Figure B-4. Maneuver brigade combat teams

HEAVY BRIGADE COMBAT TEAM

B-55. The heavy brigade combat team (HBCT) reduces complexity of deployment planning and replaces many variations of divisional armored and mechanized brigades. It contains combined arms components normally required to rapidly achieve tactical overmatch in a single formation. The HBCT is best employed against enemy mechanized and armored forces. Robust enough to fight with or without external support for limited periods, the HBCT can fight across full spectrum operations when tactically loaded.

INFANTRY BRIGADE COMBAT TEAM

B-56. The infantry brigade combat team (IBCT) reduces complexity of deployment planning and replaces many variations of divisional light, assault, and airborne brigades. It contains combined arms components normally required to forcibly enter an AO and hold key objectives for a short period of time. The IBCT is organized around dismounted infantry and is designed to operate best in high-OPTEMPO offensive operations against conventional and unconventional forces in rugged terrain. Robust enough to fight without external support for limited periods, IBCT can fight "off the ramp" across full spectrum operations when tactically loaded.

STRYKER BRIGADE COMBAT TEAM

B-57. The Stryker brigade combat team (SBCT) combines the deployability of an IBCT with the mobility of a HBCT. A SBCT can be deployed rapidly and sustained by an austere support structure for up to 72 hours of independent operations. The SBCT is manned and equipped primarily to conduct operations in a small-scale contingency and is designed with many organic elements that allow for increased flexibility during employment.

This page intentionally left blank.

Appendix C

Aircraft Characteristics

This appendix provides an overview of the basic characteristics and capabilities of aircraft organic to AHBs and GSABs.

SECTION I – UH-60 BLACK HAWK

C-1. The primary missions of the UH-60 Black Hawk aircraft are air assault, air movement, C2 support, and as required, CASEVAC.

DESCRIPTION

C-2. The UH-60A/L is a twin-engine, dual-seat, utility helicopter. The minimum required crew is a pilot and copilot but typically includes one or two crewchiefs/gunners for improved mission effectiveness. It is designed to carry 11 combat-loaded air assault troops (seats installed). It also can move a 105-millimeter howitzer and 30 rounds of ammunition. The UH-60A/L is equipped with a full instrument package and certified for instrument meteorological conditions (IMC) as well as day and NVG operations. Table C-1 provides UH-60A/L aircraft characteristics.

Table C-1. UH-60A/L aircraft characteristics

Specifications:	
Length:	64 ft 10 in rotors turning, 41 ft 4 in rotors/pylons folded
Height:	12 ft 4 in center hub, 16 ft 10 in tail rotor
Width	9 ft 8.6 in main landing gear, 14 ft 4 in stabilator
with ESSS installed:	21 ft
Main rotor and tail rotor diameter:	53 ft 8 in main rotor, 11 ft tail rotor at 20-degree angle
Cabin floor dimensions:	73 in wide x 151 in long
Cabin door dimensions:	69 in wide x 54.5 in high
Maximum gross weight:	UH-60A/L: 22,000 lbs*
Maximum cargo hook load:	UH-60A: 8,000 lbs*
Maximum cargo hook load:	UH-60L: 9,000 lbs*
Cruise airspeed:	130 kts *
Combat radius:	225 km *
Armament:	
2 x M240H (7.62 MGs)	
Optics:	
AN/AVS-6 Night Vision Goggles	
Navigation Equipment:	
Doppler/GPS, VOR, ADF, and tactical air navigation (TACAN) (HH-60 only) navigation sets	

Table C-1. UH-60A/L aircraft characteristics

Flight Characteristics:	
Max speed (level):	156 kts
Normal cruise speed:	120-145 kts
With external sling-loads:	140 kts max. Up to 8,000 lbs/120 kts max. 8,000-9,000 lbs
Additional Capabilities:	
The ESSS allows configuration for extended operations without refueling (5+ hours) (2 X 200 gallon fuel tanks) and ferry and self-deployment flights (4 X 200 gallon fuel tanks).	
The enhanced C2 console provides the maneuver commander with an airborne platform supporting six secure FM radios, one HF radio, two VHF radios, and two UHF radios.	
Can be configured with the Volcano mine dispensing system; requires 8 hours to install.	
Capable of inserting and extracting troops with FRIES/SPIES.	
Limitations:	
Use of the ESSS for fuel tanks restricts access to the cabin doors for troops and bulky cargo or litters. It also reduces the payload and maximum speed.	
Cruise speed is decreased by light, bulky sling-loads.	
* varies with environmental/mission conditions	

C-3. The UH-60M has the same characteristics as the UH-60A/L but contains a fully coupled flight director, fully integrated digital cockpit, and Integrated Vehicle Health Management System (IVHMS). The UH-60M upgrade includes the integration of electronic flight controls (fly-by-wire) and Full Authority Digital Engine Controls (FADEC). These enhancements provide the crew with enhanced situational awareness, expanded mission support capability, and improved sustainability.

Note. At the time of production of this manual, the UH-60M specifc systems, capabilities, and limitations were not finalized.

CAPABILITIES

C-4. The UH-60A/L has, but not limited to, the following capabilities:

- Countermeasure suite of IR jammers and radar warning receivers.
- Data-transfer system to upload from the AMPS data-transfer cartridge and download post-mission data.
- Internal transport of 11 combat-loaded troops with seats installed and approximately 16 combat-loaded troops with seats removed. The actual number of troops carried is limited by space and environmental conditions.
- Self-deployable range of 558 nm with the ERFS.
- Airload transportable by C-5 and C-17 aircraft.

ARMAMENT SUBSYSTEMS

C-5. The Black Hawk has provisions for gunner's window mounting of two M240H 7.62-millimeter machine guns. The subsystem is pintle-mounted in each gunner's window at the forward end of the cabin section.

AIR VOLCANO

C-6. The air Volcano is a helicopter-mounted, automated, scatterable mine-delivery system able to deliver mines day or night. The system can rapidly emplace a 278-meter, 557-meter, or 1,115- by 140-meter minefield at up to 960 mines (800 AT and 160 AP) per sortie. The AT density yields an 80 percent chance of encounter. Mines can be set to self destruct after 4 hours, 48 hours, or 15 days.

C-7. The air Volcano system limitations include—

- The UH-60 with air Volcano mounted, a full crew, and one system operator will be at high gross weight, which reduces range and maneuverability.
- Minefield emplacement is conducted at low airspeeds (80 knots or less), making the aircraft more vulnerable to detection and engagement.
- The crew cannot operate the M240H machine gun with the air Volcano installed.
- System installation requires approximately 8 hours.
- These systems require two 5-ton cargo trucks for transport; it is an engineer responsibility to provide transportation assets to move these systems.

C-8. Four types of minefields can by emplaced using Volcano: disrupt, fix, turn, and block. Refer to chapter 3 for additional information.

COMMUNICATIONS

C-9. The UH-60 A/L has the following communications systems:

- The AN/ARC-186 provides two-way voice VHF-AM/FM communications.
- The AN/ARC-164 (V) Have Quick II provides two-way voice UHF-AM communications. It provides an antijam frequency-hopping capability.
- The AN/ARC-201 (SINCGARS) provides two-way voice VHF-FM communications. It provides an antijam frequency-hopping capability.
- The TSEC/KY-58 interfaces with the ARC-186 (V), Have Quick II, and SINCGARS radios to provide secure communications.
- The AN/ARC-220 HF radio provides long-range, two-way voice and text messaging communications capabilities between other AN /ARC 220-equipped aircraft or AN/ARC-100-equipped CPs.
- The KY-100 provides secure communications for the AN/ARC-220 HF radio.

C-10. The UH-60M communication system contains the Joint Tactical Radio System and Joint Alternate Communications Suite (JACS) that includes—

- Two AN/ARC-231 multiband radios.
- Two AN/ARC-201D (SINCGARS).

Note. The UH-60M does not inlcude HF capability. Additional TSEC equipment is not required as it is imbedded in JACS.

NAVIGATION SYSTEMS

C-11. The UH-60A/L has the following navigation systems:

- The ASN-128B/D Doppler/GPS navigation set provides present position to destination navigation information in latitude and longitude or military grid reference system (MGRS) coordinates.
- The AN/ARN-89 or AN/ARN-149 (V) provides automatic direction finding capability for IFR operations.
- The AN/ARN-123 (V) or AN/ARN-147 (V) VOR/LOC/GS/MB receiving set provides navigation capability for IFR operations.

HEADS-UP DISPLAY AN/AVS-7

C-12. The heads-up display (HUD) system serves as an aid to pilots using AN/AVS-6 NVGs by providing operational symbology information directly into the NVGs. It always displays airspeed, altitude from MSL, attitude, and engine torque. It can display up to 29 symbols.

LIMITATIONS

C-13. The following are limitations of the UH-60A/L aircraft:

- UH-60A/L aircrews employ AN/AVS-6 NVGs that lack the same night capabilities as AH-64 and OH-58D TIS.
- UH-60A/L aircraft are instrument-certified but cannot operate in all environmental conditions.
- Aircraft equipped with extended-range fuel tanks may not offer the same accessibility to the aircraft cabin for loading; self-defense machine guns have a limited range of motion when ERFS kits are installed.

SECTION II – HH-60L BLACK HAWK

C-14. The HH-60L Black Hawk's primary mission is aeromedical evacuation. Secondary missions include transport of medical personnel and equipment, emergency transport of class VIII to include blood products and biologicals, PR support, and support to Title 10 U.S. Code taskings.

DESCRIPTION

C-15. The HH-60L is a twin-engine, dual seat, utility helicopter. The minimum required crew is a pilot and copilot. For aeromedical evacuation missions, the crew includes up to three medical attendants (typical configuration includes one crew chief and two medical attendants). The HH-60L is equipped with a full instrument package and certified for IMC, as well as day and NVG operations. In addition to its basic configuration, the HH-60L includes a nose-mounted TIS and kit installations allowing rescue hoist, extended-range fuel, and aeromedical evacuation operations. The interior design of the HH-60L allows for the installation of life-saving instruments and equipment for use by onboard medical attendants. Normal cabin configurations of the HH-60L can accommodate up to four primary litter patients or six ambulatory (seated) patients. However, when necessary, two STANAG litters can be placed on the floor under the forward lifts for a total of six litter patients. The unique platform design also includes oxygen distribution and suction systems, an airway management capability, and provisions for stowing intravenous solutions. The interior also features the following capabilities:

- Oxygen generating systems.
- NVG-compatible lighting throughout.
- An environmental control system.
- Medical equipment.
- Patient monitoring equipment.
- Neonatal isolettes.

Note. The HH-60M combines the MEDEVAC package of HH-60L with the avionics and airframe upgrades of the UH-60M.

Table C-2, page C-5, outlines HH-60L aircraft specifications.

Table C-2. HH-60L specifications

Length:	64 ft 10 in rotors turning, 41 ft 4 in rotors/pylon folded
Height:	12 ft 4 in center hub, 16 ft 10 in tail rotor
Width:	9 ft 8.6 in main landing gear, 14 ft 4 in stabilator
Main rotor and tail rotor diameter:	53 ft 8 in main rotor, 11 ft tail rotor at 20-degree angle
Cabin floor and door dimensions:	73 in wide x 151 in long, 69 in wide x 54.5 in high
Maximum gross weight:	22,000 lbs
Rescue hoist/cargo hook max weights:	600 lbs rescue hoist; 8,000 lbs, cargo hook
Maximum range w/ERFS:	630 nm w/400 lbs reserve
Patient capacity:	6 litter, 6 ambulatory, or combination
Crew capacity:	2 pilots, 1 crew chief, 3 medical attendants
Fuel capacity:	360 gallons and additional 400 gallons w/ERFS

CAPABILITIES

C-16. The HH-60L has, but is not limited to, the following capabilities:

- Countermeasure suite of IR jammers and radar warning receivers.
- Data-transfer system to upload from the AMPS data-transfer cartridge and download postmission data.
- Self-deployable range of 558 nm with the ERFS.
- Airload transportable by C-5 and C-17 aircraft.
- Transport of six patients and two medical attendants.
- Internally and externally loaded medical supplies.
- TIS,
- AN/ARS-6(V) Personnel Locator System (PLS).

ARMAMENT

C-17. The HH-60L is an unarmed aircraft (no gunner stations).

COMMUNICATIONS

C-18. The HH-60L has the following communication systems:

- The AN/ARC-222 provides two-way voice VHF-AM/FM air and maritime communications capability.
- The ARC-164 (V) Have Quick II provides two-way voice UHF-AM communications. It provides an antijam, frequency-hopping capability
- The AN/ARC-201 (SINCGARS) provides two-way voice VHF-FM communications. It provides an antijam frequency-hopping radio capability
- .The TSEC/KY-58 interfaces with the AN/ARC-222, Have Quick II, and SINCGARS radios to provide secure communications.
- The AN/ARC-220 HF radio provides long-range, two-way voice and text messaging communications capabilities between other AN /ARC 220-equipped aircraft or AN/ARC-100-equipped CPs.
- The KY-100 provides secure communications for the AN/ARC-220 HF radio.

NAVIGATION SYSTEMS

C-19. The HH-60L has the following navigation systems:

- The ASN-128B/D Doppler/GPS navigation set provides present position to destination navigation information in latitude and longitude or military MGRS coordinates.
- The AN/ARN-149 (V) provides automatic direction finding capability for IFR operations.
- The AN/ARN-147 (V) VOR/LOC/GS/MB receiving set provides navigation capability for IFR operations.
- AN/ASN 153 (V) TACAN provides navigation capability for IFR operations.

PERSONNEL LOCATOR SYSTEM AN/ARS-6

C-20. PLS covertly and precisely locates personnel for evacuation. This system allows aeromedical evacuation crews the ability to pinpoint personnel locations electronically rather than flying search patterns.

PILOT HEADS-UP DISPLAY AN/AVS-7

C-21. The HUD system serves as an aid to pilots using AN/AVS-6 NVGs by providing operational symbology information directly into the NVGs. It always displays airspeed, altitude (MSL), attitude, and engine torque and can display up to 29 symbols.

LIMITATIONS

C-22. The limitations of the HH-60L aircraft are—

- HH-60L aircrews employ AN/AVS-6 NVGs that lack the same night capabilities as the AH-64 TIS. The HH-60L TIS is used primarily to detect personnel to be evacuated. The TIS is not intended as a visual enhancment system for flight.
- HH-60L aircraft are instrument certified but cannot operate in all environmental conditions.
- Aircraft equipped with extended-range fuel tanks may not offer the same accessibility to the aircraft cabin for loading..

SECTION III – CH-47 CHINOOK

C-23. The primary missions of the CH-47 are air assault, air movement, and as required CASEVAC..

DESCRIPTION

The CH-47D is a twin-turbine engine, tandem-rotor helicopter. The minimum crew required for flight is a pilot, copilot, and flight engineer. Additional crewmembers/gunners, as required, may be added for improved mission effectivenss. Tactical missions normally require the addition of one or two crew chiefs. Table C-3 outlines CH-47D characteristics.

Table C-3. CH-47D characteristics

Specifications:	
Length:	98.9 ft
Height:	18.9 ft
Fuselage width:	12.4 ft
Main rotor span:	60 ft
Cargo space:	1,500 cu ft
Floor space:	225 sq ft
Maximum gross weight:	50,000 lbs

Table C-3. CH-47D characteristics

Specifications:	
Max load for forward and aft hooks:	17,000 lbs
Max tandem load for forward and aft hooks:	25,000 lbs
Max load for center hook:	26,000 lbs
Cruise airspeed:	130 kts*
Max continuous airspeed:	170 kts*
Combat radius (16,000 lbs cargo):	50 nm (90 km)*
Combat radius (33 troops):	100 nm (180 km)*
Armament:	
3 M240H 7.62 MGs (two cabin-mounted and one ramp-mounted)	
Optics:	
AN/AVS-6 Night Vision Goggles	
Navigation Equipment:	
Doppler/GPS, VOR, and ADF navigation sets	
Flight Characteristics:	
Max speed (level):	170 kts
Normal cruise speed:	120-145 kts
Additional Capabilities:	
Can be configured w/additional fuel for mobile FARE system (Fat Cow) or for ferrying/self-deployment missions. Aircraft has an internal load winch to ease loading of properly configured cargo. The CH-47D can sling-load virtually any piece of equipment in the light infantry, airborne, or air assault divisions.	
Limitations:	
Cruise speed is greatly decreased by light, bulky sling-loads.	
*Varies with factors such as temperature, wind, gross weight, internal versus external load, and time in PZ/LZ.	

C-24. The CH-47F has the same characteristics as the CH-47D but contains a fully integrated digital cockpit management system, and new flight control system. The CH-47F inlcudes improved communications suite, navigation equipment, and airframe. These enhancements provide the crew with enhanced situational awareness and improved mission support capability.

Note. At the time of production of this manual, the CH-47F specific systems, capabilities, and limitations were not finalized.

CAPABILITIES

C-25. The CH-47D has, but is not limited to, the following capabilities:

- Countermeasure suite of IR jammers, radar-warning receivers, and laser-warning detectors.
- Data-reduction transfer system to upload from the AMPS data-transfer cartridge and download post-mission data.
- Internal transport of one HMMWV or two HMMWVs externally loaded.
- Internal transport of 33 combat-loaded troops with seats installed.
- Evacuation of 24 litter patients and 2 medics.
- Self-deployable range of 1,056 nm with the ERFS
- Air transportable by C-5 and C-17 aircraft.

ARMAMENT SUBSYSTEMS

C-26. The armament subsystems are M24 and M41 machine-gun systems installed in the cabin door, cabin escape hatch, and on the ramp. Both subsystems use the M240H 7.62-millimeter machine gun. The two flexible 7.62-millimeter machine guns are free pointing but limited in traverse, elevation, and depression.

COMMUNICATIONS

C-27. The CH-47D has the following communications systems:

- The AN/ARC-186 provides two-way voice VHF-FM/AM communications
- The AN/ARC-164 Have Quick II provides two-way voice UHF-AM communications. It provides an antijam, frequency-hopping capability.
- The AN/ARC-201 (SINCGARS) provides two-way voice VHF-FM communications. It provides an antijam, frequency-hopping capability.
- The TSEC/KY-58 interfaces with the AN/ARC-186, Have Quick II, and SINCGARS radios to provide secure communications .
- The AN/ARC-220 HF radio provides long-range, two-way voice and text messaging communications capabilities between other AN /ARC 220-equipped aircraft or AN/ARC-100-equipped command
- The KY-100 provides secure communications for the AN/ARC-220 HF radio.

NAVIGATION SYSTEMS

C-28. The CH-47 has the following navigation systems:

- The AN/ASN-128B/D Doppler/GPS navigation set provides present position to destination navigation information in latitude and longitude or the MGRS coordinates.
- The AN/ARN-89 (V) provides automatic direction finding capability for IFR operations.
- The AN/ARN-123 (V) VOR/LOC/GS/MB receiving set provides navigation capability for IFR operations..

HEADS-UP DISPLAY AN/AVS-7

C-29. The HUD system serves as an aid to pilots using AN/AVS-6 NVGs by providing operational symbology information directly into the NVGs. It always displays airspeed, altitude (MSL), attitude, and engine torque and can display up to 29 symbols.

LIMITATIONS

C-30. Limitations of the CH-47D aircraft are—

- CH-47D aircrews employ AN/AVS-6 NVGs that lack the same night capabilities as AH-64 and OH-58D TIS.
- CH-47D aircraft are instrument certified but cannot operate in all environmental conditions.

SECTION IV – TYPICAL FUEL EXPENDITURE RATES, CAPACITIES, AND STANDARD LOAD CAPACITIES

C-31. Table C-4, page C-9, depicts typical rates of fuel expenditures per helicopter and fuel capacities without additional tanks.

Table C-4. Typical helicopter fuel expenditure rates and capacities

Helicopter	Average Gallons per Hour	Fuel Capacity
AH-64D	175	370
OH-58D	44	112
OH-58D (armed)	110	112
UH-60 A/L	178	362
CH-47D	514	1,030

C-32. Aircraft are capable of carrying more than is indicated on the lists in table C-5; however, safety, loading procedures, space limitations, and other factors play a great part in determining authorized loads for each helicopter, table C-6, page C-10. Environmental conditions (high altitude/high temperature decrease maximum gross weight) and configuration (internal load size/dimensions) constraints affect the ACL for each aircraft.

C-33.

Table C-5. Typical planning weights for combat equipment and vehicle

Vehicle/Equipment	Weight in Pounds
M998 HMMWV	7,535
M996 TOW HMMWV	8,095
M149 Water Buffalo (empty)	2,540
(loaded)	6,060
M101A1 ¾ Ton Trailer (empty)	1,350
(loaded)	2,850
500 Gallon Fuel Drum (empty)	275
(full)	3,625
M102 105-mm Howitzer	3,360
M119 105-mm Howitzer	4,000
M114A1 155-mm Howitzer	15,200
M198 155-mm Howitzer	15,740
M167 Vulcan (towed)	3,260
A22 Bag (loaded)	2,200
Conex, Steel (empty)	2,140
Conex, Aluminum (empty)	1,560
Conex (either) Max Load	6,500
SCAMP Crane	14,600
One Mil-Van	4,710
Electronic Shop with Wheels	3,940
Tool Set, Shop with Wheels	3,030
Shop, Portable, Aircraft Maintenance (empty)	4,220
(loaded)	5,425
M1008 Pickup (empty)	5,900
(loaded)	8,800
JD-550 Dozer	16,800

Table C-6. Typical helicopter load capacities

Type	Empty Weight Plus Crew and Fuel	Max Gross Weight	Max Sling Load
UH-60A	15,000	22,000	8,000
UH-60L	15,000	23,500*	9,000
CH-47D	30,000	50,000	26,000
* External lift missions above 22,000 pounds can only be flown with cargo hook loads above 8,000 pounds and up to 9,000 pounds			

Appendix D

Checklists, Briefings, Reports, and Formats

This appendix provides example checklists, briefings, tables, reports, and formats (table D-1 through table D-25) used by aviation units during training or combat to more efficiently accomplish assigned tasks and missions. This is not all inclusive; products are used as a guide and do not supersede unit SOPs.

SECTION I – CHECKLISTS AND BRIEFINGS

D-1. Table D-1 is an example of a predeployment and pretemporary duty checklist.

Table D-1. Sample predeployment and pretemporary duty checklist

Yes	No	N/A	Task/Action
Finance			
			Bills, recurring and nonrecurring.
			Bank accounts, checking, savings, loans. Investments and other income sources.
			Safety deposit boxes.
Legal			
			Power of attorney as needed (specific, general).
			Wills updated.
			Living wills updated.
			Spouse's social security number.
			Guardianship for children.
			Insurance policies; life, auto, home/renters, floater.
			Deeds, leases, rentals, real estate documents, management company.
			Marriage or divorce papers.
			Birth certificates, adoption papers.
			School records.
			Naturalization documents.
			Vehicle titles and registration.
			Taxes.
			Necessary court documents.
Personnel Issues			
			TDY or permanent change of station (PCS) orders.
			Emergency data cards complete.
			ID cards, copy, expiration dates, Defense Enrollment Eligibility Reporting System (DEERS) enrollment.

Table D-1. Sample predeployment and pretemporary duty checklist

Yes	No	N/A	Task/Action
Personnel Issues			
			Serviceman's Group Life Insurance.
			Passport and visa documents.
			Family care plan.
			NEO/Safe haven information.
			Personal affairs; funeral and burial instructions.
Household			
			Vehicle registration, inspection, all stickers and tags.
			Crime prevention measures/force protection information.
			Maintenance/utilities/list of who to contact for problems and repairs.
			Disaster/evacuation plan and survival kit: water, food, clothing, other personal necessities.
Communication			
			Community contact information.
			Local emergency contacts; police, fire, Red Cross, poison control, hospital, TRICARE.
			Post chaplain, Army Community Service, military police.
			Unit contact information (include phone numbers, physical address and e-mail address).
			Unit name, DIV, BDE, battalion (BN), company (CO).
			Commander, CSM/1SG, UMT, supervisor.
			FRG spouses.
			Orderly room, staff duty officer, foreign object damage.
			Rear detachment commander/officer in charge (OIC) and NCOIC.
			TDY: dates, location, phone and emergency phone.
			Personal contact information.
			Family.
			Friends.
			Immediate neighbors.
			Financial.
			Insurances.
			Emergency family and friends.
			Medical.
			TRICARE enrollment/claim process.
			Locations/providers/clinic contact information.
			Records; medical, dental, shot, other.
			Pets.
			Records.
			Veterinarian: regular and emergency.

D-2.   Table D-2 is an example of a convoy precombat inspection checklist.

Table D-2. Sample convoy checklist

	Completed
Vehicles:	
Vehicles are inspected at operating temperatures with hoods open.	
5988Es are current with all parts installed.	
Vehicle fuel will be topped off.	
All basic issue items (BIIs) present and serviceable.	
Three days rations per Soldier per vehicle.	
Five-gallon water cans topped off.	
Water buffalo sanitized and topped off.	
All supply trucks are covered.	
Complete combat life saver bag on hand (if applicable.)	
Weapons:	
Crew-served weapons functionally checked.	
.50-cal headspace and timing set.	
Functions check on all individual weapons.	
5988Es are present and current for all crew-served weapons.	
All weapons are lubricated.	
Communications:	
Radios loaded with correct frequencies. Call signs recorded.	
5998Es are all current with PMCS and manual.	
Batteries are present for dismounted radios.	
Long-range radio checks are complete.	
Digital nonsecure voice telephones are present with 2 miles of WF-16 wire per phone.	
TA-1s or TA-312s are operational with 1 roll of WD-1 per set.	
Automated net control devices are present and loaded.	
CBRN Equipment:	
5988Es are present for all CBRN equipment.	
M-8/M-22 alarms are complete with batteries and operational alarm.	
IM-93 is present and operational.	
CBRN Equipment:	
M8 and M9 paper present and attached.	
M256A1 chemical detection kit (1 per squad) on hand.	
CBRN markers are present and stocked.	
CBRN teams identified.	
Night Observation Devices (NODs):	
5988Es are present and complete for all NODs.	
15-day supply of batteries for all NODs.	
Carrying cases are complete with accessories and lens cleaning equipment.	

Table D-2. Sample convoy checklist

	Completed
Individual Solider:	
Load-bearing equipment worn in accordance with TACSOPs and properly fitted.	
Flack jacket is present/Gortex jacket if necessary.	
Flashlight present with the appropriate filter.	
Identification tags and identification card present.	
7 magazine per M-4; 3 per M-9 9-mm.	
DA Form 1156 (Casualty Feeder Card) in the first aid pouch and left pocket of the chemical protective overgarments.	
Serviceable first aid packets.	
One-quart canteen with cup and cover (extra canteen optional) present. Canteens must be filled and fitted with CBRN cap.	
All Soldiers understand the mission.	
Drivers:	
5988E with current PMCS and quality control within 72 hours.	
Dispatch signed by the driver and the company commander/XO.	
Driver has a current ULLS computer-generated license.	
Driver has sustainment graphics, control measures, and a map of the operational area.	
Leaders:	
Map with current graphics and/or strip map.	
Completed CRM.	
Leaders have appropriate FMs and MTPs.	
List of all sensitive items on company standardized sensitive items sheet.	
Current list of all vehicles organic or attached.	
Current SOI for support area and TF.	
S-2 threat assessment.	
Prepared convoy commander brief.	

D-3. Table D-3 is an example of a precombat checklist.

Table D-3. Sample precombat checklist

	Check		Check
Individual:			
Equipment packed inaccordance with (IAW) TACSOP		M8/M9 paper	
Load bearing vest (LBV) complete and serviceable		Current MOPP implemented	
• Ear plugs		Weapon at appropriate arming level	
• First aid pouch		Optical inserts	
• Ammunition pouches		Antifogging kit	
• Canteen w/water and cup		ID card	
Kevlar w/camo cover and band		ID tags (2 sets, w/2 tags, 1 set worn)	
Weapons, zero in pistol grip		MREs	
Protective mask w/carrier and hood		Drivers licenses	
Body armor as required		Challenge and password	
Flashlight w/batteries and lens filters		Shot records	
Causality feeder reports		Hot/cold weather brief	
Individual decon kit		Mission brief	
Squad Leader:			
Personnel accounted for		MOPP level known and disseminated	
Individual PCI completed		Weapons control	
Reference publications reviewed		Section status to platoon sergeant	
Uploaded by load plan		Situation briefed	
Expendable supplies on hand		MREs issued	
Sleep plan established		Ammo basic load issued	
Platoon Sergeant:			
Personnel accounted for		Sleep plan established	
Individual PCI completed		Class V issued	
Reference publications reviewed		MOPP level known and disseminated	
Uploaded by load plan		Weapons control	
Operation equipment		Platoon status to 1SG	
• Maps, updated		Situation briefed	
• Compasses		MREs issued	
• Pens.			
First Sergeant:			
Personnel accounted for		Spare equipment:	
Uploaded by load plan		• Microphones	
Expendable supplies on hand		• Headsets	
Operation equipment		• Antennas	
• Maps, updated		• Batteries	
• Compasses		SINCGARS spare battery	
• Pens.		Defensive sector diagram complete	
Individual PCI completed and verified		Range cards verified and complete	
LP/OP briefed and positioned		Camouflaged:	

Table D-3. Sample precombat checklist

	Check		Check
First Sergeant:			
Defense plan established and rehearsed		• Vehicles	
Expendable supplies on hand		• Equipment	
Communications equipment		• Positions	
Equipment accounted for:		• Glass and mirrors	
• Radios		Repack all equipment not in use	
• Microphones		Field sanitation enforced	
• Antennas		Hand washing enforced	
• Encrypting equipment		Trash kept policed	
• SOI		MEDEVAC LZ marked	
PMCS completed:		Casualty collection identified	
• Radios		Reference publications reviewed	
• Antennas		Early warning devices employed	
• Encrypting equipment		Noise and light discipline enforced	
Call Sign board		Sleep plan established	
Frequencies:		Class V issued	
• Unit		Feeding plan established	
• Next higher		MOPP level known and disseminated	
• MEDEVAC		Accountability of personnel to S-1	
• Range control		Accountability of sensitive items to S-3	
• FS		Reportable equipment status to maint officer	
TA-312s: batteries		Situation briefed	
Wire		Generator operational	
Reel handles on hand		All BIIs on hand	
SINCGARS: Batteries		Grounding rods	
Wire		Fire extinguishers	
Blank report formats		-10 manual on hand	
Coordinate pickup of equipment		PMCS performed	
Coordinate pickup of SOI		Generator topped off	
		Extra fuel and POL	
CBRN Equipment:			
Individual PCI complete		IM-93 dosimeter issued	
Chemical agent alarms operational		146 radiac meters issued	
Chemical agent alarms employed		GTA warning system issued	
PMCS performed on M8 alarm		PBT and nerve agent antidote issued	
M273 kit per chemical alarm		CBRN marking kit available	
M256/256A1 detector kit as required		Mark I kit available	
AN/VRDR-2 radiac sets on hand		Cana kit available	
Combat Lifesavers:			
Combat lifesaver bags issued		100% inventory and all supplies replenished	
Vehicle Commander:			
All BII on hand		Pens/pencils available	
Pioneer tools		Maps and overlays	

Table D-3. Sample precombat checklist

	Check		Check
Vehicle Commander:			
Fire extinguishers		Sun/wind/dust goggles	
-10 manual on hand		Compass/GPS present serviceable	
PMCS performed:		Binoculars	
Vehicle		Crew-served weapons	
Radios		Headspace and timing checked	
Vehicle topped off		Ammunition basic load	
Extra fuel and POL		Qualified gunner	
Grease pencils		Vehicle load plan verified	
Notebook available		Convoy number on vehicle	
Crew Served Weapons:			
Clean and functional		Head space and timing set (M2)	
Spare barrels, cleaning kits on-hand		Machine guns mounted	
Glove; bolt rupture extraction on hand		Function check	
Tripod w/traversing and elevation mechanism, bipod		Test fire w/permission	
		NVD, serviceable	
Driver/Vehicle Preparation:			
-10 and LO on hand		Rags	
BII/AII present and serviceable		MREs rations stowed	
First aid kit		Tools	
Fire extinguisher		Goggles	
Warning triangles		Dispatch	
PMCS performed		Vehicle hardened as required	
Vehicle topped off		Strip map on-hand	
Loaded according to load plan		Convoy route and plan briefed	
POL products including weapons oil		Camouflage nets/poles configured/stowed	
5 gallon can of water		Lights and markings covered	
5 gallon can of fuel		Convoy number on vehicle	
		Trailer properly hooked	

CHECKLIST FOR COMBAT OPERATIONS

D-4.   Table D-4 is an example of an air mission coordination meeting checklist.

Table D-4. Sample air mission coordination meeting checklist

1. Mission number:	
2. Supported unit:	
3. Supporting unit:	
4. Time required:	
5. Mission (and concept sketch):	
6. Number/type of aircraft:	
7. H-hour:	

Table D-4. Sample air mission coordination meeting checklist

8. Pickup time with rehearsal time built in:	
9. PZ location (and sketch):	
10. PZ frequency	A. Unit B. Aircraft
11. PZ call sign	A. Unit B. Aircraft
12. PZ marking (day/night)	
13. Landing heading	
14. Landing formation	
15. Door entry	
16. Number of troops total	
17. Number of troops per aircraft	
18. Number/type cargo loads	
19. Takeoff direction	
20. Takeoff formation	
21. False LZ grid	
22. Route	
23. Time of flight	
24. LZ grids (primary and alternates)	
25. LZ sketches:	
26. LZ marking (day/night)	
27. LZ frequency and call sign (if Pathfinders are available)	
28. Attack reconnaissance aviation concept	
29. LZ prep fires	
30. Landing heading	
31. Landing formation	
32. Weapons status	
33. Door exit	
34. Takeoff direction	
35. Number of turns required	
36. Abort criteria	
37. Weather call time	
38. Bump plan	
39. ABN frequency	
40. CAN/command frequencies	
41. Code words	
42. Go/No-Go criteria	
AMC initials_____	Infantry battalion S-3 Initials_____

D-5.   Table D-5 is an example of an air mission brief.

Table D-5. Sample air mission brief

Roll Call	Time Zone	Time Hack	Packet Check
_____	_____	_____	_____

References

Task Organization(Infantry Brigade TF)

1. Situation.

    a. Enemy forces (synopsis of overall enemy situation). (TF S-2)

        (1) Air IPB.

        (2) Enemy air capability.

        (3) Enemy ADA capability.

            (a) Type/location.

            (b) Night capability/range.

            (c) Weather/NOTAMs.

SR:	SS:
MR:	MS:
Max % illum:	Illum. range (during air assault, sucha as 0% - 45%):
NVG window:	Ceiling/visibility:
MAX temp:	MAX density altitude/pressure altitude:
End evening nautical twilight (EENT):	Begin morning nautical twilight (BMNT):

    b. Friendly forces (TF S-3).

        (1) Mission higher HQ (include commander's intent).

        (2) BDE/BN Infantry scheme of maneuver. (TF S-3)

2. Mission. (AVN TF S-3).

    a. Brigade/Battalion commander's intent. (AATFC)

    b. Conditions for air assault. Conditions for ice.

    c. Mission risk assessment. (TF S-3)

    d. Aviation mission. (AVN S-3)

Table D-5. Sample air mission brief

3. Execution.

    a. Aviation commander's intent. (AMC)

    b. Concept of the aviation operation. (AVN TF S-3)

    c. AVN tasks to subordinate units. (AVN TF S-3)

    d. Fires. (AVN TF FSO)

        (1) FA. Annex I (FS graphics)

            (a) Purpose of supporting fires.

            (b) Unit/location.

            (c) Priority of fire.

            (d) SEAD information/targets.

            (e) LZ prep.

        (2) Close air support. (ALO)

            (a) Purpose/mission.

            (b) Coordinating altitude.

                Rotary wing.

                Fixed wing.

            (c) #, type, and time of sorties available.

            (d) Call signs and frequencies.

        (3) Attack reconnaissance aviation. (Attack Recon S-3/CDR)

            (a) Mission.

            (b) Concept.

            (c) Attack BPs/ABF sectors/routes in and out.

    e. Staging plan. Annex A (PZ Diagram) (AATF XO)

        (1) Name/number.

        (2) Coordinates.

        (3) Load time.

        (4) Takeoff time.

Table D-5. Sample air mission brief

(5) Markings.

(6) Control.

(7) Call signs/frequencies.

(8) Landing formation.

(9) Heading.

(10) Hazards/go arounds.

(11) Supported unit bump plan. (Annex A-1 coordinating instructions)

(12) PZ arrival times.

f. Air movement plan. (Assault S-3/Mission lead)

    (1) Routes/corridors. Annex B (Route Card)

        (a) Ingress primary/alternate.

        (b) Egress primary/alternate.

        (c) Others.

    (2) En route hazards.

    (3) Abort criteria.

        (a) Weather.

        (b) Aircraft available.

        (c) Time.

        (d) Mission essential combat power.

        (e) Mission criticality.

        (f) Enemy.

    (4) Penetration points.

    (5) En route formation/rotor separation/angle/airspeeds (as per crew brief).

    (6) Deception measures/false insertions.

    (7) Air movement plan. Annex D

    (8) Cargo doors.

    (9) External lighting. (SOP)

Table D-5. Sample air mission brief

(10) ROZ locations.

   (a) Air assault C2.

   (b) ATK C2.

   (c) QUICKFIX.

(11) MEDEVAC/CASEVAC aircraft plan.

(12) Aircraft decontamination plan.

g. Landing plan. Annex C (LZ diagram) (Assault S-3/Mission lead)

   (1) Name/number.

   (2) Coordinates.

   (3) LDG times (as per AMT).

   (4) Markings.

   (5) Control.

   (6) Call signs/frequencies.

   (7) LDG formation/direction.

   (8) LZ abort criteria. (based on GTC guidance)

   (9) Go arounds. (flight/single ship, as per crew brief)

   (10) Departure. (as per crew brief)

h. Laager plan. (Assault S-3/Mission lead)

   (1) Name/locations.

   (2) Times/REDCON status.

   (3) Security plan.

   (4) Scatter plan.

   (5) Call forward plan.

i. Extraction plan. (Assault S-3/Mission lead)

j. Coordinating instructions. (Aviation) (Assault S-3)

   (1) MOPP level/CBRN warning status.

   (2) M240H control status.

Table D-5. Sample air mission brief

(3) ADA status.

(4) IFF procedures/times.

(5) Chaff/ALQ 144 employment.

(6) NVG-specific procedures. (SOP)

(7) Vertical helicopter instrument recovery procedure/IIMC. (as per crew brief)

(8) Mission contingencies. (SOP)

    (a) DAPP/SAR/emergency aircrew extraction.

    (b) Downed aircraft/SERE/DART.

    (c) BDAR.

(9) Spare aircraft procedures.

(10) Special aircraft equipment/preparation.

(11) PPC.

(12) Mission brief sheet.

(13) Risk assessment form (completed/signed).

(14) Safety considerations/hazards.

(15) OPSEC considerations (SOI, kneeboard sheets, maps).

(16) Weather decision plan/times.

(17) Debrief location/time.

k. Coordinating instructions. (AATF) (AATF S-3)

4. Service Support.

a. Class I (1 case meals, MREs/5 gallons water/survival kits) (TF S-4)

b. Class III/V. (III/V platoon leader)

(1) Minimum fuel. (as per crew brief)

(2) Basic load.

(3) FARP/rapid refuel point.

Table D-5. Sample air mission brief

c. Class VIII (HSSO)
(1) CCP. (record locations of company CCPs)
(2) Evacuation plan/hospital location.
d. MEDEVAC/CASEVAC plan. (HSSO)
5. Command and Signal. (AVN TF S-3).
a. Command.
(1) AC2. (as per ACO, this AMB, and established tactical flight procedures)
(2) AATFC/location.
(3) AVN TF AMC/location.
(4) ABC/location.
(5) Aviation chain of command. (as per serial chain of command)
b. Signal. (AVN TF S-6)
(1) Commo card day (Annex ____).
(2) Execution matrix (Annex ____).
(3) Code words.
Mission Brief Back
Final Questions
Commanders Comments

D-6. Table D-6 is an example of a pickup zone/landing zone kneeboard diagram

Table D-6. Sample pickup zone/landing zone kneeboard diagram

PRIMARY PZ DIAGRAM		PRIMARY LZ DIAGRAM
ALTERNATE PZ DIAGRAM		ALTERNATE LZ DIAGRAM
PZ name/grid coordinates	PZ elevation/LZ elevation	LZ name/grid coordinates
PZ formation	PZCO freq/call sign	LZ formation
Alternate PZ name/grid coordinates	Chalk aircraft, entry/exit PZ: LZ:	Alternate LZ name/grid coordinates
PZ landing direction/touchdown point marking, takeoff direction	PZ wind direction LZ wind direction	LZ landing direction: Primary LZ: Alternate LZ:
PZ time/load/weight: Lift 1: Lift 2: Lift 3:	Onboard fuel versus minimum fuel for lift: PZ fuel lift 1: / PZ fuel lift 2: / PZ fuel lift 3: /	Take-off direction: Primary LZ: Alternate LZ: Collection point for CASEVAC

D-7.   Table D-7 is an example of a personnel recovery planning checklist

Table D-7. Sample personnel recovery planning checklist

	Go/No-Go
Date-time group (DTG) Notified:	
Premission planning:	
Record event on appropriate incident form	
Determine PR plan of action	
Complete PR worksheet	
Obtain current intelligence brief	
Obtain ISOPREP, authentication data, and EPA	
Determine threat level	
Obtain weather brief	
Study terrain/obtain sea conditions	
Determine survival equipment	
Determine CBRN contamination	
Determine medical status	
Special considerations	
Complete PR planning:	
PR plan (forces, timing, locations)	
Comm plan/flight following including backups	
Rescue forces informed	
Support forces requested (as requested)	
OSC appointed /notified	
Coordination complete with all PR forces	
Mission Execution:	
Monitor mission progress	
Start times	
Keep component rescue coordination center (RCC)/ intelligence, surveillance, and reconnaissance cell (ISRC) advised of actions	
Arrival times at scene	
Arrange for transport of injured (as required)	
Obtain additional PR forces/support (as required)	
Complete reports (as required)	
Closing Actions:	
Rescue personnel debriefed	
INTEL debriefed (as required)	
Component RCC/ISRC notified of mission results	
Rescued personnel status confirmed	
Paperwork complete	
PR Precombat Checks/Precombat Inspection:	
Medics kit inventoried, splints, IV bags, sufficient for full up crew of downed aircraft (UH-60 = four personnel, AH-64 and OH-58 = two personnel).	
Commo cards accurate? (prepared by RCC)	
Location of Level I and II care known, freqs and approach paths into C Med. known?	
Contingency plans for early departure from battle, return crossing of PP if cross-FLOT?	

Table D-7. Sample personnel recovery planning checklist

PR Precombat Checks/Precombat Inspection:	
Aircrew knowledge of adjacent airspace coordination measures.	
Personnel qualified/trained/rehearsed.	
Weapons PCC/PCI.	
Battle graphics on maps.	
Safing procedures for downed aircraft.	
Personnel should be trained on use of all survival equipment including forest penetrator and horse collar.	
Emphasis should be placed on letting the hoist cable ground itself before touching.	
Ensure completion of DD Form 1833 (Isolated Personnel Report [ISOPREP]).	
Ensure PRC-112 radios are programmed correctly with frequencies and isolated personnel code.	
	Go/No-Go
Airspace Coordinating Measures:	
Coordination for PPs in cross-FLOT.	
Location of Level II care, communication, and familiar with landing site at Level II care.	
Knowledge of airspace available and ability to coordinate passage through adjacent airspace.	
Enemy situation.	
Friendly situation.	
Air routes.	
Individual PR Related Requirement:	
All aircrew personnel should wear on their person the following equipment: • A survival vest with combat survivor/evader locator (CSEL) or PRC-112 radio. • Strobe light with IR cover. • 6 chemlights. • Signal mirror.	
Ensure they have completed DD Form 1833.	
Ensure PRC-112 radios are programmed correctly with frequencies and isolated personnel code.	
Security team personnel should be equipped with the following nonstandard items: • Crash rescue (quickie) saw. • Crowbars. • Crash axes. • Rappel ropes. • STABO harnesses. • Aviator flak vests. • SABRE radios (w/headsets). • PRC-112s. • Additional back boards and medical supplies.	
	Go/No-Go
AMC:	
Appoint an OSC. • Usually wingman (will have location and condition information). • If not wingman relay vicinity and condition if known. • Consider station time and weapons load.	
Ensure OSC authenticates the downed aircrew IAW SPINS and pass used/compromised authentication data to higher.	
Find PRC-112 CSEL codes (PLS codes) and ISOPREP data from S-2 and pass to RMC/OSC.	

Table D-7. Sample personnel recovery planning checklist

	Go/No-Go
AMC:	
Coordinate and monitor PR radio nets.	
Manage flow of aircraft to and from the objective area.	
On Scene Commander:	
Authenticate isolated personnel. • Record all used: • Call sign _____ • Authentication used _____	
Locate isolated personnel and pass initial information to the AMC via the RMB. • # of isolated personnel _____ • Location: Grid/LL is transmitted secure only • MGRS Grid _____ • Latitude/longitude (L/L) N_____ E _____ • Search and rescue dot (SARDOT)/DAPP • Bearing: _____ Range _____ (from isolated personnel to SARDOT/DAPP)	
Conduct a threat assessment of the objective area (Avoid highlighting the isolated personnel's location). • Avoid/Suppress/Kill • Enemy positions _____ • Neutralize enemy IAW ROE • Set-up assets to sanitize the SAR unit route • Isolated personnel EPA _____ • Isolated personnel communications plan _____ • Remind them when to transmit/listen • Limit transmissions < 5 sec	
Determine the health/condition of the isolated personnel and pass status to the AMC. • Rabbit or Turtle _____ • Condition	
Evaluate: Why did aircraft go down? _____ Check all assets for: • Station time _____ • Ordnance _____ • What is needed/on the way? _____ • Reset Bingo (don't overfly) _____ • Weather options	
Rescue Mission Commander:	
Complete all necessary information in the RMB.	
Determine Isolated Personnel's available signaling devices.	
Conduct a thorough threat assessment: • Recommend ingress and egress routes • Inform RESCORT of threat positions so they can be circumvented. • Request additional support if required.	
Make Go/No-Go recommendation based on information gathered at the objective area.	
Brief replacement RMC/RESCORT using the RMB.	
Prepare isolated personnel for pickup.	
Re-authenticate the isolated personnel after OSC changeover only if situation warrants.	

Table D-7. Sample personnel recovery planning checklist

SARIR TEMPLATE		INFO: ALPHA	DTG
Line 1	Call sign		
Line 2	Aircraft type		
Line 3	Nationality		
Line 4	Bailout location		
Line 5	Source Time Altitude Winds		
Line 6	Ground location		
Line 7	Source Time		
Line 8	DTG of incident		
Line 9	Cause of incident		
Line 10	Details		
Line 11	Conditions of isolated person		
Line 12	Last contact		
Line 13	Reported by Method Authenticated yes or no		
Line 14	Authentication used		
Line 15	Situation AD Ground		
Line 16	SAR code/PLS 112 CSEL code		

D-8.   Table D-8 is an example of a search and rescue situation summary report.

Table D-8. Sample search and rescue situation summary report

Line 1	DTG
Line 2	Unit (unit making report)
Line 3	Mission number (enter the JPRC SAR mission number)
Line 4	Status (SAR status: completed or terminated if SAR activity has ceased and will not be resumed at a later time; suspended, if SAR activity is discontinued and objective is not recovered)
Line 5	Call sign (call sign of disabled or lost aircraft, ship, submarine, or other)
Line 6	Type (type of disabled or lost aircraft, ship, submarine, or other)
Line 7	Location (universal transverse mercator or six-digit grid coordinate with MGRS grid zone designator of SAR incident)
Line 8	Personnel (number of personnel involved in incident)
Line 9	Personnel status (status of personnel involved in incident (recovered))
Line 10	Narrative (free text for additional information required for clarification of report)
Line 11	Authentication (report authentication)

D-9.   Table D-9 is an example of a rescue mission brief.

Table D-9. Sample rescue mission brief

Survivor Information	
Call sign:	
Number of survivors:	
Location - circle appropriate GRID L/L Range/Bearing SARDOT/DPP GPS	
Condition/injuries	Walking (yes or no)
Equipment (communication/signal)	
Authentication complete (yes/no)	Method
Recovery Area Brief	
Threats	
Elevation	
Description	
RESCORT plan	
Initial point	
Ingress	
Egress	
Ordinance	
RESCORT tactics	
Interior	Exterior

D-10. Table D-10 is an example of a landing zone survey checklist.

Table D-10. Sample landing zone survey checklist

Survey Date:		LZ #:		LZ Name:	
GPS Coord:			MGRS Grid:		
Landing Area					
Type:	[ ] Helipad	[ ] Field	[ ] Road	[ ] Other	
Surface:	[ ] Level	[ ] Sloped	[ ] Rocky	[ ] Dusty	[ ] Wet
Wind Indicator:		[ ] Wind Sock	[ ] None	[ ] Other	
Lighting:	[ ] Chemlite	[ ] Bean Bag	[ ] Inverted Y	[ ] None	[ ] Other _____
LZ Obstacles					
	[ ] Towers	[ ] High Grass	[ ] Brush	[ ] Trees	[ ] Buildings
	[ ] Poles	[ ] Wires/Height		[ ] Other_____	
Approach Information					
LZ Long Axis:_____ (Degrees Magnetic)			LZ Size: (Meters) _____ X _____		
Approach heading:			Departure heading:		
Number/type aircraft:					
UH-60	CH-47		OH-58	AH-64	
Flight route					
Unaided night operations:			NVD operations:		
[ ] Yes [ ] No			[ ] Yes [ ] No		
Accessibility					
[ ] Ground/emergency vehicles			[ ] Other		
Considerations:					
[ ] Near housing area		[ ] Noise abatement		[ ] Other	
Restrictions/Remarks: (out of ground effect, in ground effect (IGE), number and type A/C, Day Only.)					
LZ sketch/photo: (attach to this document)					
Distribution:					
[ ] Reading file			[ ] Detachment operations files		
Surveyor:					
Risk:					
[ ] Low		[ ] Medium		[ ] High	
*** This form is intended for use at field site landing areas, not helipads***					

SECTION III – REPORTS AND FORMATS

D-11. Table D-11 is an example of a helicopter flight status report.

Table D-11. Sample helicopter flight status report

Unit making report.
DTG of report.
LINE 1: Departure/takeoff DTG.
LINE 2: Number of aircraft departing.
LINE 3: Departure location.
LINE 4: OIC.
LINE 5: Number of passengers and location of manifest.
LINE 6: Planned primary and alternate destinations.
LINE 7: Planned arrival times.
LINE 8: Delay status.
a. Delay DTG.
b. Delay location.
c. Number and type of aircraft delayed.
d. Number and grade of passengers delayed.
e. Reason for delay.
f. Expected length of stay and contact information.
g. Delay departure DTG.
h. Alternate departure information (vehicle, DTG for departure, route ETA and location).
LINE 9: Arrival DTG.
LINE 10: Remarks.

D-12. Use the weather advisory/watch report (table D-12) to send flash weather information that will effect current unit operations.

Table D-12. Sample weather advisory/watch report

LINE 1: DTG.
LINE 2: Unit making report.
LINE 3: Report line.
LINE 4: Summary of warning.
LINE 5: Time of watch (DTG from-to DTG/as of DTG of watch).
LINE 6: Area effected.
LINE 7: Narrative/remarks, free text for additional information required for clarification of report.
LINE 8: Report authentication.

D-13. Use the following report (table D-13) to update convoy status.

Table D-13. Sample convoy status report

LINE 1: DTG.
LINE 2: Unit making report.
LINE 3: Convoy commander.
LINE 4: Convoy unit number.
LINE 5: Number of wheeled vehicles.
LINE 6: Number of personnel.
LINE 7: Route being used and alternate proposed.
LINE 8: Starting point, include first vehicle to DTG and last vehicle DTG.
LINE 9: Resting points.
a. DTG of arrival and departure at/from resting point.
b. Number of vehicles arrived and number of vehicles departing.
c. Number of personnel arrived and number of personnel departing.
LINE 10: RP including DTG of first vehicle to cross and last vehicle to cross RP.
LINE 11: CP.
LINE 12: Convoy closing DTG.
LINE 13: Accidents/breakdowns.
a. Type/bumper number/unit of broken down vehicles/equipment.
b. Location or broken vehicles/equipment.
c. Estimated time to continue operations.
LINE 14: Sensitive items status.
LINE 15: Narrative/remarks.
LINE 16: Authentication.

D-14. Table D-14 is an example of an unexploded ordnance report.

Table D-14. Sample unexploded ordinance report

LINE 1: DTG item was discovered.
LINE 2: Reporting unit and location (grid or directions from landmark).
LINE 3: Contact method between witness and responding EOD team (RF, call sign, POC, phone number, meeting place.).
LINE 4: Type of ordnance (dropped, placed, projected, thrown). Give description of item and quantity, if more than one.
LINE 5: CBRN contamination in the area. Be as specific as possible.
LINE 6: Resources threatened. Facilities, routes.
LINE 7: Impact on mission. How the threat from the unexploded ordnance (UXO) affects your mission.
LINE 8: Protective measures that you have taken to protect personnel or equipment.
LINE 9: Recommended priority for response by EOD technicians. Priorities: • **IMMEDIATE.** UXO stops unit's maneuver and mission capability or threatens vital critical assets. • **INDIRECT.** UXO slows maneuver or mission capability or threatens mission critical assets. • **MINOR.** UXO reduces unit's maneuver and mission capability or threatens noncritical assets of value. • **NO THREAT.** UXO has little or no affect on unit's mission or assets.

D-15. Table D-15 is an example of a medical evacuation nine-line report.

Table D-15. Sample medical evacuation nine-line report

LINE 1: Location of pickup site (full grid such as 34T EN43532501):_____	
LINE 2: Frequency/call sign at pickup site (30.75 is mandatory): 30.750 _____	
	Call sign of personnel at pick up site.
LINE 3: Number of patients by precedence.	
	Urgent–to save life, limb, or eyesight within 2 hours. Evacuate within 2 hours.
	Urgent surgery–must receive surgical care within 2 hours.
	Priority–evacuate within 4 hours.
	Routine–evacuate within 24 hours.
LINE 4: Special equipment (Circle one if needed):	
	None.
	Hoist.
	Extraction equipment.
	Ventilator.
LINE 5: Number of patients by type:	
	L: Number of litter patients.

Table D-15. Sample medical evacuation nine-line report

	A: Number of ambulatory patients.
LINE 6: Security of pickup site:	
	N: no enemy troops.
	P: possible enemy troops.
	E: enemy troops in area (caution).
	X: enemy troops in area (armed escort required).
LINE 7: Method of marking pickup site:	
	Panels.
	Pyrotechnics.
	Smoke signals.
	None.
	Other: _____
LINE 8: Patient nationality and status:	
	U.S. military.
	U.S civilian.
	Non-U.S. military, specify_____
	Non-U.S. civilian, specify_____
	EPW, nationality_____
	Other, specify_____
LINE 9: PZ CBRN status (wartime) terrain description (peacetime).	

D-16. Table D-16 is an example of a warning order.

Table D-16. Sample warning order

1. Situation.
Brief description of the enemy and friendly situations, attachments, and detachments to the company.
2. Mission.
Use the restated mission from mission analysis.
3. General Instructions.
   a. Special teams or task organization within the company.
   b. Uniform and equipment common to all (changes from SOP; MOPP level or additional equipment).
   c. Special weapons, ammunition, or equipment (different from SOP) (Amor piercing incendiary rounds, internal fuel tanks).
   d. The tentative time schedule is formed on the basis of mission analysis including the following:
- Earliest time of move.
- Time and place of OPORD.
- Probable execution time.
- Inspection times and items to be inspected if different from SOP.
- Rehearsal actions and times (actions at the objective, and SPINS for sections or platoon aircraft).

   e. Additional general instruction as needed or IAW SOP.
4. Special Instructions.
   a. To subordinate leaders:
- 1SG.

Table D-16. Sample warning order

> - Platoon leaders.
> - SIP/IPs.
> - PCs.
> **5. Attachments.**
>   a. To persons helping prepare OPORD (SOP).
>   b. As needed or IAW SOP.
>   c. Acknowledgement. All subordinates verify receipt of WARNO to ensure required personnel are notified.

D-17. Table D-17 is an example of an operation order.

Table D-17. Sample operation order

> **Task Organization:**
>
> 1st PLT(-) 2nd PLT
>
> **1. Situation.** (The task organization for the mission is stated at the start of the OPORD so that the subordinates know what assets they will have during the operation.)
>
> **a. Enemy situation.**
>
> - Composition, disposition, and strength.
> - Recent activities.
> - Capabilities.
>
> The enemy's most probable COA. A sketch or enemy overlay is normally included to clarify this description.
>
> **b. Friendly situation.**
>
> - Mission and concept for the aviation battalion or TF.
> - Mission for the ground tactical units supported.
> - Mission for any units supporting the aviation battalion or TF that may impact on the company mission.
>
> **c. Attachments and detachments.** Changes to the task organization during the operation. For example, if the task organization changes during a phase of the operation, it would be indicated here.
>
> **2. Mission.** The mission essential task(s) and purpose(s). It normally includes who, what, when, where and why. The where is described in terms of terrain features/grid coordinates. If objective names are used, they are secondary references and placed in parenthesis. Commanders must understand the GTP to effectively determine essential and implied company/troop task.
>
> **3. Execution.**
>
> **a. Concept of the operation.** This paragraph describes how the company/troop intends to accomplish its mission. At company/troop level, a maneuver and fires subparagraph will always be included. When needed to clarify the concept or to ensure synchronization, additional subparagraphs, such as engineering, intelligence, EW and counter ai operations, may be included. The operation overlay/concept sketch is referenced here.
>
> - **Maneuver.** The maneuver paragraph should be focused on the decisive action. At company/troop level, a maneuver paragraph that assigns the missions to each platoon and/or section and identifies the main effort normally, requires no additional clarification. If it should, the commander may clarify it in the concept of the operation paragraph (paragraph 3a).
> - **Fires.** This paragraph describes how the commander intends for the fires to support his maneuver. It normally states the purpose to be achieved by the fires, the priority of fires for the company, and the allocation of any priority targets. A target list, fires execution matrix, or target overlay may be referenced here.
> - **Engineering.** Often, especially in defensive operations, this paragraph is required to clarify the commander's concept for preparing obstacles, mines and fortifications. When the company is supported by engineer equipment or units, the commander states his guidance for employing these assets here. He may do this by stating his priority for the engineer effort (survivability, countermobility, and mobility) and the priority for supporting his subordinates, (1st platoon, 2nd platoon).
>
> **b. Tasks to maneuver units.** This paragraph lists each of the platoons' tasks/limitations. Each of these subordinate units will have a separate paragraph.

Table D-17. Sample operation order

c. Tasks to combat support units. This paragraph lists the tasks and limitations for support units. Each unit will have a separate paragraph. **d. Coordinating instructions.** These are the tasks and limitations that apply to two or more subordinate units. It they do not apply to all the subordinate units, and then those units that must comply are clearly stated. **4. Service Support.** This paragraph provides the critical logistics information required to sustain the company during the operation. **a. General.** It provides current and future trains locations. **b. Materiel and services.** It may have a separate subparagraph for each class of supply, as required. **c. CASEVAC.** **d. Miscellaneous.** **5. Command and Signal.** **a. Command.** This paragraph states where the C2 facilities and key personnel will be located during the operation and adjustments to the unit SOP, such as a change to the succession of command. **b. Signal.** It provides critical communication requirements such as radio listening silence in effect forward of the LD, signals for specific events or actions, emergency/visual signals for critical actions and SOI information. **6. Acknowledge.** Use the message reference number. **7. Annexes.** A-Intell/Intell overlay(s). B-Operation overlay/concept sketches. C-As required, such as air assault execution matrix, AMT.

D-18. Table D-18 is an example of a company warning order.

Table D-18. Sample company warning order

Air Mission Commander			
Task Org			
Sit Overview			
Proposed Mission			
1. Situation			
a. Enemy Forces (Cell 1)			
Unit		Task	
		Purpose	
Most dangerous COA			
Most likely COA			
b. Friendly Forces (Cell 3-AMC)			
Battalion Mission			
Battalion Intent			
c. Weather and Terrain (Cell 2)			

Table D-18. Sample company warning order

Air Mission Commander					
2. Mission (Cell 3-AMC)					
a. Fires (Cell 4)					
b. Tasks to Maneuver Units (Cell 3)					
c. Tasks to Maintenance Team					
A/C Required		Hours Required			
Preflight Time		Weapons Configuration			
Takeoff		Return to Base			
Rotor Stables		Aux Requirement			
d. Coordinating Instructions (Cell 5)					
4. Service Support (Cell 6)					
5. Command and Signal (Cell 7)					
a. Command					
Key leader locations	BN CDR	XO	S-3	CSM	Co CDR	1SG
b. Signal (Brief Commo Card)					
6. Risk Assessment(Cell 3)					
7. AMC					
Questions					
Next critical time					

D-19. Table D-19 is an example of a company operation order.

Table D-19. Sample company operation order

Air Mission Commander				
Roll Call				
Team	Call sign	A/C	PC	Pilot
Roll call		Packet inventory		Area of interest
Time hack		Map orientation		AO
Task org				
Sit overview				
1. Situation				
a. Enemy Forces (Cell 1)				
Unit		Task		
		Purpose		
Defense		Offense	Objective	
Area		Attack	Avenues of approach	
Mobile		Recon	Formations	
Staging		Security	Rate of March	
Most dangerous COA				
Most likely COA				
Enemy action on contact				

Table D-19. Sample company operation order

Air Mission Commander

Equip	Qty	Min Alt	Rng	Exp Time	APR 39	AVR 2	RFI	Night		Remarks

ASE and FCR Settings

Equipment	Setting	Defeat	Detect

Other Significant Enemy Capabilities

CBRN	0
Jamming	0
Radar detection	0
Reinforcements	0
Night fighting capabilities	0

Intelligence Collection

Asset		Asset	
Call sign		Call sign	
Frequency		Frequency	
Priority		Priority	
DTG		DTG	
Location		Location	

b. Friendly Forces (Cell 3 - AMC)

Brigade mission	
Brigade intent	
Battalion mission	
Battalion intent	
Ground units in AO	
Aviation units in AO	
To our Left	
To our Right	

Table D-19. Sample company operation order

Air Mission Commander							
To our Front							
To our Rear							
c. Weather and Terrain (Cell 2)							
Takeoff and En route		Objective			Return to Base		
Winds		Winds			Winds		
Ceiling		Ceiling			Ceiling		
Vis		Vis			Vis		
Altimeter		Altimeter			Altimeter		
PA		PA			PA		
DA		DA			DA		
Sig WX		Sig WX			Sig WX		
Light Data	BMNT	SR	SS		EENT	ILLUM	EO
	MR	MS	IR X-OVER				
Tactical Considerations							
Backscatter		Winds (ABF)			Key terrain		
Ceilings (HF)		Go-No Go terrain			Hazards		
Winds (Smoke)		IR crossover			Dust		
Trafficability		Cover/conceal			Obstacles		
FCR clutter							
2. Mission (Cell 3-AMC)							
Mission							
Intent							
3. Execution							
a. Concept of the Operation							
(1) Scheme of Maneuver (Refer to Map)							
(2) Fires (Cell 4)							
Artillery							
Unit		Unit					
Type		Type					
PAA		PAA					
Location		Location					
Range		Range					
Call sign		Call sign					
Frequency		Frequency					
Task		Task					
Purpose		Purpose					

Table D-19. Sample company operation order

Air Mission Commander			
Method		Method	
Priority		Priority	
Allocation		Allocation	
Restrictions		Restrictions	
Effects		Effects	
SEAD			
Ingress		**Egress**	
Location		Location	
Type		Type	
Route		Route	
Trigger		Trigger	
TRP		Time		TRP		Time	
TRP		Time		TRP		Time	
TRP		Time		TRP		Time	
TRP		Time		TRP		Time	
TRP		Time		TRP		Time	
TRP		Time		TRP		Time	
TRP		Time		TRP		Time	
TRP		Time		TRP		Time	
TRP		Time		TRP		Time	
Coordination Measures			
CFL		**DTG**		**FSCL**		**DTG**	
CAS			
Unit		Unit	
Type		Type	
Call sign		Call sign	
IP/location		IP/location	
Ordnance		Ordnance	
Station time		Station time	
Fighter check-in		Fighter check-in	
Frequency		Frequency	
Killbox		Killbox	
EW			
Asset		Asset	
Type		Type	
DTG		DTG	
Location		Location	

Table D-19. Sample company operation order

Air Mission Commander				
b. Tasks to Maneuver Units (CELL 3)				
Team 1	Task			
	Purpose			
	Task			
	Purpose			
Team 2	Task			
	Purpose			
	Task			
	Purpose			
Team 3	Task			
	Purpose			
	Task			
	Purpose			
c. Tasks to Maintenance Team				
A/C required		Hours required		
Preflight time		Weapons configuration		
Takeoff		Return to Base		
Rotor stables		Aux requirement		

d. Coordinating Instructions (Cell 5)

CCIR	PIR			
	FFIR			

Concept	A/S	ALT	Formation	Movement Tech
Takeoff to SP				
SP to PP				
PP to RP				
RP to OBJ				
OBJ to SP				
SP to PP				
PP to RP				
RP to tactical assembly area (TAA)				

Fire Distribution

	Primary	Alternate	Trigger	Shift
Gun1				
Gun2				
Gun3				
Gun4				
Gun5				
Gun6				
Gun7				

Table D-19. Sample company operation order

Air Mission Commander						
MOPP Level						
ADA Status						
FCR ROE						
Lead Change						
Abort Criteria		A/C				
		WX				
Actions on Contact						
Lost Commo						
Reports						
Bypass Criteria						
ROE						
Downed Aviator Recovery		Word of the day			DAPP	
		Number of the day			DAPP	
		Duress			DAPP	
		Pickup Times			DAPP	
		SAR satellite-aided tracking			DAPP	
A/C Destruction						
Special Msn Equip						
Bump Plan						
ATO						
IIMC Recovery	Friendly	MSA		XFLOT	MEA	
		Team or CO			Route	
		Heading			Separation	
		Approach			Climb Loc	
		Contact			Contact	
BDA Reports						
Out Front BS		Location		Type		
ROZ		Location		Time		
Coordinating Alt						
Success Criteria						
Target Priorities						
Egress Criteria						
Rally Procedures						
PL Plan		Prior FLOT				
		XFLOT				
CASH		Location		CASH		Frequency
SPINS						
Timelines	Rehearsal		REDCON 1		RP	
	Run-ups		Takeoff		Time of Target	
	Final Update		SP		Egress	
	Commo		PP			

Table D-19. Sample company operation order

Air Mission Commander			
Weapons Load	Team 1	Team 2	Team 3
Bingo			
Winchester			
Named Area of Interest Responsibility			

A2C2			
TAA w/Sketch		**Forward Assembly Area w/Sketch**	
Call sign		Call sign	
Frequency		Frequency	
ACPs		ACPs	
Traffic Pattern		Traffic Pattern	
Landing Direction		Landing Direction	
Landing Point		Landing Point	
Hazards		Hazards	
Reporting Points		Reporting Points	
Scatter Plan		Scatter Plan	

4. Service Support (Cell 6)							
Status							
A/C	Weapons	Fuel	ASE	AUX	Avionics		Remarks

A2C2			
FARP w/Sketch		**JFARP w/Sketch**	
Callsign		Callsign	
Frequency		Frequency	
Points		Points	
ACPs		ACPs	
Traffic Pattern		Traffic Pattern	
Landing Direction		Landing Direction	
Landing Point		Landing Point	
Takeoff Direction		Takeoff Direction	
Hazards		Hazards	
Reporting Points		Reporting Points	
Scatter Plan		Scatter Plan	
Class 3/5 Avail		Class 3/5 Avail	
Hot Gas			
Cold Gas			

5. Command and Signal (Cell 7)	
a. Command	
Battalion combat operations center (COC)	
Co COC	
TAC Loc	

Table D-19. Sample company operation order

Air Mission Commander						
Key Leader Locations	BN CDR	XO	S-3	CSM	SAFETY	1SG
b. Signal (Brief Commo Card)						
AMPS Card	MSN1	WPTs	CTRLMs	Targets	Routes	Phase Lines
	MSN2	WPTs	CTRLMs	Targets	Routes	Phase Lines
Commo	Nets	IDs	HQ	TACFIRE	A/C Spec	Others
IFF	Mode 1	Mode 2		Mode 3		Mode 4
SOI Change over						
6. Risk Assessment (Cell 3)						
Brief risk assessment method						
Questions						
Questions						
Confirmation Brief			Next Critical Time			

D-20. Table D-20 is an example of a flounder report.

Table D-20. Sample flounder report

Initial Report		
1	Location and type of aircraft	
2	Injuries requiring immediate attention	
3	Reason aircraft went down	
Follow-on Report		
4	Tail number of aircraft	
5	DTG aircraft went down	
6	Proword: Sierra=secured November=not secured	
7	Call sign of downed aircraft	
8	Personnel: Number onboard Number wounded in action/killed in action/missing in action Perched=Survivors at site Flown Coop=Survivor's Escape and Evasion	
9	Aircraft Status: Damage assessment COMSEC status	
10	Threat situation at site	
11	Call sign of sender	
12	Remarks	

This page intentionally left blank.

Glossary

1SG	first sergeant
A&L	administrative and logistics
A/C	aircraft
AC2	airspace command and control
A2C2S	Army airborne command and control system
AA	assembly area
AAA	antiaircraft artillery
AAFARS	advanced aviation forward area refueling system
AAFES	Army and Air Force Exchange Service
AAR	after action review
AATF	air assault task force
AATFC	air assault task force commander
ABC	air battle captain
ABCS	Army battle command system
ABF	attack by fire
ABN	air battle net
ABTF	aviation battalion task force
ACL	allowable combat load
ACO	air control order
ACP	air control point
AD	air defense
ADA	air defense artillery
ADE	assistant division engineer
AFTTP	Air Force technical training publication
AGSE	aviation ground support equipment
AH	attack helicopter
AHB	assault helicopter battalion
AHC	assault helicopter company
AIC	airspace information center
AKO	Army Knowledge Online
ALO	air liaison officer
ALSE	aviation life support equipment
ALSO	aviation life support officer
ALSS	aviation life support system
AM	amplitude modulated
AMB	air mission brief
AMC	air mission commander
AMCM	air mission coordination meeting

AMCOM	Aviation and Missile Command
AMO	aviation materiel officer
AMPS	Aviation Mission Planning System
AMT	air movement table
ANCD	automated network control device
AO	area of operations
AP	antipersonnel
APD	Army Publishing Directorate
AR	Army regulation
ARB	attack reconnaissance battalion
ARFOR	Army forces
ARMS	aviation resource management survey
ARP	aircraft repair platoon
ASB	aviation support battalion
ASC	aviation support company
ASE	aircraft survivability equipment
ASI	additional skill identifier
ASL	authorized stockage list
AT	antitank
ATC	air traffic control
ATCCS	Army Tactical Command and Control System
ATHP	ammunition transfer holding point
ATM	aircrew training manual
ATO	air tasking order
ATP	aircrew training program
ATS	air traffic services
BAE	brigade aviation element
BAO	brigade aviation officer
BAS	battalion aid station
BCOTM	battle command on the move
BCT	brigade combat team
BDA	battle damage assessment
BDAR	battle damage assessment and repair
BDE	brigade
BDZ	base defense zone
BFT-A	Blue Force Tracking-Aviation
BII	basic issue item
BLOS	beyond line of sight
BMNT	begin morning nautical twilight
BN	battalion

BP	battle position
BS	bench stock
BSA	brigade support area
C2	command and control
CAB	combat aviation brigade
CAC	command aviation company
CAN	combat aviation net
CAS	close air support
CASEVAC	casualty evacuation
CBAT	computer-based ASE training
CBRN	chemical, biological, radiological, and nuclear
CCA	close combat attack
CCIR	commander's critical intelligence requirements
CCP	casualty collection point
CDR	commander
CEOI	communications-electronics operating instructions
CH	cargo helicopter
CNR	combat net radio
CO	company
COA	course of action
COC	combat operations center
COLT	combat observation laser team
COMMEX	communications exercise
COMSEC	communications security
CONUS	continental United States
COP	common operational picture
CP	command post
CRM	composite risk management
CRP	component repair platoon
CSAR	combat search and rescue
CSEL	combat survivor/evader locator
CSM	command sergeant major
CSR	controlled supply rate
CTA	common table of allowances
CTASC	corps/theater automated data processing service center
CTL	commander's task list
D3A	decide, detect, deliver, and assess
DA	Department of the Army
DAAS	defense automatic addressing system
DAPP	downed aviator pickup point

DART	downed aircraft recovery team
DCU	dispensing control unit
DD	Department of Defense
DEA	Drug Enforcement Agency
DEERS	Defense Enrollment Eligibility Reporting System
DEW	directed-energy weapon
DIDEA	detect, identify, decide, engage, and assess
DMC	distribution management center
DOD	Department of Defense
DODAAC	Department of Defense Activity Address Code
DODD	Department of Defense Directive
DOS	days of supply
DOTD	Directorate of Training and Doctrine
DP	decision point
DS	direct support
DTG	date-time group
EA	engagement area
EENT	end evening nautical twilight
ELINT	electronic intelligence
EMT	emergency medical treatment
EO	electro-optical
EOD	explosive ordnance disposal
EPA	evasive plan of action
EPW	enemy prisoner of war
ERFS	extended range fuel system
ESR	external supported recovery
ESSS	external stores support system
ETE	estimated time en route
ETM	electronic technical manual
EUH	electronic utility helicopter
EW	electronic warfare
EWO	electronic warfare officer
FA	field artillery
FARE	forward area refueling equipment
FARP	forward arming and refueling point
FASCAM	family of scatterable mines
FBCB2	Force XXI Battle Command Brigade and Below
FCR	fire control radar
FEDLOG	Federal Logistics
FI	flight instructor

FID	foreign internal defense
FLOT	forward line of own troops
FM	field manual; frequency modulated
FMI	field manual interim
FMT	forward maintenance team
FOB	forward operating base
FORSCOM	United States Army Forces Command
FRAGO	fragmentary order
FRIES	fast rope insertion/extraction system
FS	fire support
FSC	forward support company
FSCL	fire support coordination line
FSCOORD	fire support coordinator
FSMT	forward support MEDEVAC team
FSO	fire support officer
FTX	field training exercise
G-2	Assistant Chief of Staff, Intelligence
GCA	ground controlled approach
GPS	global positioning system
GS	general support
GSAB	general support aviation battalion
GTC	ground tactical commander
GTP	ground tactical plan
HA	holding area
HBCT	heavy brigade combat team
HELOCAST	helicopter cast and recovery
HEMTT	heavy expanded mobility tactical truck
HF	high frequency
HHC	headquarters and headquarters company
HICHS	helicopter internal cargo handling system
HIDACZ	high-density airspace control zone
HMMWV	high-mobility multipurpose wheeled vehicle
HQ	headquarters
HSC	headquarters and support company
HSS	health service support
HSSO	health service support officer
HUD	heads-up display
HvyHC	heavy helicopter company
IATF	individual aircrew training folder
IAW	in accordance with

IBCT	infantry brigade combat team
ICM	improved conventional munition
ICS	internal communications system
IED	improvised explosive device
IFF	identification friend or foe
IFR	instrument flight rules
IGE	in ground effect
IIMC	inadvertent instrument meteorological conditions
ILAP	Integrated Logistics Analysis Program
IMC	instrument meteorological conditions
IMDC	isolated, missing, detained, or captured
INTREP	intelligence report
IP	instructor pilot
IPB	intelligence preparation of the battlefield
IPC	initial planning conference
IR	infrared
ISOPREP	isolated personnel report
ISR	intelligence, surveillance, and reconnaissance
ISRC	intelligence, surveillance, and reconnaissance cell
JAAT	joint air attack team
JACS	Joint Alternate Communications Suite
JIM	joint, interagency, and multinational
JP	joint publication
JPRC	joint personnel recovery center
J-SEAD	joint suppression of enemy air defenses
JSTARS	Joint Surveillance Target Attack Radar System
JTF	joint task force
kph	kilometers per hour
km	kilometer
L/L	latitude/longitude
LAN	local area network
LAR	logistics assistant representative
LBV	load bearing vest
LD	line of departure
LNO	liaison officer
LOC	lines of communications
LOGPAC	logistics package
LOGTAADS	Logistics Army Authorization Document System
LOS	line of sight
LP	listening post

LRP	logistics release point
LRS	long-range surveillance
LRSD	long-range surveillance detachment
LRU	line replaceable unit
LSA	logistics support area
LZ	landing zone
MAC	maintenance allocation chart
MDMP	military decisionmaking process
MEA	minimum en route altitude
MEDEVAC	medical evacuation
MEF	marine expeditionary force
METL	mission essential task list
METT-TC	mission, enemy, terrain and weather, troops and support available, time available, and civil considerations
MGRS	military grid reference system
MOC	medical operations cell
MOPP	mission-oriented protective posture
MP	maintenance test pilot
mph	miles per hour
MR	moonrise
MRE	meal, ready to eat
MS	moonset
MSA	minimum safe altitude
MSE	mobile subscriber equipment
MSL	mean sea level
MTF	medical treatment facility
MTOE	modified table of organization and equipment
MWO	modification work order
NAVAID	navigational aid
NCM	nonrated crewmember
NCO	noncommissioned officer
NCOIC	noncommissioned officer in charge
NEO	noncombatant evacuation operations
nm	nautical mile
NMP	National Maintenance Program
NOD	night observation device
NOE	nap-of-the-earth
NOTAM	notice to airman
NSC	network support company
NSFS	naval surface fire support
NVD	night vision device

NVG	night vision goggle
O&I	operations and intelligence
OCONUS	outside the continental United States
OH	observation helicopter
OIC	officer in charge
OP	observation post
OPCON	operational control
OPLAN	operation plan
OPORD	operation order
OPSEC	operations security
OPTEMPO	operational tempo
OSC	on-scene commander
P4T2	problem, plan, people, parts, time, and tools
PAA	position area for artillery
PBO	property book officer
PBUSE	property book and unit supply enhanced
PC	pilot in command
PCC	precombat check
PCI	precombat inspection
PCS	permanent change of station
PEO	peace enforcement operations
PGM	precision guided munition
PIR	priority intelligence requirements
PKO	peacekeeping operations
PLL	prescribed load list
PLS	personnel locator system
PMCS	preventive maintenance checks and services
POC	point of contact
POL	petroleum, oils, and lubricants
PPC	performance planning card
PR	personnel recovery
PRCC	personnel recovery coordination cell
PRO	personnel recovery officer
PSYOP	psychological operations
PZ	pickup zone
PZCO	pickup zone control
QA	quality assurance
QRF	quick reaction force
RCC	rescue coordination center
REDCON	readiness condition

RESCORT	rescue escort
RF	radio frequency
RFI	request further information
RMB	rescue mission brief
RMC	rescue mission commander
ROE	rules of engagement
ROI	rules of interaction
ROZ	restricted operations zone
RP	release point
RSR	required supply rate
RTO	radio telephone operator
RX	reparable exchange
S-1	personnel staff officer
S-2	intelligence staff officer
S-3	operations staff officer
S-4	logistics staff officer
S-6	command, control, communications, and computer operations (C4OPS) staff officer
S-9	civil affairs staff officer
SA	situational awareness
SAMS	Standard Army Maintenance System
SAMS-1	Standard Army Maintenance System- Level 1
SAMS-2	Standard Army Maintenance System- Level 2
SAMS-E	Standard Army Maintenance System–Enhanced
SAR	search and rescue
SARDOT	search and rescue dot
SARIR	search and rescue incident report
SARSS	Standard Army Retail Supply System
SARSS-1	Standard Army Retail Supply System-Level 1
SARSS-O	Standard Army Retail Supply System-Objective
SATCOM	satellite communications
SBCT	Stryker brigade combat team
SDDCTEA	Surface Deployment and Distribution Command Transportation Engineering Agency
SEAD	suppression of enemy air defenses
SECM	shop equipment contact maintenance
SERE	survival, evasion, resistance, and escape
SI	standardization flight instructor
SINCGARS	Single Channel Ground and Airborne Radio System
SITREP	situation report
SJA	staff judge advocate

SKOT	sets, kits, outfits, tools, and special tools
SO	safety officer
SOF	special operations forces
SOI	signal operating instructions
SOP	standing operating procedure
SP	standardization instructor pilot
SPIES	special patrol infiltration/exfiltration system
SPINS	special instructions
SPOTREP	spot report
SR	sunrise
SS	sunset
SSA	supply support activity
STAMIS	Standard Army Management Information System
STANAG	standardization agreement
STX	situational training exercise
SU	situational understanding
TAA	tactical assembly area
TAC	theater aviation command
TACAN	tactical air navigation
TAC CP	tactical command post
TACFIRE	Tactical Fire Direction System
TACOPS	tactical operations
TACSAT	tactical satellite
TACSOP	tactical standing operating procedure
TACT	tactical aviation control team
TC	training circular
TDY	temporary duty
TF	task force
TLP	troop leading procedures
TIS	thermal imaging system
TM	technical manual
TOE	table of organization and equipment
TRADOC	Training and Doctrine Command
TRP	target reference point
TTP	tactics, techniques, and procedures
U.S.	United States
UAS	unmanned aircraft system
UH	utility helicopter
UHF	ultrahigh frequency
ULLS	Unit Level Logistics System

ULLS-A	Unit Level Logistics System-Aviation
ULLS-S4	Unit Level Logistics System-Supply
UMT	unit ministry team
UXO	unexploded ordinance
VHF	very high frequency
WARNO	warning order
WFF	warfighting functions (Army)
WPT	waypoint
XO	executive officer

This page intentionally left blank.

References

These publications are sources for additional information on the topics in this FM. Find most JPs at http://www.dtic.mil/doctrine/doctrine.htm. Most Army publications are found online at http://www.army.mil/usapa.

SOURCES USED

These are the sources quoted or paraphrased in this publication.

JOINT AND MULTISERVICE PUBLICATIONS

FM 4-20.197. *Multiservice Helicopter Sling Load: Basic Operations and Equipment {MCRP 4-11.3E, Vol I; NTTP 3-04.11; AFMAN 11-223(I), Vol I; COMDINST M13482.2B}.* 20 July 2006.

FM 10-450-4. *Multiservice Helicopter Sling Load: Single-Point Load Rigging Procedures {AFJMAN 11-223, Vol II; COMDTINST M13482.3A; MCRP 4-23E, Vol II; NWP 3-04.12}.* 30 May 1998.

FM 10-450-5. *Multiservice Helicopter Sling Load: Dual-Point Load Rigging Procedures.* 30 August 1999.

JP 4-0. *Doctrine for Logistic Support of Joint Operations.* 6 April 2000.

JP 4-03. *Joint Bulk Petroleum and Water Doctrine.* 23 May 2003.

ARMY PUBLICATIONS

AR 95-1. *Flight Regulations.* 3 February 2006.

AR 700-138. *Army Logistics Readiness and Sustainability.* 26 February 2004.

CTA 8-100. *Army Medical Department Expendable/Durable Items.* 17 December 2004.

CTA 50-900. *Clothing and Individual Equipment.* 1 September 1994.

CTA 50-970. *Expendable/Durable Items (Except Medical, Class V, Repair Parts, and Heraldic Items).* 28 January 2005.

FM 1. *The Army.* 14 June 2005.

FM 3-0. *Operations.* 14 June 2001.

FM 3-04.104. *Tactics, Techniques, and Procedures for Forward Arming and Refueling Point.* 3 August 2006.

FM 3-04.111. *Aviation Brigades.* 21 August 2003.

FM 3-04.120. *Air Traffic Services Operations.* 16 February 2007.

FM 3-04.126. *Attack Reconnaissance Helicopter Operations.* 16 February 2007.

FM 3-04.140. *Helicopter Gunnery.* 14 July 2003.

FM 3-04-203. *Fundamentals of Flight.* 7 May 2007.

FM 3-04.500. *Army Aviation Maintenance.* 23 August 2006.

FM 3-04.513. *Battlefield Recovery and Evacuation of Aircraft.* 27 September 2000.

FM 3-05.210. *Special Forces Air Operations.* 31 August 2004.

FM 3-06.11. *Combined Arms Operations in Urban Terrain.* 28 February 2002.

FM 3-09.32. *(J-FIRE) Multiservice Procedures for the Joint Application of Firepower {MCRP 3-16.6A; NTTP 3-09.2; AFTTP(I) 3-2.6}.* 29 October 2004.

FM 3-34.210. *Explosive Hazards Operations.* 27 March 2007.

FM 3-50.1. *Army Personnel Recovery.* 10 August 2005.

FM 4-0. *Combat Service Support.* 29 August 2003.

FM 4-02.2. *Medical Evacuation.* 8 May 2007.

FM 5-0. *Army Planning and Orders Production.* 20 January 2005.

FM 6-0. *Mission Command: Command and Control of Army Forces.* 11 August 2003.

FM 7-1. *Battle Focused Training.* 15 September 2003.

FM 7-93. *Long-Range Surveillance Unit Operations.* 3 October 1995.

FM 10-1. *Quartermaster Principles.* 11 August 1994.

FM 23-10. *Sniper Training.* 17 August 1994.

FM 90-4. *Air Assault Operations.* 16 March 1987.

FMI 5-0.1. *The Operations Process.* 31 March 2006.

TC 1-210. *Aircrew Training Program Commander's Guide to Individual, Crew, and Collective Training.* 20 June 2006.

TC 1-400. *Brigade Aviation Element Handbook.* 27 April 2006.

TM 750-244-1-5. *Procedures for the Destruction of Aircraft and Associated Equipment to Prevent Enemy Use.* 12 November 1971.

DOCUMENTS NEEDED

These documents must be available to the intended users of this publication.

DA Form 1156. *Casualty Feeder Card.*

DA Form 2028. *Recommended Changes to Publications and Blank Forms.*

DA Form 7573. *Aircraft Survivability Equipment (ASE) Risk Assessment Worksheet Survivability Risk Analysis.*

DA PAM 25-30. *Consolidated Index of Army Publications and Blank Forms.* 1 January 2007.

DA PAM 25-33. *User's Guide for Army Publications and Forms.* 15 September 1996.

DD Form 1833. *Isolated Personnel Report (ISOPREP).*

READINGS RECOMMENDED

These sources contain relevant supplemental information.

AR 200-1. *Environmental Protection and Enhancement.* 28 August 2007.

AR 385-10. The *Army Safety Program.* 23 August 2007.

AR 600-55. *The Army Driver and Operator Standardization Program (Selection, Training, Testing, and Licensing).* 18 June 2007.

ARTEP 1-111-MTP. *Mission Training Plan for the Aviation Brigade.* 27 October 2005.

ARTEP 1-113-MTP. *Mission Training Plan for the Assault Helicopter Battalion.* 29 December 2005.

ARTEP 1-118-MTP. *General Support Aviation Battalion.* 17 January 2006.

ARTEP 1-126-MTP. *Mission Training Plan for the Attack Reconnaissance Helicopter Battalion/Squadron.* 8 March 2006.

ARTEP 1-500-MTP. *Mission Training Plan for the Aviation Intermediate Maintenance (AVIM) Battalion and Company.* 1 April 2002.

Department of Defense Directive (DODD) 2000.12. *DOD Antiterrorism (AT) Program.* 18 August 2003.

DA PAM 385-40. *Army Accident Investigation and Reporting.* 1 November 1994.

DA PAM 385-64. *Ammunition and Explosives Safety Standards.* 15 December 1999.

DA PAM 710-2-1. *Using Unit Supply System (Manual Procedures).* 31 December 1997.

DA PAM 710-2-2. *Supply Support Activity Supply System: Manual Procedures.* 30 September 1998.

Electronic Manual (EM) 0007. *(O) FEDLOG.* 1 December 2007.

FAA. *Aeronautical Information Manual (AIM)*. 16 February 2006.

FAA. *Air Traffic Bulletin Issue 99-5*. Fall 1999.

FAA. *North Atlantic International General Aviation Operations Manual (NAIGAO)*.

FAA. *Notices to Airman Publication (Class II) (NOTAMS)*.

FAA. *Pilot/Controller Glossary (P/CG)*.

FAA Order 3120.4. *Air Traffic Technical Training*. 22 June 2005.

FAA Order 7000.5. *Submissions for Air Traffic Publications*. 18 October 2001.

FAA Order 7010.1. *Air Traffic Control Safety Evaluations and Audits*. 1 October 2005.

FAA Order 7110.10. *Flight Services*. 30 August 2007.

FAA Order 7110.65. *Air Traffic Control*. 30 August 2007.

FAA Order 7210.3. *Facility Operation and Administration*. 30 August 2007.

FAA Order 7210.56. *Air Traffic Quality Assurance*. 15 August 2002.

FAA Order 7340.1. *Contractions*. 15 March 2007.

FAA Order 7350.7. *Location Identifiers*. 25 October 2007.

FAA Order 7400.2. *Procedures for Handling Airspace Matters*. 15 March 2007.

FAA Order 7450.1. *Special Use Airspace Management System*. 21 June 1999.

FAA Order 7610.4. *Special Operations*. 18 January 2007.

FAA Order 7900.5. *Surface Weather Observing*. 11 May 2001.

FAA Order 7930.2. *Notices to Airmen (NOTAMs)*. 15 February 2007.

FM 1-02. *Operational Terms and Graphics*. 21 September 2004.

FM 1-100. *Army Aviation Operations*. 21 February 1997.

FM 2-0. *Intelligence*. 17 May 2004.

FM 3-04.240. *Instrument Flight for Army Aviators*. 30 April 2007.

FM 3-04.303. *Air Traffic Services Facility Operations, Training, Maintenance, and Standardization*.
3 December 2003.

FM 3-04.508. *Aviation Life Support System Maintenance Management and Training Programs*.
23 April 2004.

FM 3-04.300. *Flight Operations Procedures*. 26 April 2004.

FM 3-04.301. *Aeromedical Training for Flight Personnel*. 29 September 2000.

FM 3-04.508. *Aviation Life Support System Maintenance Management and Training Programs*.
23 April 2004.

FM 3-05.60. *Army Special Operations Forces Aviation Operations*. 30 October 2007.

FM 3-06. *Urban Operations*. 26 October 2006.

FM 3-06.1. *Aviation Urban Operations Multi-Service Tactics, Techniques, and Procedures for Aviation Urban Operations {MCRP 3-35.3A; NTTP 3-01.04; AFTTP(I) 3-2.29}*. 9 July 2005.

FM 3-07. *Stability Operations and Support Operations*. 20 February 2003.

FM 3-07.31. *Peace Operations Multi-Service Tactics, Techniques, and Procedures for Conducting Peace Operations {MCWP 3-33.8; AFTTP(I) 3-2.40}*. 26 October 2003.

FM 3-11.3. *Multiservice Tactics, Techniques, and Procedures for Chemical, Biological, Radiological, and Nuclear Contamination Avoidance {MCWP 3-37.2A; NTTP 3-11.25; AFTTP(I) 3-2.56}*.
2 February 2006.

FM 3-11.5. *Multiservice Tactics, Techniques, and Procedures for Chemical, Biological, Radiological, and Nuclear Decontamination {MCWP 3-37.3; NTTP 3-11.26; AFTTP(I) 3-2.60}*.
4 April 2006.

FM 3-13. *Information Operations: Doctrine, Tactics, Techniques, and Procedures.* 28 November 2003.

FM 3-21.20. *The Infantry Battalion.* 13 December 2006.

FM 3-21.38. *Pathfinder Operations.* 25 April 2006.

FM 3-50.3. *Multi-Service Tactics, Techniques, and Procedures for Survival, Evasion and Recovery {NTTP 3-50.3; AFTTP(I) 3-2.26}.* 20 March 2007.

FM 3-52.2. *Multi-Service Tactics, Techniques, and Procedures for the Theater Air Ground System {NTTP 3-56.2; AFTTP(I) 3-2.17}.* 10 April 2007.

FM 3-90.6 *The Brigade Combat Team.* 4 August 2006.

FM 3-100.4. *Environmental Considerations in Military Operations {MCRP 4-11B}.* 15 June 2000.

FM 3-100.12. *Risk Management for Multiservices Tactics, Techniques, and Procedures {MCRP 5-12.1C; NTTP 5-03.5; AFTTP(I) 3-2.34}.* 15 February 2001.

FM 4-01.011. *Unit Movement Operations.* 31 October 2002.

FM 4-01.45. *Multi-Service Tactics, Techniques, and Procedures for Tactical Convoy Operations {MCRP 4-11.31H; AFTTP(I) 3-2.58; NTTP 4-01.3}.* 24 March 2005.

FM 4-30.31. *Recovery and Battle Damage Assessment and Repair {MCRP 4-11.4A}.* 19 September 2006.

FM 5-19. *Composite Risk Management.* 21 August 2006.

FM 5-34. *Engineer Field Data {MCRP 3-17A}.* 19 July 2005.

FM 5-103. *Survivability.* 10 June 1985.

FM 6-20. *Fire Support in the AirLand Battle.* 17 May 1988.

FM 7-0. *Training the Force.* 22 October 2002.

FM 10-67-1. *Concepts and Equipment of Petroleum Operations.* 2 April 1998.

FM 17-95. *Cavalry Operations.* 24 December 1996.

FM 20-3. *Camouflage, Concealment, and Decoys.* 30 August 1999.

FM 34-2-1. *Tactics, Techniques, and Procedures for Reconnaissance and Surveillance and Intelligence Support to Counterreconnaissance.* 19 June 1991.

FM 34-60. *Counterintelligence.* 3 October 1995.

FM 34-130. *Intelligence Preparation of the Battlefield.* 8 July 1994.

FM 55-30. *Army Motor Transport Units and Operations.* 27 June 1997.

FM 55-450-2. *Army Helicopter Internal Load Operations.* 5 June 1992.

FM 63-23 *Aviation Support Battalion.* 6 June 1996.

FM 71-100. *Division Operations.* 28 August 1996.

FM 71-100-3. *Air Assault Division Operations Tactics, Techniques, and Procedures.* 29 October 1996.

FM 100-8. *The Army in Multinational Operations.* 24 November 1997.

FM 100-9. *Reconstitution.* 13 January 1992.

FMI 3-35. *Army Deployment and Redeployment.* 15 June 2007.

FMI 3-04.155. *Army Unmanned Aircraft System Operations.* 4 April 2006.

HQDA Letter 525-07-1. *Personnel Recovery.* 20 March 2007.

JP 3-0. *Joint Operations.* 17 September 2006.

JP 3-01. *Counter Air and Missile Threats.* 05 February 2007.

JP 3-09. *Joint Fire Support.* 13 November 2006.

JP 3-09.1. *Joint Tactics, Techniques, and Procedures for Laser Designation Operations.* 28 May 1999.

JP 3-09.3. *Joint Tactics, Techniques, and Procedures for Close Air Support (CAS).* 3 September 2003.

JP 3-50. *Personnel Recovery.* 05 January 2007.

JP 3-52. *Joint Doctrine for Airspace Control in the Combat Zone.* 30 August 2004.

JP 4-02. *Health Service Support.* 21 October 2006.

Maneuver Support Center (MANSCEN) Safety Office. *Commander and Staff Risk Management Booklet.* 6 January 1999.

MANSCEN Safety Officer. *Small Unit Risk Management Booklet.* 6 January 1999.

Surface Deployment and Distribution Command Transportation Engineering Agency (SDDCTEA) Pam 55-19. *Tiedown Handbook for Rail Movements 6th edition.* September 2003.

SDDCTEA Pamphlet 55-20. *Tiedown Handbook for Truck Movements.* July 2001.

SDDCTEA Pamphlet 55-21. *Lifting and Tiedown Handbook for Helicopter Movements 4th edition.* June 2006.

SDDCTEA Pamphlet 55-22. *Lifting and Lashing Handbook for Marine Movement.* August 2005.

SDDCTEA Pamphlet 55-23. *Tiedown Handbook for Containerized Movements 2nd edition.* September 2003.

SDDCTEA Pamphlet 55-24. *Vehicle Preparation Handbook for Fixed Wing Air Movements.* September 2002.

SDDCTEA Pamphlet 70-1. *Transportability for Better Deployability.* August 2005.

SDDCTEA Pamphlet 700-2. *Logistics Handbook for Strategic Mobility Planning.* September 2002

SDDCTEA Pamphlet 700-4. *Vessel Characteristics for Shiploading.* August 2001.

SDDCTEA Pamphlet 700-5. *Deployment Planning Guide.* May 2001.

SDDCTEA Pamphlet 700-6. *Large, Medium-Speed Roll-on/Roll-off (RORO) (LMSR) Ships Users' Manual.* September 2002.

Soldier Training Publication (STP) 1-15D13-SM-TG. *Soldier's Manual and Trainer's Guide for MOS 15D, Aircraft Powertrain Repairer, Skill Levels 1 and 3.* 27 October 2004.

STP 1-15M13-SM-TG. *Soldier's Manual and Trainer's Guide for MOS 15M, UH-1 Helicopter Repairer, Skill Levels 1, 2, and 3.* 26 October 2004.

STP 1-15T13-SM-TG. *Soldier's Manual and Trainer's Guide for MOS 15T, UH-60 Helicopter Repairer, Skill Levels 1, 2, and 3.* 6 January 2005.

STP 1-15U13-SM-TG. *Soldier's Manual and Trainer's Guide for MOS 15U, CH-47D Helicopter Repairer, Skill Levels 1, 2 and 3.* 29 October 2004.

STP 1-93C1-SM-TG. *Soldier's Manual and Trainer's Guide, MOS 93C, Air Traffic Control, Skill Level 1.* 1 April 2002.

STP 1-93C24-SM-TG. *Soldier's Manual and Trainer's Guide, MOS 93C, Air Traffic Control, Skill Levels 2/3/4.* 04 April 2002.

STP 1-93P1-SM-TG. *Soldier's Manual and Trainer's Guide for MOS 93P, Aviation Operations Specialist, Skill Level 1.* 1 October 2002.

STP 1-93P24-SM-TG. *Soldier's Manual and Trainer's Guide, MOS 93P, Aviation Operations Specialist, Skill Levels 2/3/4.* 1 October 2002.

TC 1-237. *Aircrew Training Manual, Utility Helicopter, H-60 Series.* 12 October 2007.

TC 1-238. *Aircrew Training Manual, Attack Helicopter, AH-64A.* 23 September 2005.

TC 1-240. *Aircrew Training Manual, Cargo Helicopter, CH-47D.* 12 September 2005.

TC 1-248. *Aircrew Training Manual, OH-58D, Kiowa Warrior.* 12 April 2007.

TC 1-251 *Aircrew Training Manual, Attack Helicopter, AH-64D.* 14 September 2005.

TC 1-600. *Unmanned Aircraft System Commander's Guide and Aircrew Training Manual.* 23 August 2007.

TM 1-1500-204-23-1. *Aviation Unit Maintenance (AVUM) and Aviation Intermediate Maintenance (AVIM) Manual for General Aircraft Maintenance (General Maintenance and Practices) Volume 1.* 31 July 1992.

TM 1-1500-328-23. *Aeronautical Equipment Maintenance Management Policies and Procedures.* 30 July 1999.

TM 1-1520-237-10. *Operator's Manual for UH-60A Helicopter, UH-60L Helicopter, and EH-60A Helicopter.* 17 April 2006.

TM 1-1520-237-S. *Preparation for Shipment of Army Model Helicopters UH-60A, UH-60L, EH-60A, HH-60A, HH-60L UH-60M andHH-60M .* 1 November 2007.

TM 1-1520-240-10. *Operator's Manual for Army CH-47D Helicopter.* 30 June 2006.

TM 1-1520-241-S. *Preparation for Shipment of CH-47D Helicopter.* 30 June 2004.

TM 1-1520-252-S. *Preparation for Shipment of MH-47E Helicopter.* 28 June 1995.

TM 1-1520-253-10. *Operator's Manual for Army Models UH-60Q Helicopter, HH-60L Helicopter.* 17 April 2006.

TM 10-4930-247-13&P. *Technical Manual Operator's, Unit and Direct Support Maintenance Manual Including Repair Parts and Special Tools List for HEMTT Tanker Aircraft Refueling System Model HTARS100 and Model HTARS101.* 28 February 1994.

TM 750-244-1-3. *Procedures for the Destruction of Aviation Ground Support Equipment (FSC 1700) to Prevent Enemy Use.* 14 December 1971.

U.S. Army Aviation Center. *Aviation Liaison Officer (LNO) Handbook.* July 2001.

U.S. Army Transportation School, Fort Eustis, VA. *Unit Movement Officer (UMO) Deployment Handbook Reference 97-1.*

WEBSITES RECOMMENDED

Reimer Digital Library used to access military publications online (www.train.army.mil).

DOD Dictionary of Military Terms and Definitions (www.dtic.mil).

Active FM–Army Doctrine and Training Publications (www.army.mil/usapa/doctrine).

Air War College References, on and offline (www.au.af.mil).

AKO. Online medium to access e-mail, publications, current events, links to other military organizations and special project groups. (www.us.army.mil).

Army Doctrine Online (http://www.tradoc.army mil/doctrine/).

Army Homepage (www.army mil).

Army Publishing Directorate (APD) Home Page (www.apd.army.mil).

Center for Army Lessons Learned (CALL) Public Web Page. Gathers and provides information on lessons learned by Soldiers conducting military operations. Information is available for downloading and provisions are established for special requests (http://call.army mil/).

Fort Rucker (The Home of Army Aviation). Online interface providing information regarding installation, Army aviation, units and directorates, current events and points of contact (http://www.rucker.army.mil/).

Joint Electronic Library Welcome (www.dtic mil/doctrine).

TRADOC Homepage (www monroe.army mil).

Warrant Officer Career Center (http://usawocc.army.mil/).

Index

By Order of the Secretary of the Army:

GEORGE W. CASEY, JR
General, United States Army
Chief of Staff

Official:

JOYCE E. MORROW
Administrative Assistant to the
Secretary of the Army
0731902

DISTRIBUTION:

Active Army, Army National Guard, and U.S. Army Reserve: To be distributed in accordance with the initial distribution number (IDN) 110713, requirements for FM 3-04.113.

www.ingramcontent.com/pod-product-compliance
Lightning Source LLC
Chambersburg PA
CBHW081407270326
41931CB00016B/3401